WHITE
BEAR

WHITE BEAR

Encounters with the Master of the Arctic Ice

CHARLES T. FEAZEL

Henry Holt and Company / New York

Published by Henry Holt and Company, Inc.,
115 West 18th Street, New York, New York 10011.
Published in Canada by Fitzhenry & Whiteside Limited,
195 Allstate Parkway, Markham, Ontario L3R 4T8.

Library of Congress Cataloging-in-Publication Data
Feazel, Charles T.
White bear : encounters with the master of the arctic ice /
Charles T. Feazel—1st ed.
p. cm.
ISBN 0-8050-1153-6 (alk. paper)
1. Polar bear—Arctic regions. I. Title
QL737.C27F43 1990
599.74′446—dc20   90-34133
CIP

Henry Holt books are available at special discounts
for bulk purchases for sales promotions, premiums,
fund-raising, or educational use. Special editions
or book excerpts can also be created to specification.
For details contact:
Special Sales Director, Henry Holt and Company, Inc.,
115 West 18th Street, New York, New York 10011

FIRST EDITION

Designed by Katy Riegel

Printed in the United States of America
Recognizing the importance of preserving
the written word, Henry Holt and Company, Inc.,
by policy, prints all of its first editions
on acid-free paper. ∞

1 2 3 4 5 6 7 8 9 10

Permission to quote or paraphrase at length from the following is gratefully
acknowledged: A Kayak Full of Ghosts, copyright © 1987 by Lawrence Millman,
reprinted by permission of Capra Press; Lords of the Arctic, copyright © 1983 by
Richard C. Davids and Dan Guravich, reprinted with permission of Macmillan
Publishing Company; Polar Bears, copyright © 1988 by Ian Stirling, reprinted with
permission of The University of Michigan Press. Portions reproduced from Kingdom
of the Ice Bear by Hugh Miles and Michael Salisbury with the permission of BBC
Enterprises Limited.

Unless otherwise noted, all photographs are copyright © Charles T. Feazel.

FOR JAN, CHRIS, AND KYLIE

Contents

Photographs follow page 114.

Acknowledgments

Anyone reading this book will recognize the contributions of many people. Most are quoted or acknowledged in some way, but there are others whose assistance is less visible, though just as valuable. Sandra Dijkstra and Laurie Fox first convinced me to write a book. Scott Carlberg was always there with encouragement and helpful suggestions to make it more readable. Ben Powell read the text critically and truly went the extra mile, all the way to northern Manitoba, to share a bear-watching experience neither of us will ever forget. My editor, Channa Taub, showed me how to turn a collection of anecdotes into a flowing narrative. Larry Watson's persistence enabled me to meet bears in their own element in the Beaufort Sea icepack. Joe Carter, M.D., guided me through medical literature, and biologist Dave McIntosh did the same in his field. Mike Beedell provided a wonderful introduction to the Hudson Bay shoreline. Ingebjørg Mjåland Ellen translated from Norwegian to English a fascinating description of the bears of Svalbard by Erik Nyholm. Rosa Armitage and Bob Heil helped with the illustrations. Finally, I thank all the wildlife biologists, zoo experts, arctic veterans, government officials, and other polar bear specialists who helped me understand the world of the white bear.

WHITE
BEAR

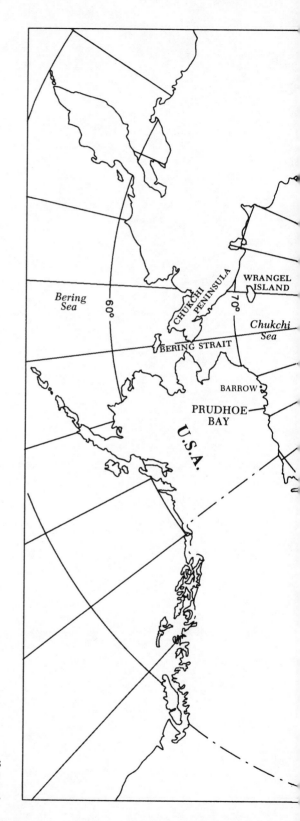

Map of the Arctic regions
that encompass the world of
the polar bear.

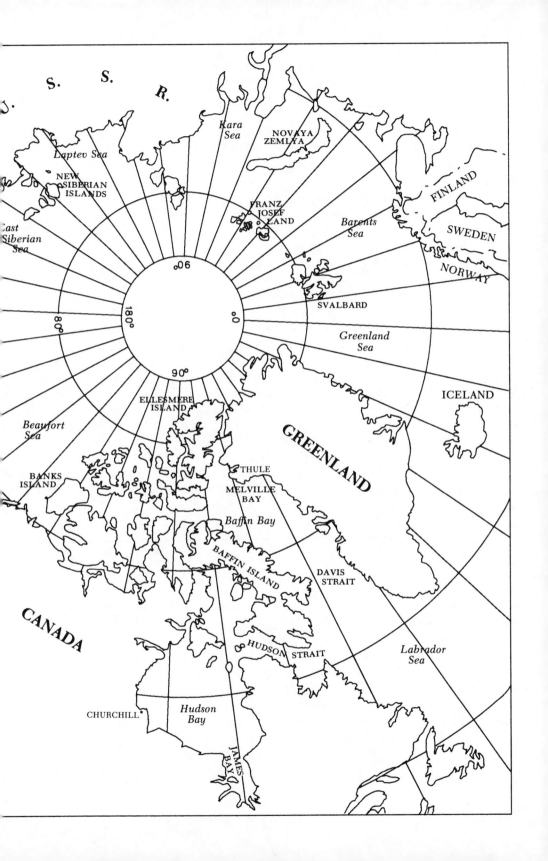

ONE

North of
the North Slope

THE ICE BENEATH my boots is fifteen feet thick. I've come north to survey it, to probe its secrets in the name of science. Covered with snow, the frozen slab is as solid and familiar—and as cheerless—as a prairie in winter. Under the ice, unseen and half-forgotten, lies black water a thousand feet deep. Death water. Liquid, yet I'm walking on it. Water so cold that a man missing here is presumed dead in less time than it takes to organize a search.

How could they search, anyway, if I were to slip through a snow bridge that covers an unsuspected crack? I imagine men peering down a blue-white crevice with black water rising nearly to the surface. "Yup, that must be where he went in. No use looking for him by now." And the search would be over.

A turn-of-the-century explorer, Vilhjalmur Stefansson, wrote, "Too many Arctic travellers suffer real agonies because they are haunted by the spectre of their own death: if you are not worried about it, it won't haunt you." I tuck the thought of an icy death away in a hidden, dank, moldy corner of my mind. The icescape regains its safety. Besides, I've got more immediate worries, more gruesome fates to ponder than simply slipping into numbing oblivion. I'm concerned now not about a cold, lingering death, but about a quick, violent one. Where there is arctic sea ice, there are seals. Where there are seals, there is also Nanook, the white bear.

I'm supposed to be studying the ice. Arctic science demands a concentration that's hard to deliver. I keep looking over my shoulder. In the snow behind me is a double line of circular depressions, a trail left by paws the size of dinner plates. Somewhere beyond the ice ridges lurks the master of the Arctic, the only predator that purposefully stalks humans.

He is called by many names. To the polar Eskimos, he is *Nanook*, both a spirit and a very real part of their world. They also know him as "the eternal vagabond" or "he who is without shadow." To the Cree Indians living near Canada's James Bay, the bear is *Wahbesco*. To the ancient Greeks, he was simply the sea bear. To whalers of the last century, he was "the farmer," out walking in icy fields that were his alone to tend. To modern scientists, he is *Ursus maritimus*. By any name he is a formidable adversary.

With his extraordinary sense of smell, if the bear is downwind, he knows exactly where I am. My nose is no help: I have no idea where he is. There's a tightness in my chest. My labored breathing coats my face mask with exhaled moisture, forming icicles that decorate my face from mouth to eyebrows. The windchill plummets below − 80° F as the wind screams across the polar icecap and whips away into the darkening sky any chance I might have of hearing the bear's approach.

In the blowing snow and gathering gloom I have little hope of seeing a half-ton mountain of white fur until it gets within about fifty feet. Too close. A leap, a pounce, a bone-crushing paw swipe, and the elegant precision of scientific research would dissolve into brief, bloody chaos. The ultimate ignominy: after all those years of burgers and fries, to end up as fast food myself.

Yesterday I watched a bear kill a seal. I shouldn't have. Like the strength-sapping cold, the memory seeps inward, displacing all focus on my scientific mission. The scene was a grim lesson in arctic efficiency. Shuffling along through the snow, the big she-bear looked peaceable enough. Then scenting, through more than two feet of snow cover, a seal's breathing hole in the ice, she froze. The bear shape I'd seen moving against a backdrop of white disappeared in the invisibility of ultimate camouflage. Suddenly, rearing up on her hind legs, she towered, motionless, a silent, menacing apparition almost eight feet tall. She waited. Then, with a dive so fast that the eye couldn't follow, she plunged nose first into the snow. A great cloud of white powder exploded into the still air, mercifully obscuring the seal's final agonies. With her massive jaw and thick neck muscles, the bear crushed the seal's skull and lifted its 150-pound body clear of the water. The power of the upward jerk pulled her prey through the narrow opening in the ice, and broke most of the seal's bones. Swinging her long, snakelike neck from side to side, the bear flayed the seal, leaving the meat for the foxes who would scavenge after she'd finished. She ate only the blubber, the seal's insulating fat, protection against inanimate dangers but also the seal's undoing—a polar bear's favorite meal. The bloody carcass, sleek as a red torpedo, slithered across the snow, a grotesque puck in a deadly game.

In warmer climes I've been in the water with sharks. I fear the white bear infinitely more. More than fear, I *respect* it. It is respect for our kinship. We, Nanook and I, are warm-blooded, sentient creatures. I appreciate the bear's mammalian intelligence, his superb adaptation to this environment, where I am the intruder. The bear is a terribly efficient predator, and I am the prey. In the tropical sea chances are very good that a shark will ignore me. In the winter icepack chances are very good that a bear will investigate my presence.

My senses rush back to reality. A warning echoes across the ice. Our armed guard—those of us in the survey party call him Bear Bait—is firing shots. The crack of his rifle, muffled by the wind's roar, snaps us to full alert. No one in the ice party knows what's happening, but we're all apprehensive.

We begin to cluster in small groups, casually at first, as if each of us has suddenly thought of some pressing matter to discuss with the others. We gather around sleds, plywood crates, or snowmobiles, as if these totems will offer protection from Nanook, the white bear.

Nothing with us on the ice except the rifle would stop a

determined one-thousand-pound polar bear, but we take comfort in small precautions. One of our team carries a flare pistol—the rest of us jeer: we want to be far away if he infuriates a bear by singeing its muzzle in a final, desperate move. Another has carried a peanut-butter sandwich for weeks in his parka. He's convinced that an attacking bear will stop to sniff it if he drops it on the ice, and he will gain a few precious seconds. All of us plan routes back to our base of operations, the immense ship that rests nearby in "icedock," where wooden ladders lead upward to the safety of the main deck.

The sailors laugh about the time a bear got between the ice party and the ship during last year's project. Two men tried a dangerous end run: one got to the ladder first, but the other was on deck first. The second man stormed right over his companions as they clambered up the ladder.

A grizzled arctic veteran offers the best advice, tongue in bearded cheek: "All you need is a short baseball bat. When the bear comes, hit your buddy in the leg and run for the ship."

"I don't have to outrun the bear," he laughs, "I just have to outrun you!" Small comfort to those of us who aren't built for speed.

This time we're lucky. Word comes from the icebreaker: the guard was given permission to test-fire his weapon. They'd forgotten to tell us. "Our apologies to you folks on the ice."

The polar bear is protected by international agreements. Anyone—even Bear Bait—killing a bear had best be prepared to justify his actions. This probably means that before Bear Bait feels entitled to fire, he'll have his choice of two targets: Nanook on top, me underneath.

Polar bears have enjoyed the law's protection for only a few years. Man's interaction with polar bears is a saga that continues to evolve. It began in prehistoric times. Over thousands of years the Eskimo people learned to coexist with bears in what scientists call a dynamic steady state: the Eskimos would win some of the time, and kill a few bears, and the bears would win some of the time, and kill a few Eskimos.

When European explorers first ventured into the Arctic, the alien environment they found was something to be feared. This view evolved rapidly into the Victorian model of macho-exploration: all of nature was to be conquered. Thus most turn-of-the-century descriptions of polar bear encounters end with something like "I put one well-aimed Mannlicher bullet into the huge beast's heart, and our harrowing adventure came to an end." This man-was-meant-to-win attitude, the Hemingway syndrome, persisted through the early days of arctic development, until only a few decades ago. Establishment of the Distant Early Warning (DEW) Line radar stations during the 1950s and preliminary probing for petroleum during the 1960s marked the end of the explorers' reign and saw the rise to power of technocrats and engineers. Bears, however, were still viewed as a menace. Today's views are reflected in an understatement that appeared in the journal *Polar Record* about Jean Louis Etienne, a French physician who made a solo trek to the North Pole in 1986, man-hauling a sledge over the ice. At 84° north latitude, "Etienne saw fresh tracks of two polar bears but fortunately never met any; he had found a gun and cartridges too heavy to carry."

Etienne's enlightened (many would say *naive*) view of polar bears as nonthreatening illustrates conflicts that are still developing. Those who have spent years working in the Arctic, whether they are native hunters or oil-rig roughnecks, share a pragmatic outlook. They speak with disgust of "eco freaks" or "tree huggers" who never leave the lower forty-eight states yet presume to know what's best for the Arctic. "The only polar bears those folks see," says a rough-hewn arctic veteran, "are at the zoo, where they look cuddly and playful. I know better—I lost my best friend to a bear." On the other side of the argument, environmentalists rail against the rape of the Arctic by people they see as driven only by corporate greed. These defenders of wilderness have pressed their often reluctant governments for more stringent regulations. Through their efforts the bears and other denizens of the North may well have been spared from extinction.

A curious cultural about-face has occurred during the past three decades as the native people of the northern regions have adopted southern clothing, habits, and possessions (notably rifles and snowmobiles). At the same time people far to the south experienced an awakening awareness and respect for the dignity of native cultures during the 1960s and for the environment during the 1970s. While white culture has been learning to co-exist with nature and adopt what it reveres as the "native" view of the environment, the natives across most of the arctic regions have done just the opposite, becoming increasingly "white" in their outlook. They have learned to use the legal processes of lands far to the south to defend their right to hunt bears, whales, seals, and walrus, and to strengthen their claims to lands rich in oil and ore.

The bears, of course, don't know the difference. Increasingly, though, instead of the certainty of death from the barrel of a rifle, they face only the momentary indignity of being tranquilized, tattooed, tagged, measured, marked with dye, and then released, a bit groggy, perhaps missing a tooth (extracted to determine the bear's age), but otherwise unharmed. The need for such studies—designed to learn more about bears for their own protection—is growing. Although they aren't classified as an endangered species, polar bears are protected as an international resource. Bears know nothing of human boundaries: they cross at will from Siberia to Alaska, or from Alaska to Canada. North of Norway, they rule the islands of Svalbard with a territorial claim more ancient, more valid than that of the Soviet and Norwegian colonists who for years disputed ownership of the land. Once Nanook was truly the king of the top of the world. Recently, though, his world has changed. The polar bear is now beset by snowmobiles, drilling rigs, helicopters, and pollution where previously all he had to face was a solitary hunter and his dogs. To survive as a species, Nanook needs protection.

An individual bear, however, is clearly in command of his world and needs no help from anyone. "Certainly not from me," I mutter, as my thoughts return to the work at hand. Today I'm serving as the rodman for an ice surveyor who's trying to avoid having his eyeball freeze to the telescope of his transit. The wind, ripping across the prairie-flat sheets of ice, bends the fiberglass pole back over my head at a 45-degree angle. Defying any attempt to read its markings, the rod thrashes like a palm tree caught in a hurricane. Science on the ice is so unlike science in the laboratory, so foreign to the world occupied by 99.9 percent of the human beings on earth, that when we review the day's work, the survey chief remarks, "Dammit, there's just no way to convince someone down south what it's like. You have to *be* here."

Only after we're back aboard the icebreaker, safe and warm, do the bears come. I like their sense of timing. Over the ship's intercom the familiar "toowhee" of the bosun's pipe is followed by an announcement that few warm-water sailors will ever hear: "Now hear this—two polar bears on the ice off the port quarter, distance twenty-five yards." Scientists and crew scramble on deck, pulling on parkas, winding cameras on the run. (During a summer cruise off Greenland, when we sighted a polar bear drifting leisurely aboard an ice floe, the ship's executive officer grumbled, "The quartermaster can't hear commands to the helm for the clicking of all those damned cameras!")

Out of the November darkness they materialize, ghostly, white, and massive. No specters these, but powerful physical beings. Two bears, mother and yearling son. They approach from downwind, snaking their necks from side to side, probing the air, homing in on the scent of man. Showing no fear, they approach the icebreaker, rear up on their hind legs, and rest their huge forepaws against the steel sides of the ship. High enough to be safe, we look down into lustrous, intelligent eyes and expressive faces. It's an exhilarating closeness.

Suddenly a crewman remembers the accommodation ladder, a stairway lowered to the ice on the starboard side of the vessel. "You realize those bears can get on deck any time they want, just by walking around to the other side?" A sobering thought. Each of us silently charts a course through a sturdy door to safety belowdecks. Fortunately the bears are content to remain on the ice. If they wanted their run of the ship, no one would argue.

For two days they remain near the icebreaker, hunting seals. At least four arctic foxes, magnificent in white winter coats, dodge between them, snapping at the seal meat. One fox lets boldness overcome survival sense. He nips too close. In a flash the mother bear crushes the small body beneath her paw. The fox lies silent in the snow, his beautiful fur smeared with crimson, a grim reminder to all who would treat the bears lightly. Those who share the ice with Nanook walk the very edge of life itself.

TWO

Land and Sea of the Midnight Sun

How FOOLISH IS man's view of his own valor. I fancied myself an intrepid explorer, fazed by nothing from pole to equator. This self-image was shattered during my first ten seconds in the Arctic. My first reaction to this world I'd come so far to savor was fear. I was under attack by a huge furred creature galumphing toward me at incredible speed down the gravel runway. I didn't know what it was. As it came closer, this dark, disorganized mass resolved itself into the largest dog I have ever seen, before or since. An immense, friendly Newfoundland, it was the size of a small pony, a mountain of shagginess as high as my waist, with a slobbery tongue that alternately hung—huge, pink, and dripping—and disappeared into a cavernous mouth.

"He sleeps underneath our transmitting station," said a young electronics technician, "even when it's sixty below outside."

I asked if the dog seemed as happy during the winter as he was in August. "Yeah," said the technician. "He can't come inside anyway—I don't think he'd fit through the door."

"When we go out to feed him," said the Coast Guardsman,

"it's as still as a tomb and twice as cold. You can throw a cup of hot coffee into the air and hear it tinkle—frozen—when it hits the ground."

Behind him the buildings spoke with eloquent silence of winters endured. Their insulating walls were twelve inches thick. The buildings were connected by boxlike passages so no one would have to venture outside during blizzards. Outside the structures, hand ropes offered pedestrians guidance during whiteouts, arctic snow and fog storms of such blinding intensity that in them it's easy to become totally disoriented only a few feet from safety. The structures were held together with pins positioned for instant release in case of fire, man's greatest fear in the Arctic. "When all the water is frozen," I learned from a veteran of five arctic winters, "you don't fight fires—you just pull the building apart so the flames can't spread."

The summer thaw had exposed tools lost in snowbanks and foundations in need of repair. Only a few weeks of warmth were available for the work. With the shortening days came hints of the returning cold. Construction went on around the clock. Even though the sun never really sets during the summer, daytime temperatures rose and fell slightly. By the evening twilight I found ice covering the meltwater ponds. Like an unstoppable train grinding slowly closer, the cold was coming.

"Don't let today fool you," the young technician said. "Up here, we have only two seasons: July and winter."

This arctic deep freeze is the kingdom of the white bear. His realm encompasses all the cold lands and seas at the top of the globe. Polar bears are marine mammals, as comfortable in the water as walrus, whales, and seals. They live in, on, and beside the Arctic Ocean (although they have been spotted, drifting on ice floes, well to the south). Bears wander (or drift) as far south as Labrador, Newfoundland, Lake Winnipeg, Kamchatka, Hokkaido, and northern Norway. They travel as far as one hundred miles inland. One of the best-studied concentrations of polar bears in the world lives entirely outside the Arctic, on the western shore of Hudson Bay, well south of latitude 60° north. Some polar bears live in the James Bay region, at the same latitude as London or Berlin. Bears do not live in antarctic regions—despite the sketches of cartoonists who draw polar bears sharing the ice with penguins (these artists stretch the truth across the icecaps, literally poles apart).

The absence of polar bears from antarctic waters causes a curious contrast in behavior between northern and southern seals. In the Arctic the main danger to seals is from polar bears, who hunt them when they lie on top of the ice. In antarctic waters danger lurks in the sea: the leopard seal is the predator to be feared, and it attacks smaller seals in the water. A veteran of icebreaker cruises to both regions describes the difference: "Up north, when the ship crunches through the ice, the seals slip into the water. They know that danger comes from above and that sounds transmitted through the ice signal threats. In the south, seals wait until the ship is almost on top of them before they leave the safety of the ice. In fact, I'm afraid we may have squashed a few seals who didn't get out of the way."

The two regions, north and south, though at first glance similar (they are both, of course, cold, remote, and sparsely populated), are fundamentally different. The arctic region is an ocean surrounded by land; the antarctic, a continent surrounded by water. The distinction means much more than colors on a map. The distribution of land and sea controls the climate: much colder temperatures are reported from the Antarctic, where the mercury has dipped to $-129°$ F, the lowest temperature ever recorded on earth. The Arctic Ocean, cold as it is, is warmer than Antarctica's rocky mountains, and it moderates the temperatures of the northern regions. Water is the best place on Earth to store heat. This property makes the oceans vast thermal regulators, whose effects reach far inland. Even so, arctic winter temperatures often drop to 60 degrees below zero, and $-90°$ F has been recorded at Verkhoyansk, in the interior of Siberia.

One aspect of life—and only one—becomes simpler in the Arctic than in more temperate lands. For those of us continually bewildered by temperatures reported in Celsius and Fahrenheit, it's comforting to know that 40 degrees below zero reads the same on either scale. A small matter, perhaps, but at 40 below, you take what few comforts you can.

Long before the Arctic was explored, ice bears were said to live at the North Pole. They were called *polar* bears long before the North Pole was "discovered." In our own time the name has been verified: polar bears are indeed found at the Pole. When the nuclear submarine *Skate* surfaced through the ice near the North Pole and a lookout scrambled up through the hatch, the first thing he spotted was a bear—no doubt the most surprised polar bear in history.

The name of the region is a gift from Nanook: *arktos* is the Greek word for "bear." Greeks, and later, Romans, pointed north by finding a constellation in the night sky that we call the Big Dipper. They named it the Great Bear. The northern regions became *Arktikos*, "Country of the Great Bear." Thus, in turnabout fashion, the bear wears the name of the Pole, and the Arctic wears the name of the bear.

The Arctic contains three poles: (1) the "cold pole," where the lowest arctic thermometer readings are recorded, located in central Siberia and more a region than a specific site; (2) the north magnetic pole, located in Canada's Arctic Islands, west of Greenland, a continually shifting nomad, where a compass needle points straight down; and (3) the true North Pole, an imaginary spot that can't be located on the earth's surface at all, because it lies in a field of mobile ice with no land nearby.

The North Pole is an abstraction, a concept defined by Greek mathematicians three thousand years before Robert E. Peary first planted a flag. Peary's flagpole, set in the ice, moved with the wind-drifted floe; by the time he returned to civilization to claim his mark in history, his mark was no longer at the Pole, which he'd sought for so long. (Recent evidence suggests that he may never have gotten there at all.)

The North Pole is a mystical place; it exerted such a powerful pull on nineteenth-century explorers that they risked everything in its pursuit. Legends of splendid treasures and rumors of a Northwest Passage to the Orient drew earlier adventurers to the Arctic, but after the 1850s, the Pole itself became the goal. All glory, it seemed, would fall to the first to reach the northernmost point on the globe. From a modern perspective it all seems rather pointless, but the Pole continues, even today, to be a place of compelling mystery, a spot whose very name fires the imagination and chills the soul. Over most of the Northern Hemisphere, men, women, and children point to the North Star, Polaris, and tell of its earthly sister, the North Pole. And any child who's heard of Santa Claus can tell you where he lives.

The Pole still draws explorers, from adventurers who brave the rigors of skis, dogsleds, or snowmobiles to passengers seated comfortably aboard transpolar commercial jets, who pause from leisurely meals to glance out the aircraft windows and shudder as the pilot describes the frigid scene below. Exceptionally hardy golfers can even slice and hook from the top of the world, according to the latest travel brochures. For a place that is literally no place, the Pole has a remarkable following. It is the best-known least-visited spot on the earth.

Because the earth's axis—a line through the planet connecting North and South poles, around which we rotate each day—is tilted, the North Pole spends part of the year (summer) inclined toward the sun and part of the year (winter) facing away from it.

A tilted axis offsets the path of the sun's rays across the globe. At the Pole itself the year consists of one long "day": six months of light, six of darkness. Some 1,630 miles farther south, at latitude 66.5° north, the effect is still apparent but diminished. For one twenty-four-hour day in the dead of winter, the sun never rises; for one twenty-four-hour summer day, the sun never sets (the British Empire had nothing on an arctic summer). This latitude, like the Pole itself, has a magical grip on the human mind. So important is this geographic abstraction, this boundary drawn on maps of the earth but related to celestial mechanics—significant because its effects could be read in the sun's motions by primitive people long before their shamans, seers, and scientists could explain the phenomenon—that long ago it was given a name. All things important to humans have names. The imaginary line encircling the earth at 66.5° north of the equator is called the *Arctic Circle.*

This line of demarcation that encompasses Nanook's world

is crossed with great ceremony aboard ship. Any sailor who submits to indignities prescribed by Boreas Rex and his royal court is proclaimed a "true and trusty brine-encrusted blue-nose." My circle crossing included obeisance to the king and his queen, and kissing the belly of the Royal Baby, a rotund chief boatswain's mate whose navel had been smeared with engine-room grease. After a haircut from the royal barber (which took three weeks to grow back to normal), I crawled through a trough of galley slops and was hosed down with frigid seawater. The Arctic Circle, once crossed, is not easily forgotten.

A different definition of the arctic environment relies on the northern limit of trees (but even in the "treeless" tundra there are ground-hugging varieties of plants that grow to tree height in warmer settings). Still another definition is based on climate: meteorologists define the arctic realm as that area north of a line of 50° F average temperatures during the warmest month of the year. Regardless of how it's defined, the Arctic wears impressive titles. My favorite descriptive term for the Far North—simply because it rolls from the tongue with such eloquent elegance—is *hyperborean*.

To the polar Eskimos, or Inuit, this area is *nunassiaq*, "the beautiful land." It is a region still largely unknown, even in this age of satellite reconnaissance. Only as recently as 1968 did surveyors of David Humphreys's aborted polar expedition confirm Robert Peary's 1900 discovery of Kaffeklubben Ø (Coffee Klatsch Island), north of Greenland, as the northernmost piece of land in the world. Only in 1978 did surveyors from the Danish Geodetic Institute discover a still more northerly island—a patch of gravel rising barely above the sea north of Kaffeklubben. They named it Oodaaq, for one of Peary's 1909 companions to the Pole. It nudges unobtrusively into the Arctic Ocean as the last outpost of the land, at 83°40′32.51″ north latitude.

Within the Arctic lie innumerable surprises. A summer sun that rolls like a brilliant gold coin around the horizon instead of arcing overhead. Coal and dinosaur bones that record past subtropical times. Mammoth tusks beneath the sea, marking former dry-land migration routes. Icebergs, daughters of the mighty glaciers, that plow the ocean floor with their toes as they drift, leaving furrows fifteen feet deep. Ancient lichens that grow only 1 day each year and lie dormant the other 364 because the climate is so hostile. Nuclear submarines that play deadly games of hide-and-seek beneath the ice. Optical illusions called sundogs that flank the sun's disk during ice fogs. Double and triple mock moons. Mirages, caused by layers of cold air, that show land where there is no land. Above all, the true symbols of the Far North, the silent, shifting curtains of the aurora borealis, the Northern Lights.

The Arctic is a special world, described by a sixteenth-century explorer as "the place of greatest dignitie" on earth and by an experienced arctic traveler of this century as "the most horrible part of the world." It is a place of contrast. Water dominates the scene, in the form of snow, compacted snow called *firn* or *névé*, glacial ice, sea ice, icebergs, seawater, meltwater, lakes, streams, rivers, clouds, fog, and ice crystals that hang suspended in the air like light-shattering prisms. Even so, the high Arctic is truly a desert. The farthest north gets very little precipitation, because cold air can't hold much moisture. The polar desert is as dry as the Sahara; it receives less than ten inches of precipitation each year. Deserts are, by definition, largely deserted. The interior of the Greenland icecap is as empty—as devoid of life—as any spot on the planet.

In the Arctic Ocean the contrast between summer and winter is reflected in the water's surface. For a few weeks of summer the edge of the pack ice retreats poleward and large areas of open water host an abundance of life, including millions of seabirds. In autumn, as the temperature of the saltwater drops to 28° F, tiny ice crystals form at the ocean's surface, giving the water a greasy appearance. As the air temperature falls a skin of flexible ice covers the sea, a layer only an inch or two thick. Waves that ripple the remaining open water are subdued by the ice but can still tear the sheets into fragments. Floating, jostling, and splashing one another, the tiny, flat ice islands acquire raised edges and rounded outlines. They resemble overturned Frisbees. These albino lily pads, these frozen flap-jacks, are known as pancake ice.

Eventually, when the air temperature drops well below zero, the entire ocean surface freezes to a depth of ten to twelve feet. Multiyear ice that survived the summer with only super-ficial melting is rafted with new floes in a jigsaw puzzle that covers thousands of square miles. Circumpolar winds push and drag at the ice. The sheets split apart, exposing the black water that lurks silently beneath. These water-filled cracks are called *leads*. In winter the liquid is ephemeral: within hours the ice has reclaimed the spot and frozen over the opening, forming an opaque cataract that covers the ocean's dark eye. It is this white covering that makes the Arctic so cold. It reflects more than 70 percent of the sun's light and heat back into space. The icepack also functions as a gigantic lid, covering the sea and preventing the sun's rays from warming the water, or the ocean from warming the air.

The ice moves in a clockwise drift around the Pole. At various times in the past this pattern has been documented by ships frozen in the ice, riding as passengers on the immense turntable at the top of the globe. From 1893 to 1896 Fridtjof Nansen's *Fram*, deliberately frozen into the icepack as an oceanographic experiment, drifted from Siberia to the Greenland Sea. Earlier the ship *Jeanette*, caught in the ice in 1881 north of Russia's Lena River delta while seeking a Northwest Passage, emerged in pieces aboard drifting floes off the southwestern coast of Greenland.

Ice that makes this circuit is the true *polar pack*. Ice that remains frozen to the shoreline or grounded on the seafloor is termed *fast ice*. In between, where massive frozen walls and icy pinnacles grind past one another in an awesome display of nature's power, is the *shear zone*.

As the flat sheets of ice crunch into adjacent floes, titanic forces crumple their edges into *pressure ridges*, collision bound-aries where jumbled ice rubble is fused into elongated mounds with deep roots that reach downward like the keels of ships. The superstructures of pressure ridges rise twenty, thirty, forty, or more feet above the frozen surface. The keels extend down even deeper. In the arctic icepack in winter, the flat surface of the ice cover is unrelenting: pressure ridges are a relief to the eye, offering the only reprieve from flatness and whiteness. To surveyors and explorers, pressure ridges are adversaries to be conquered. To anyone on the ice, pressure ridges mean danger: behind any one of them, unheard and unseen, polar bears may pace the snow-covered surface.

The debris field of a high pressure ridge is an almost impenetrable pile of blocks, each slab tens of feet across, stacked in chaotic disorder, strewn like a giant handful of pale dominoes. Its beauty depends on whether you admire it from afar or struggle from one side of it to the other, dragging a sledge laden with two hundred pounds of supplies.

In the spring leads open again, and the cycle of arctic life begins anew. Whales migrate north as soon as they find enough leads to permit them to surface and breathe, for as mammals they are prisoners of the air. Seals can winter in the Arctic, because they use the claws on their front flippers to scrape breathing holes from beneath the ice, but whales must find open leads. Even the narwhal, the unicorn of the sea, who uses his ivory tusk to fight for females, doesn't break ice with it.

As the sun returns, meltwater lakes form atop the floes, fresher than seawater, because salt was largely excluded from the ice during the fall freeze. On land the spring thaw brings forth profuse vegetation. Hundreds of species of flowering plants and thousands of kinds of mosses and lichens thrive even on the northernmost land areas. New-formed lakes are home to millions of insects, including enough mosquitoes to daunt even the hardiest explorers.

What never thaws in the Arctic is permafrost, permanently frozen soil that lies just a few inches below the surface and extends over a thousand feet down. The earth freezes from the top down and thaws only at depths where the planet's interior is warmer than the freezing point of water. Permafrost, more than frigid air temperatures, makes arctic life difficult for modern man. From Eskimo igloos, wonderfully insulated by the air trapped in the snow, to modern structures with freezer doors to keep the cold out, not in, man's engineering creations have allowed him to thrive in extreme cold. What he can't do well, however, is dig into, drill through, or build on permafrost. Only since the discovery and development of the Prudhoe Bay oil fields have engineers found ways to keep deep structures warm and the surrounding permafrost cold at the same time.

Permafrost-frozen plumbing is no joke. I have been acutely embarrassed as a guest at an arctic radar installation when I've watched the contents of the toilet rise and overflow the bowl because of a frozen line that everyone but me had been warned about. Above-ground plumbing and heating ducts, oil pipelines, and other necessities of civilized life are a consequence of the permafrost and must seem strange complications to older Eskimos. They remember that the only concern with frozen ground was burial of the dead (which even today must often be delayed until spring). Eskimos use the permafrost to their advantage, as a deep freeze for storing seal and whale meat through the warmer months.

Permafrost is harder than many rocks: in its way, it *is* a rock. All the solid forms of water are rocks. Geologists will tell you that snow is a sediment; compacted snow, a sedimentary rock. Because the snow and ice of a glacier flow and recrystallize, glacial ice is a metamorphic rock. Sea ice and pond ice are igneous rocks, because they form by the cooling of a molten liquid. It seems odd to think of water—such a familiar, everyday substance—as progenitor of an igneous rock. The polar territories play such games with our senses, toy with our temperate experiences, and confuse our concepts based on a warmer world.

The northern regions, cold as they are, are recovering from a much colder time. Although some parts of Alaska and Siberia were never covered by glaciers during the four great Pleistocene ice ages, many of the northern lands were buried by ice one, two, or even three miles thick. As the great continental ice sheets melted, sea level rose, flooding coastal areas worldwide. Drowned shorelines are common in temperate and tropical regions. Northern shorelines, however, notable for their ice-gouged fjords, are rising out of the sea. Why this gigantic uplift of glaciated terrains?

Geologists speak of *isostatic rebound*, the recovery of huge continental areas from having sunk into the earth's crust, pushed down by the weight of all that ice. If you unload heavy cargo from a ship, the hull floats higher in the water. The continents, relieved of their icy burden some ten to fifteen thousand years ago, are still rising, still floating higher. Beaches that once graced the shoreline now hang suspended on the walls of fjords, ten, fifty, or a hundred feet above the water.

Glacial evidence is everywhere in the Arctic. The ground is covered with ice-dropped stones, with outwash sands from glacial streams, and with debris plucked from surrounding hills and crushed to flourlike fineness by relentless grinding at the base of the ice sheets. The sculptured surface left behind recalls the ice ages as a not-so-distant memory.

Crossing this terrain is difficult in winter, almost impossible in summer, except in areas of open water where boats can maneuver. When snow covers the land, traveling is done by dogsled or snowmobile—there are no roads through most of the arctic regions. Except in sporting events, however, dogsleds are rare today in the Arctic, although in Greenland and parts of Canada dogs are still used for winter transportation along the coast. Snowmobiles have their uses, but something important has been lost with the disappearance of dog teams from the north country. With dependence on gasoline comes the danger of being caught in a blizzard without it.

Dogs had many uses. Cut free from their sled traces, they could encircle a bear and hold him until the hunter arrived. They could provide companionship, and they lifted the hunter's spirits with their voices on the trek. Dogs could even be used as food by desperate nomads in an unforgiving world. The snowmobile offers none of these benefits; it is a cold, impersonal mass of steel and plastic, fast and efficient when it's running right, cantankerous and useless when it's not.

When a snowmobile engine snarls, bears usually turn and run. When the machine sits quietly in the snow, however, Nanook may investigate. Larry Brooks, an engineer with years of arctic experience, tells of an expedition to study multiyear ice floes in the Chukchi Sea west of Point Barrow, Alaska. Working from the icebreaker *Polar Sea*, the scientific party had armed

Coast Guard enlisted men posted on bear watch. "We had bears ambling through there a lot that time of year," Brooks reports, matter-of-factly. "While we were laying out ice-survey stakes, one walked into the middle of our operation. We retreated to the safety of the ship. The bear investigated most of our equipment, sniffed the marker flags, knocked a few of them down, and sauntered over to our snowmobile. He sniffed about the snow machine for a minute, and then became fascinated by its leather seat. He ripped off the seat cover and ate it. The bear walked a few yards, spit up the remains of the cover, and ambled off. I guess if it wasn't made out of seal hide, it wasn't worth eating."

Traveling beyond snowmobile range across the vast frozen landscape means flying with a special breed of aviator. In the Arctic, especially, the pilot's creed—"There are old pilots and bold pilots, but there are no old, bold pilots"—acquires a deadly seriousness. Any pilot who is equally at home landing a Twin Otter on frozen sea ice or a Hercules C-130 on a gravel beach is someone I'd trust to fly me anywhere. These are men I've seen running, screaming, and laughing like maniacs in blue-lipped nakedness through frigid waterfalls that tumble directly off the glaciers. They could out-macho Indiana Jones, but they're meticulous fliers, checking everything twice, leaving nothing to chance. The history of polar exploration is filled with grim tales of men who took chances, of expeditions ill prepared, of leaders overzealous in the pursuit of unattainable goals. The Arctic doesn't allow many mistakes.

If you want to know about bears, ask an arctic pilot. He's seen more bears and bear tracks than anyone on the ice or on board a ship. He'll have stories to tell. "I never leave the chopper," a helicopter pilot told me, "while the scientists are on the ice and there's a bear nearby. And I always keep the rotor turning."

More than once he's had researchers diving into his aircraft's open door with a bear in pursuit. "One time, I thought we'd had it. The bear followed the men to the helo and reached up as we were taking off—like he wanted to grab the skid under my feet. When we lifted off, he was sure surprised. With one paw in the air, it looked like he was waving good-bye."

Nonchalant arctic fliers seem to relish their passengers' discomfort. I had my first such encounter on the way to Greenland, flying up Canada's northeastern shoreline. I knew we were in for an exciting landing when the crew chief passed cheerily among us, saying, "Gentlemen, you may wish to loosen any tight clothing and remove sharp objects from your pockets"—words designed to inspire confidence in white-knuckle passengers. The huge C-130 lumbered toward a stretch of beach on Baffin Island's eastern shore where a runway had been bulldozed smooth and outlined with 55-gallon drums—the ubiquitous totem of "civilized" man in the Arctic. Over the end of the runway, while we were still several feet in the air, the pilot reversed the pitch on the propeller blades. We fell like an immense rock. Our wheels plowed a furrow over a foot deep in the soft beach—the 'dozer had to smooth the sand again before we could take off. "Exact minimum length," the pilot said with considerable pride, relishing our anxious expressions. "We'll be off again as soon as I work up my nerve."

When I stepped out of the airplane, leaving a warm, familiar, high-tech world for the cold, alien, untamed habitat of the white bear, the Arctic hit me with a frontal assault on the senses. Brilliant sunlight caromed off blue-white ice and sprang in rainbow colors from a meadow full of blossoms. On other days the light seeped through a fog of such palpable density that I marveled at the pilot's skill in bringing the plane safely to earth.

In winter the arctic shock to the senses is felt rather than seen. Wind rips at my clothing and hammers hair across my face. The cold seeks entry through the slightest chink in my insulating armor. Like a knight preparing for battle, I check every detail, then check it again. I dash in street shoes, carrying my boots, to the lee of a Quonset hut—or forget the storm flap that covers my parka zipper—and I'm reminded of my folly in the first seconds of exposure. The enemy is the cold, and I underestimate it at my peril.

The most powerful sense, capable of stirring the deepest memories, is smell. It's also the hardest to put into words. The smell of the Arctic depends, like so many other sensations, on the season. Unfortunately, most visitors never get sufficiently far from the trappings of civilization to experience the smell of the

Arctic. They'll tell you the overriding scent of the north country is the stink of diesel exhaust—the effusion from countless generators, Sno-Cats, heavy trucks, drilling rigs, and ships' engines. Getting away from such contaminants may be as difficult as a day's hike or as simple as a few steps to windward.

Winter in the polar icepack, or on the Greenland icecap, brings an almost total absence of smell. Wrapped in multiple layers, hoods, face masks, and scarves, I've been far more aware of my own body odors than of any external scents. There are only two worlds that matter in the Arctic—inside and outside. This concept is portable: there's a very strong sense when cocooned in cold-weather gear that I'm sealed in a cozy room, and it's far more comfortable—and safer—to keep my nose "in here with me" than "out there." Because my nose is so confined, so swathed in clothing, the odor of the Arctic mimics the wintertime smell of elementary school classrooms: it's the odor of wet wool. However, icepack scents exist for those attuned to them—polar bears and Eskimo hunters are adept at sniffing out the *aglus*, or breathing holes, of seals (male seals, in particular, emit a strong, unpleasant odor)—but overall the ice is the nearest approximation on earth to an absolutely odorless environment.

Summer in the Arctic brings smells of freshly thawed earth, of flowers, of swamp muck, of all the refuse and sewage strewn about native villages during the cold months. Archaeologists excavating ancient Eskimo sites suffer the odors of innumerable dog droppings, thawing for the first time in a thousand years. In Greenland near villages the summer odors are overwhelmed by the absolutely indescribable stench of fish, sun dried on wooden frames set high so the dogs can't get to the meat. Man's best friend must be content with the drippings that ooze from the oily split fish and fall to the ground below. Arctic travelers with a refined sense of smell are advised to visit during the colder months.

More immediate than smell is the sense of sound. Sound in the Arctic echoes a song title: it's the sound of silence. There are, to be sure, the cries of birds in summer, the rumble of icebergs calving from the fronts of glaciers, the shriek of the wind, the gurgle of waves against the small icebergs known as growlers, and the continuous cracks and groans from the shifting icepack, but the silence of the Arctic is what finally gives dimension to its immensity.

If you get far enough from man's engines, generators, and humming wires, the silence is loud enough to be heard—a physical impossibility: something from nothing. In summer the blue sky stretches endlessly overhead, the sun gilds every pinnacle, and the absence of sound brings peace. In winter all contrasts are studies in black and white, and the dry sounds echo the absence of color. Like the temperature, they are more harsh, more threatening, even in their silence. Nanook himself is silent. Silent as he comes, silent in his stalk. Silence is the sound of death approaching.

One sound in the Arctic that is, above all, reassuring is the whup-up-up-up of a helicopter returning to pick up our survey crew stranded ashore for several days by bad weather. The radio crackles to life. "I can make out the ridge you're camped on," the pilot calls, "but I can't see you. Try lighting a flare." A moment later the fire-spitting tube ignites. I wave it overhead, making giant sweeps. The pilot spots a moving, bright orange dot against the dark rocks. A smoke plume trails off downwind, to help him gauge the breezes at his landing site. "Tallyho!" the radio squawks, and the surveyors smile, the anxiety of our situation a thing of the past. No C rations tonight; we'll get a real meal aboard ship, followed by a hot shower and a soft mattress.

A friend who travels extensively by dogsled, far removed from the noises that most of us find familiar, reports satisfaction at becoming attuned to the rhythms of the Arctic: subtle changes in the wind's intensity, the exultant hiss of sled runners over smooth ice, the pleasing crunch of boots in the snow.

The Arctic is a place of isolation: it has been called, with good reason, "the lonely land." Summer loneliness is pleasant, but winter isolation brings normal minds to the brink of insanity. In the arctic storm known as a whiteout, a man is as completely alone with himself as he will ever be: no sight, no smell, no sound—nothing, absolutely nothing, beyond the length of his mittened hand. Diffuse sunlight seeps through, seeming to come from all directions at once. No reference points. No shadows. No depth perception. Only in such a setting, divorced from reality, when all the senses stretch to desperate limits but are soon exhausted by the effort—each, in turn, sensing nothing—do you really *feel* the Arctic.

Written descriptions of science often seem dry and sterile—you'd think the research must have performed itself, without human interference. In the Arctic that's just not true. So much effort is expended every field day in satisfying basic human needs that the actual time devoted to science can be astonishingly small. *Food* assumes a high priority. Rations are increased to gluttonous proportions north of the Arctic Circle, because the body needs more calories to fuel its internal furnace. *Clothing* attains a monumental importance that it never acquires back in the southern world. Not fashion but function. Parkas, coveralls, sweaters, hoods, face masks, insulated long johns, wool socks, and inflatable "bunny boots" are carefully inspected for even the slightest gap that will allow entry of the cold air. Frostbite is a very real enemy.

Arctic experiences are filed away as distinct memories, their sharp edges blurred little by the passage of time. The feeling of the summer-soft tundra sucking at my boots. Sharp stilettos of ice stabbing skyward on the tops of glaciers between depressions where dark specks of dust had melted their way into the surface—a hand-slashing menace. Majestic vistas: hundreds of miles containing absolutely no sign of human passage. The shared agony of my partner's frostbitten eyeballs. My feeling of vulnerability, set ashore with only a .45 pistol for protection. My first meeting with Greenland kayakers, paddling their sleek sealskin boats, clad in trousers sewn from polar bear fur. (It was at that moment that this book was conceived, though I didn't know it for years to come.) The incongruity of lifeboat drills on a ship surrounded by a frozen ocean. Meltwater streams flowing beneath glaciers, carving blue ice caves with hidden waterfalls. My wonder at watching a 727 jet land on top of the sea, on a runway bulldozed smooth atop an ice floe. And more vivid, more painful than all the others, the cold. Biting, stinging, slashing cold. Creeping, seeping cold. Deadly cold.

With the cold, and magnifying it to deadly dimensions, comes the wind. Wind so forceful that it wrenches measuring instruments off their mountings. Wind that pushed a nineteenth-century scientist back more than twenty times as he tried to crawl on hands and knees toward an observation hut atop an icy ridge. Wind that snatched away a twentieth-century meteorologist who became disoriented in a blizzard. He was staggering in near-zero visibility from one building to another nearby: his companions found his body weeks later, blown several miles away across the frozen surface.

Finally, the Arctic is a place of emptiness. In summer daylight with all its attendant colors, the open space is exhilarating. North country light brings forth—especially from photographers—descriptions rare in other settings: fabled, dazzling, unreal, biblical. In winter the darkness conceals the vistas but magnifies the emptiness. Every building, every rock, every snowbank assumes a grayish purple identity. Mercury-vapor lights dispel the gloom but enhance the ghostly color. Like stars come to earth, they perch atop tall poles—the only vertical features in the horizontal arctic landscape—and cast cones of blue-white light on the snow-swept scene below. One of the best descriptions of an arctic winter was penned by survivors of the Hall Expedition of 1871: "The face of the earth was in the last degree bleak and desolate."

Not everyone shares this grim view of northern winters though. Farley Mowat, who has a gift for description that transports you directly into the arctic scene, has written, "The northern people are happy when snow lies heavy on the land. They welcome the first snow in autumn, and often regret its passing in the spring. Snow is their friend. Without it they would have perished or—almost worse from their point of view—they would long since have been driven south to join us in our frenetic rush to wherever it is that we are bound."

Eskimos, Inuit, Greenlanders, Lapps, and all the northern peoples of Eurasia learned long ago that they can survive, and even prosper, in the arctic winter. They look forward to the coming of the cold, because it hardens the spongy earth and makes overland travel possible. After freeze-up the noxious clouds of mosquitoes no longer swarm about arms and faces.

Light summer clothes made in Taiwan or Korea are discarded in favor of warm parkas made of caribou hide or trousers sewn with great skill from polar bear skin. Far from fearing the cold, the people of the Arctic are nourished by it. They thrive in the midst of ice and snow.

I write these words from the warmth of a temperate office. While I enjoy the changing colors of autumn, I know that in the treeless Arctic the rhythms of change are more intense but the colors are all variants of one: white. At the transmitting station that marked my introduction to the arctic world, the sun has already disappeared below the horizon. Its cheering rays won't be seen again for more than a hundred days. The huge Newfoundland dog lies curled beneath the building, wrapped in a deepening blanket of snow that shelters him from the icy blast of the polar winds.

And in the gathering gloom, in the pack ice now frozen into solid sheets, there are bears. Hundreds of bears. Thousands of bears. Masters of darkness. White ghosts in the black night. No human, nothing in nature, challenges their supremacy: in the darkness of winter, the ice belongs to Nanook.

THREE

White Bears
in a White World

Nanook is a marine mammal, more at home in the frigid waters of the Arctic Ocean than he is on dry land. Swimming with powerful webbed, paddlelike forepaws for propulsion, and trailing his hind legs as steering rudders, a polar bear can swim tirelessly all day at a steady pace of six miles an hour. Polar bears have been spotted swimming several hundred miles from the nearest land or ice floe. They can apparently swim for days without hauling out to rest.

Nanook appears effortless in the water. The bear shape cuts through the sea like the bow of a ship. Compared with other bears, polar bears are elongate, with stocky bodies behind their long necks and no humps at the shoulders. They have long, bowed forelegs that join with no chest between them. Seen from above or from the side, a bear's profile is a wedge, tapered toward the head, which appears undersized compared with the body. This shape is highly efficient in the water. It has an additional advantage: it makes an approaching bear less visible to his prey. The long neck extends the head well forward of the shoulders. This positions the nose—Nanook's primary detection system—where it can sweep from side to side and interpret faint scents borne on the arctic wind. This architecture also gets the bear's huge canine teeth well out in front of his body, so they can grasp a seal through its breathing hole, several feet deep in the ice and snow. The wedge shape also makes a bear stable on his hind legs. The standing position that zoo visitors find so comical is a behavioral adaptation that allows the bear a better view and scent in his natural setting.

Polar bears are the largest predators that stalk the earth. Adult males average about 1,000 pounds, females, half that weight, although pregnant females with well-developed fat reserves tip the scales at 1,100 pounds. Large, dominant males exceed 1,500 pounds. A male bear tagged and released by Canadian researchers weighed almost 2,000 pounds. One male, stuffed and on display in the Anchorage air terminal, is reported to have weighed over 2,200 pounds when killed (but this figure is disputed by bear experts). This bear stands just over eleven feet tall, dwarfing huge oil-rig roughnecks who trudge past it on their way to jobs at Prudhoe Bay.

When walking on all fours, Nanook is the size and weight of a small truck; when he stands on two legs, he seems to reach the sky. The claws of a large male can rake almost fourteen feet overhead. If he wished Nanook could slap a giraffe in the face. In the bear family only grizzlies are larger, but they are omnivores; they eat almost everything. This leaves Nanook supreme, at the top of the heap, largest of the land-dwelling meat eaters, or carnivores. Grizzlies range freely through parts of the Arctic but appear to avoid the coastline. Possibly even the mighty grizzly bear fears Nanook.

Nanook's scientific name, *Ursus maritimus*, means simply "maritime bear." For a short period in the middle of this century, the polar bear was considered sufficiently distinct from other bears of the genus *Ursus* to be given his own separate identity: *Thalarctos maritimus*. In recent years, however, he has regained the name *Ursus* because—at least in captivity— polar bears can interbreed with other *Ursus* bears and produce fertile offspring. Such hybrid cubs show many characteristics of their polar bear parent, including body and head shape, a white coat at birth, and good swimming abilities. Some hybrids' coats darken as they mature. The female offspring of such unions have been successfully crossbred back to polar bears, demonstrating both the viability of the hybrid and the close relationship of the two *Ursus* parent species.

A male bear is a *boar*; a female bear, a *sow*—horribly inelegant labels for creatures of such power and majesty. Most people who encounter them describe polar bears as simply bears and she-bears, or just male and female. Yet to most of us in the Arctic, all polar bears seem compellingly male. Thus when I write of the generic polar bear, I write of Nanook and describe *his* shaggy coat, *his* actions, or *his* food, knowing full well that I slight over half the world's polar bear population. Even so, *anything* that outweighs me by more than five to one seems like it ought to be male.

N anook is a creature of surprises. Confounding first impressions, a polar bear reveals his secrets gradually. First, a polar bear's fur is not white (nor even pale yellow, as many bears appear) but *transparent*. Second, the hairs of his coat aren't solid but rather *hollow*. Third (and perhaps most surprising), beneath his white-clear coat, the bear's skin is *black*. Fourth, living in and on the ice-choked waters of the Arctic Ocean, Nanook has the problem not so much of keeping warm in his frigid world but of *overheating*.

These four interwoven surprises form part of the polar bear's superb adaptation to the most hostile physical environment on earth. A bear must contend with near-freezing seawater, with ice and snow, and with an air temperature range of over 150° F, spread equally above and below zero. In addition, his food supply is uncertain from day to day, depending on ice conditions. The miracle is that Nanook not only survives in such extremes but prospers.

The bear's strategy for coping with this environment begins beneath his skin. Between skin and muscle is the *subcutaneous* layer. In the polar bear a layer of insulating subcutaneous fat, distributed across the back and surrounding the broad rump, stores food during times of poor hunting, adds buoyancy in the water, and provides a very effective thermal blanket. The bear's blubber insulates him so well from his surroundings that water may freeze solid in his fur, while beneath his frosty shell he remains comfortable. The layer of fat, often three to four inches thick, is capped by Nanook's dark skin. From the hide grow transparent hairs two to six inches long (though much longer at the backs of his legs). His hair has no insulating value in the sea, but the longest guard hairs shed water when the bear shakes, dog fashion, upon emerging onto the ice.

In an evolutionary adaptation as old as the Ice Age, Nanook uses a principle of the Electronic Age. To transmit sunlight from his outer fur to his dark skin, where its warmth can be absorbed, the bear employs highly sophisticated fiber-optics technology. Images from scanning electron microscopes, which magnify bear hair several thousand times, reveal an empty core in the center of each strand. The inner walls of this central tube are rough. Like the etched surface of frosted glass, they appear white because they reflect and scatter light that the clear hair has permitted to enter the long cavity. Each hair functions as a light trap, a conduit that takes the sun's rays—which have traveled 93 million miles to get to the bear's outer coat—the last few inches to his dark skin.

This energy-capturing system is more efficient than anything human engineers have been able to assemble. A very good man-made solar energy system changes about 40 percent of the sun's radiation into heat. Nanook's hair is 95 percent effective. Scientists are now using polar bear fur as a pattern for designing solar devices. Researchers at Northeastern University have shown that by adding hairlike fibers to flat-plate collectors they can increase the efficiency of their system by 50 percent. The designer also gained another advantage; unlike flat plates, which must turn mechanically to track the sun, a hairy collector is independent of sun angle. The fur light pipes will trap sunshine coming from any direction.

Polar bears are sun worshipers. In northern Manitoba during the waning days of autumn, I watched white bears bask in the last warm rays of the sun. They savored the light; they luxuriated in the warmth. Stretching languorously, yawning, sprawling on the ground, they seemed aware that the moment would soon pass. Like bearskin rugs before a fire, they absorbed the heat and relished its last hour. The cold was coming.

A truly white bear would reflect the sun's energy and not be warmed. A bear covered with transparent light guides, however, wears a portable greenhouse. His coat pulls warmth from one of the coldest places on earth—actually, warmth that is not of this world at all—and pipes it more efficiently than steam heat to a skin capable of absorbing it.

Nanook's greenhouse, is, at times, literally green. In a paper with an eye-catching title, "The Greening of Polar Bears in Zoos," scientists R. A. Lerwin and P. T. Robinson described the appearance of healthy green bears. Zookeepers had interpreted the discoloration of their fur as algae growing on the surface of the bears' coats, but microscopic examination revealed that the algae were thriving inside the hollow centers of the stiff guard hairs that comprise the animals' outer coats. The freshwater blue-green algae had apparently entered the *medullae*, or central cavities, through short tubes leading from the center of each hair to its outer surface. The growth didn't seem to harm the bears in any way—perhaps it even improved their camouflage for the leafy world surrounding their zoo abodes.

Researchers tracking polar bears find them difficult to see against a background of ice and snow. Various attempts have been made to photograph them with infrared film, on the theory that living creatures give off heat and should show up against a cold background. This technique works well in more temperate locations, but in the Arctic both seals and bears are so well insulated that their exterior temperatures are as cold as their surroundings. They don't show up in infrared photos. Another attempt, at the other end of the visible spectrum, produced better results. Ultraviolet photos, researchers surmised, might show animals that absorb UV radiation against a background that reflects it. The scientists were right. Ultraviolet photos show black polar bears against a white backdrop. Polar bear skin is, in fact, one of nature's most efficient UV absorbers. Ultraviolet light penetrates clouds, so Nanook's efficient solar collection system works even on overcast days. Solar engineers could learn a lot from the king of the Arctic.

Beneath his skin a polar bear maintains a temperature of 98.6° F, as do most mammals, humans included. The difference between a bear's internal temperature and the temperature of his skin can be well over 75° F. The blubber blanket is highly effective at keeping the cold out. Unfortunately for an active bear, it also keeps the heat in. A major problem, even in the frigid Arctic, is getting rid of excess heat. A polar bear loses heat primarily through the pads on his feet (although these are surrounded by fur, which provides traction on ice), the tissue surrounding his claws, the short-furred areas of his face, his ears and nose, his mouth (by panting like a dog), the insides of his hind legs, and his shoulders. Immediately behind his shoulders, in the center of the bear's back, is a special radiator: several square feet of muscle and a network of blood vessels release excess heat, particularly during the warm summer months.

Other adaptations to the arctic world include the bear's short, furry ears and tail, well supplied with warming blood vessels; his relatively short, stocky legs (compared with those of other bears); and his large body size, which gives the low ratio of surface area to body mass that is essential to conserving heat. All these special means of dealing with the cold are lumped under a biological category with a daunting label: *thermoregulation.* All warm-blooded creatures have thermoregulation systems or thermoregulatory behavior, but the demands of Nanook's physical environment are extreme and call for extreme responses. According to physiologists, a polar bear's insulation combines the best features of the blubber of sleek-skinned marine mammals and the fur of the land dwellers.

Thermoregulation is a delicate art: an animal must carefully balance food intake and energy expenditure. Studies of polar bear physiology show that *Ursus maritimus* needs more than twice as much energy as most mammals to move at a particular speed; this requirement may be a consequence of his massive build. Walking bears triple their resting heart rates. Getting around in the Arctic requires an effort, and such work uses precious energy. A polar bear compensates by lying around a lot and hunting by waiting, motionless, for his seal dinner to come to him. Nanook is most efficient when doing nothing at all.

A bear builds his insulating layer of fat by eating the blubber of seals. Like firewood that you cut with your own saw, often called the wood that warms you twice, the fat that keeps the seal snug when immersed in frigid seawater is swallowed, digested, and reprocessed to warm Nanook. A diet of fat provides a particularly effective source of heat, because fat metabolizes to produce only energy, water, and carbon dioxide. There are no other waste products from pure fat that require excretion. This means better conservation of body heat, because wastes stored in the body absorb heat, which is lost when they pass outside. Thus, the sun's warmth absorbed through the skin is passive heat that only augments a bear's main heating furnace, stoked by the metabolism of seal blubber. Sunlight in the Arctic is ephemeral, but fat can be stored. The sun shines on a bear when he needs it least—when his environment is above freezing—and not at all during the coldest winter months. A polar bear may have to live for half a year without a meal during the ice-free season, when he can't hunt effectively. Accumulating a thick reserve of blubber is *the* essential activity of late summer and early fall for pregnant females, who spend the winter months curled deep in a snow den and may go eight months without food.

The diet of polar bears consists almost exclusively of the skin and blubber of ringed seals (*Phoca hispida*). Polar bears also eat, when they chance on them, bearded seals (*Erignathus barbatus*), harp seals (*Pagophilus groenlandicus*), and hooded seals (*Cystophora cristata*). Bears prefer suckling seal pups, but they also eat subadult and full-grown seals after the spring seal birthing season. With a stomach capacity of 150 pounds, Nanook could, if he wished, eat an entire seal at one sitting, but after gobbling the blubber, he usually leaves the rest of the carcass behind. Scientists who study the nutritional requirements of arctic animals report that one seal provides a bear with energy for eleven days. Such a belly store is important in a world where the next meal is uncertain and depends on the bear's hunting skill, the shifting of the icepack, and the subice wanderings of the seals.

Nanook has some variety in his diet and has been known to eat young walrus; fish; foxes; stranded dead whales; small whales, such as belugas, that he can kill; mussels; seabirds; eggs; and seaweed. On land polar bears occasionally eat berries, grass, musk-oxen, caribou, flightless molting geese, rodents, or whatever culinary treasures present themselves at human garbage dumps. Overall, though, Nanook dines almost exclusively on seals, making him the northernmost carnivore in the world.

Competing for that title is the arctic fox (*Alopex lagopus*). Foxes are found wherever polar bears wander. They wait impatiently for a chance to snatch scraps of seal meat after the bears eat the blubber. Bears usually tolerate the foxes' boldness but can grow impatient themselves, whirling to bellow a throaty warning or lashing out with massive paws. An arctic fox, however, depends for its winter survival on the white bear's leavings and won't be dissuaded. In summer there are plenty of hares, lemmings, and birds, but during the cold months food is scarce. In desperate times the foxes survive by eating the bears' droppings.

Surveying glaciers on the coast of Greenland, I was approached one summer day by an arctic fox, superbly camouflaged in a coat of gray fur. He was surrounded by boulders dropped centuries ago by melting glaciers—rocks of exactly the same matte gray finish. Creeping up on me, the little fox was there—and then he wasn't. I spotted him again. Gone. Only after my eye and brain adjusted to his camouflage did I see that he was there all the time. He was so well disguised, so boulderlike when he stood still, that only in the quick blur of motion was he visible at all. Gray on gray, with two glistening black eyes. The same creatures in winter strut proudly in sleek, fluffy white coats so thick that the animals look more than twice as large as summer foxes. In the dark winter months, when their entire world is snow covered, the foxes are whiter than bears and, in their own way, just as majestic. With bushy tails and thick ruff collars, they gleam, whiter than white, out of the darkness when man's lights probe the night. And, as in summer, their black eyes shine with intelligent expression.

Unlike the foxes—or the arctic hare, lemmings, weasels, ptarmigan, or other animals of the North that change color with the seasons—Nanook keeps his white coat, his magnificent pelage, the year round. Hunting in the summer involves stalking seals on floating ice or approaching through the water between white floes, so a snowy covering is still an advantage during the warmer months. Nanook owes much of his regal appearance, and his universal appeal, to his white-robed dignity. Like the powdered wig of an English magistrate, the beautiful white fur makes Nanook seem larger than life. Dazzling blue-white, or slightly yellow-brown, he is a supreme being, his dramatic appearance only enhanced by three breaks in the seamless pattern: two dark eyes and an ebony nose. Many authors have written that a polar bear is aware of his black nose and will cover it with a white paw while hunting seals, to make the snowy camouflage complete. Modern bear observers, however, have never seen this behavior and think it unlikely.

Other popular images of polar bears are also mistaken. Glass sculptors show Nanook fishing, scooping salmon like other bears. Not so. Polar bears do eat fish on occasion, but most often they scavenge dead, floating fish rather than catch their own. The same glass artisans are fond of carving icebergs of towering crystal, complete with etched or gilded bears. I have seen thousands of genuine icebergs drifting leisurely along the coasts of Greenland and Canada but never one with a furry white passenger. Others have reported seeing bears climb aboard icebergs, but this is undoubtedly rare behavior. (An explorer once surprised a pair of polar bears mating in a cave, high up the side of an iceberg. He feared the male bear might attack, but Nanook seemed interested only in romance.) Bears do ride flat floes of sea ice—frozen seawater. These slabs float low in the water, with a freeboard of only a few feet. A bear can easily scramble aboard them. In contrast, icebergs calve in thundering splendor from the floating tongues of thick glaciers and have vertical faces that often rise more than a hundred feet above the water. Although these steep sides moderate somewhat as bergs melt, crack, or roll over, icebergs are difficult to board, even for men with crampons and ice axes leaping from inflatable boats or large ships. Nanook's claws and stiff-haired, non-skid footpads might help, but he'd have to start submerged, and there is little incentive for him to try. His ability to jump from the water, though, is prodigious, and many a seal's life has ended with a terrifying final vision of a bear leaping seven to eight feet into the air from a swimming start.

Where seals are plentiful at the edges of the ice, bears thrive.

If the seal population dwindles, life for Nanook becomes a precarious struggle. If seal hunting is good, a bear may live twenty or thirty years. Longevity in the wild is hard to estimate, but some captured bears have been twenty-five years old. In captivity they live even longer: a bear in England's Chester Zoo lived to be forty-one. The age of an individual bear is revealed by his teeth. New layers are added every year to each tooth's *cementum*—the thin zone surrounding the tooth's roots. When a tooth is removed from an anesthetized bear, it is taken to the laboratory and sliced with a diamond-impregnated saw. The cut surface, when polished, reveals layers. Like the rings of a tree stump, these *annuli*, or growth bands, are concentric. Also like tree rings, they tell a story. A bear carries his history in his mouth. Unfortunately for researchers, the history of a polar bear is more dimly written than the stories of other bears, because the polar bear's annuli are less distinct. Determining Nanook's exact age is more art than science.

All bears have feet designed for *plantigrade* walking, meaning they put their feet down flat on the ground, like humans. Most other large creatures (hoofed animals, dogs, and even elephants) walk on their toes. Plantigrade walkers stand flat-footed. The plantigrade stance makes it easy for bears to stand upright. Polar bears often rise on their hind legs and occasionally even walk short distances on two feet. Their immense paws—the front feet are up to twelve inches across, the hind feet slightly smaller—have five toes, ending in formidable claws two to three inches long. Behind the claws are black leathery pads with white fur between them. These pads are well supplied with blood vessels and form an important part of the bear's thermoregulation system. Nanook must, after all, keep his feet from freezing when walking on snow and ice, yet he must also conserve heat. It's a delicate balance. A bear's feet provide a multipurpose tool kit. In addition to their role as heat exchangers, they are paddles for swimming, shovels for scooping snow, axes for chopping holes in the ice, and daggers for killing.

How does a bear walk across smooth ice without slipping? Scientists from a British medical panel on accident prevention asked that question, citing statistics suggesting that slipping is the most frequent cause of human injuries requiring a doctor's treatment. The investigators suggested designs for non-skid shoe soles based on polar bear footpads. Examining the bottoms of Nanook's feet, the scientists found them densely covered with protrusions, or *papillae* (Latin for nipples), each about a millimeter across. These fingerlike bumps give the soft, flexible footpad the texture of coarse sandpaper. Using the high magnification of a scanning electron microscope, the researchers also discovered small circular depressions on the soles of polar bear feet. The role played by these minute pits is uncertain, but their resemblance to the suction-cup treads on basketball shoes is compelling. The investigators concluded that a barefoot bear foot, with rough-surfaced pliable pads, offers an excellent grip on rough ice and the best possible grip on smooth ice.

A bear places his foot flat on the ice, ensuring good contact and reducing the tendency to slip. When climbing he can also rock his foot forward to dig in his claws like a mountaineer's crampons. The bear's claws deserve the nickname given to such spikes: mountain climbers call them foot fangs.

Polar bears walk with a shuffling gait that keeps their body weight spread over the ice, an advantage when the frozen surface is only inches thick and barely supports them without breaking. When bears run, they pace like thoroughbreds, with a grace all their own (though no one is likely to confuse the two). The legs on one side move together; then the legs on the other side. As a healthy, fat bear runs, insulating blubber ripples beneath his coat and shaggy waves surge across his back and along his flanks. Picture a flamboyant prizefighter, arrogant in his heavy fur coat, mugging for the camera. He shudders, flexing and releasing his muscles, and his coat ripples in sympathetic vibration with his barely contained power. So it is with Nanook's massive white covering as he runs. Like the fighter, a bear wears his coat loosely about immensely strong shoulders and forearms well muscled for sparring with his fellow bears, swimming, and grabbing prey.

Although he's not built for speed, a bear can sprint for short distances at better than thirty-five miles an hour. He can easily outrun a man, especially a man flailing through snow. This fact, so clean, so innocuous on the written page, is burned indelibly into the conscious and subconscious mind of every person who works on the ice. I've seen bears move that fast, but, fortunately, never toward me.

The fastest bears are subadults without a thick store of blubber. Older, fatter bears move quickly but soon become overheated. The behavior that many explorers interpreted as intense curiosity and absence of fear—a bear sitting down in the midst of a chase to face his attackers—is really a desperate attempt to cool down. The bear may be highly stressed, a point that modern ecologists and photographers must keep in mind. An overheated bear may not appear to be suffering, but he certainly is.

Polar bears are also agile climbers. Scientific observers have watched them scale a thirty-five-foot ice wall or leap eighteen feet from a flat floe onto an iceberg. This ability haunts zoo designers. Mark Rosenthal, curator of mammals at Chicago's Lincoln Park Zoo, consulted other zoo officials and wildlife biologists when planning a new polar bear enclosure. "An important question we asked the experts," Rosenthal told me, "is 'How far can a bear *porpoise*, or jump out of the water?' They told me the highest they'd seen was 103 inches. We don't know if this is usual—if that was an average bear—or if they were watching The Olympic Bear.

"There's an old saying among zoo planners," Rosenthal continued, " 'As excitement increases, barriers weaken.' Can an excited bear jump higher? We don't know. What I do know is that the one time it happens could be a tragic time."

The Lincoln Park Zoo exhibit is designed with safety in mind. The public views the bears from above, but through glass panels, so there can be no dangerous leaning over the bears' rocky enclosure. A built-in alarm system is in place for the safety of keepers, who also carry walkie-talkies. When workers must be outside with the bears, they carry cans of repellent. Doors to the exhibit are doubled, double-locked, and rigorously checked. Rosenthal leaves nothing to chance.

Beneath the fur, beneath the skin, beneath the blubber and muscle, a polar bear's skeleton reveals kinship with other bears, and with dogs as well. The skull is over a foot long and carries 42 teeth, formidable weapons. When a bear opens his mouth, the prominent canine teeth add to his fearsome appearance. Combined with strong incisors, the canines—longer than those of any other bear—are evidence of his grab-and-lift hunting style. His clean jerk and dead lift with his teeth put human weight lifters to shame. The canine teeth do the killing: with numerous quick bites to a seal's head and neck, a polar bear ensures the death of his prey. Small cheek teeth are for tearing into meat, but a bear most often peels his seals like bananas and gulps huge sheets of skin and blubber without much chewing.

A polar bear's face is remarkably doglike. Anyone who has ever owned a German shepherd will recognize Nanook's facial expressions. The snout of a polar bear is elongate, in contrast to the shorter nose and dished face of other bears. The long nose warms the icy air before it can chill the bear's lungs. The nose also gets the business end of a bear's jaw—those huge canine teeth—deep into a seal's breathing hole.

The muzzle, the one part of a bear that no one wants to see up close, is the feature that distinguishes individual bears. Because it is covered sparsely with short hair, the muzzle's dark skin shows through, and the muzzle appears in varying shades of gray. Scars earned in disputes over food or females form prominent dark gashes amid the white hairs of mature males' muzzles. Narrow, unscarred faces identify young females. Older females may bear some scars, but their faces still retain a slender, graceful appearance. A face with a broad, heavy outline is the mark of a male bear. Subadult males lack fighting scars, but mature male bears wear reminders of many battles over prospective mates. Like dueling scars on the cheeks of Teutonic noblemen, the dark slashes bespeak a code of honor, a pattern of instinctive behavior whose origins are lost in the icy mists.

Old bears move slowly, their joints stiff with age. When angered, though, even the oldest whirls around with surprising fury, teeth and claws at the ready. The oldest, largest bears are often the worst tempered, having survived a thousand challenges by lesser bruins. Their teeth and bones have been broken in confrontations long forgotten. The bones knit back together;

the teeth remain jagged stumps or empty sockets. More painful from the perspective of human empathy—I shudder to think of it—is the plight of the old males. Male polar bears carry a penis bone, or *baculum*. In older bears even this structure may be broken, evidence of the ardor of mating or the violence of battle.

Female bears have four nipples, positioned near the midline of the belly. The milk they produce is creamy white, like everything else in the bear world, and very rich, averaging 32 percent fat but ranging as high as 48 percent (richer, in fact, than the high-fat milk of whales). Human mothers nurse their young with milk that averages 3.8 percent fat, so bear milk is nearly ten times richer. Bear milk also contains 10 to 12 percent protein, essential for growing cubs.

Mother bears may nurse their cubs for more than two and a half years, during which they equip their young with the insulating fat they need to survive in the cold. Barry Lopez wrote of polar bear milk in *Arctic Dreams*, "Those who have tasted of it say it tastes like cod liver oil and smells of seals or fish." *Those who have tasted it?* How many people can make such a claim? Surely behind this ultimate machismo experience lies one of the least-populated categories of human beings. Polar bear milk? The very thought recalls ribald jokes about newcomers to the arctic world. Tasted it? One such epicure is Eugen Schumacher, who studied polar bears in the late 1960s for the World Wildlife Fund. Sticking his finger into a sample of the milk drawn from a tranquilized bear, Schumacher reported, "Not bad . . . it tastes like nuts. But it's very rich."

Nanook has better eyes than most of his bear relatives and can see in air or water. His eyes appear black from far away; up close, they are a gentle golden brown. His retinas are especially adapted to hunting in the dark of winter: they are backed by a reflective layer like the shiny interior of an automobile headlight. Called the *tapetum*, it intensifies light and gives the bear good vision in dim conditions. Nanook's eyes are almost as large as human eyes but better adapted to a wide range of light conditions. He must hunt in near darkness through much of the year yet be able to function in the brightness of the summer sun reflected off myriad ice pinnacles and snowbanks. His eyes are wide spaced, but they face forward, giving good binocular vision. Polar bears have excellent depth perception and distance vision. Their eyes are adapted to tracking moving objects; they see stationary targets less easily.

A bear relies heavily on his sense of smell. In the polar bears this sense is finely developed. Like a radar or laser tracking system on a missile, a polar bear's nose guides him over many miles in a straight line to his target. On the way to his objective, a bear will crash through brush, swim across meltwater ponds, or destroy houses without a second thought. In a test of the scents available to Nanook's nose, Ian Stirling experimented on the ice with a Labrador retriever. The dog could sniff out a seal's breathing hole, beneath three feet of snow, at distances exceeding half a mile. Stirling, speculating that a bear's nose is even more sensitive, wrote, "This means that when a bear tests the wind, it must be checking a veritable smorgasbord of smells."

A polar bear hears his world through small but sensitive ears. There's not much to hear, other than the shriek of the wind and the cracking and groaning of the ice. Against this constant background he can detect the whoosh of a seal, rising to breathe beneath the snow, or the squeak of a tiny vole or lemming deep in its tundra tunnel. Many arctic explorers were surprised that polar bears showed little reaction to the sound of firearms. Modern researchers studying various bear deterrents report the same observation. Cracks and booms are common sounds in the bear's world, as the ice floes split, jostle, and continually readjust their jigsaw patterns. Nanook is not easily intimidated—least of all by familiar sounds.

The end of this tale is the end of the tail, at the end of the bear. Nanook, like bears in general, has a tail that is almost no tail at all. A short, furry flap of skin, it is well insulated against the cold. If bears had a sense of humor, they'd delight in the irony of the two-legged, tailless creatures who invade their icy world and then complain that "we're up here freezing our tails off." But that's another tale . . .

FOUR

Life amid
the Icepack Floes

It's NINE O'CLOCK on a gray, windswept November morning in Alaska's Beaufort Sea. The violent, steady gale roaring over the polar pack drives the windchill well below $-75°$ F. On the tab of my parka zipper, a small thermometer dangles, useless. Its readings plunged offscale yesterday, and the tiny instrument never recovered from the shock.

Facing such a forbidding world, sensible men would long since have retreated to the warmth of our ship's inner spaces, but no one shows any desire to leave the open deck. In fact, the crowd of parka-bundled figures huddled at the lee rail is growing. What holds our attention so firmly are three white figures in the snow about 30 yards away. We're watching bears.

The fascination these animals generate is powerful. In zoos they always draw crowds. In the arctic icepack the attraction is far stronger. I usually find myself lethargic, rather than invigorated, after about thirty minutes in the bitter wind, but polar bears near the icebreaker keep us out here for hours. Even after I lift off the deck in a helicopter and watch the ship shrink in the distance, my gaze is drawn to the bears, to the red patches of snow where they've eaten their kills, and to the lines of their pawprints in the snow. Humans are mesmerized by the white bear.

I'm intrigued both by the bears and by the human response to them. Bear behavior in many ways parallels human behavior, and the bears elicit the same responses from people that we show one another: fear, anger, curiosity, empathy, fascination.

Investigations of Nanook's private life once relied on tales told by explorers, whalers, and sport hunters (who had their own prejudices about these "dangerous villains"). Other tales came from native hunters, keen observers but imaginative storytellers. To further complicate matters, their observations were often mistranslated. And the natives were eager to please: many an explorer was told what his native hosts believed he wanted to hear. Native spirit tales were confused with genuine happenings. With polar bears, however, reality is so fascinating that no embellishment is needed.

A bear's day begins whenever he awakens. Nanook sleeps seven to eight hours a day—that is, each twenty-four hours, for the concept of a "day" is without meaning in the high Arctic. He sleeps wherever and whenever he pleases. When a storm fills the air with blowing and drifting snow, a bear may lie down with his back to the wind and let the snow drift over him as he sleeps through the blizzard. When the summer sun shines warm on his fur, he dozes in pits dug deep in the shoreline sand. Mothers with cubs dig sleeping pits atop high ridges for much the same reason early settlers on the prairie built hilltop homes— so they can see danger approaching. Bears doze off after a full meal. Bears who wait at the edges of the ice for a seal to surface may appear intensely involved in the hunt when in fact they have nodded off, losing only a little dignity in the process.

During their waking hours, bears of all ages are constantly on the move. They swim often, to cool off or apparently for sheer pleasure. Emerging from the water, they shake like dogs, throwing flat, wide arcs of water in all directions. To dry off, they roll in the snow. On land they seem random but steady wanderers. Cubs are forever tumbling with each other or tottering along behind their mother. The mother bear may keep them moving until they drop, exhausted, and fall asleep, giving her time for serious hunting alone. Adult males, young and old, and cubless females range the ice in seemingly aimless patterns, unless some interesting odor presents itself. At such a moment they turn and home in unerringly, although the source of the scent may be miles away. Tracks in the snow reveal the very instant that a bear's curiosity was aroused. From a path of random shuffling, tracing broad loops and reversals, the now deliberate footprints mark an arrow-straight course across the jumbled icepack.

A hunting polar bear stalks the zone of active ice, where the white floes jostle continually, where new leads of open water appear daily, and where young, inexperienced seals congregate. The bear uses a number of strategies—probably more than any other predator. If native tales are to be believed (and many are substantiated by scientific observation), Nanook even uses tools in pursuit of his favorite meal, the ringed seal. Native hunters tell of bears that push ice or snow blocks ahead of them as they slither close to the breathing holes seals have scraped from beneath the ice. Bears build walls of snow to hide behind and they use blocks of ice to smash through the icy crust that covers a breathing hole.

More than two million ringed seals live in the arctic region, eating fish, crustaceans, and microscopic zooplankton. Over five feet long, they weigh up to 200 pounds. From midfall through April the seals stay in the water and rise through the ice cover to breathe at *aglus*, holes they've scraped from beneath the ice with their claws. These aglus are inverted funnels, as small as six inches across at the ice surface, carved into ice as thick as six feet. In the winter snow and ice may crust over the top of an aglu, but a seal keeps the main tube open. A single seal may use as many as six breathing holes and may share its aglus with other seals. Subice arguments over "breathing rights" are undoubtedly common. Beneath the snows of winter but safe above the water's lapping reach, the seal enlarges a den, or haul-out lair, often in the lee of a pressure ridge. A shelf of ice leads away from the breathing hole, and a snow roof arches overhead. In a side chamber, a mother seal gives birth to a pup weighing about ten pounds. On smooth ice slight mounds mark the surface locations of aglus. They resemble icy volcanoes, formed from the frozen overflow of water pushed ahead of the seals as they rise to the surface. In winter these mounds are covered by drifted snow.

Throughout the warmer months the seals bask on the ice, always near a floe's edge, with the sheltering water close by. Like polar bears they seem to relish the warmth of the summer sun. Having hauled themselves out on the ice, the seals nap for about a minute, then rise on their front flippers for a six- to eight-second look around. Such vigilance is necessary, for the seals are the prey of both white bears and human hunters. With accurate hearing, they are alert to any unusual sound telegraphed through the ice. Their huge eyes detect the slightest moving shadow. If a seal spots anything out of the ordinary, it pops up for a better look. If alarmed, it slips quickly into the water.

Summer makes seal hunting difficult for polar bears. Without the ice, or with just a few white chunks floating in a broad expanse of water, a bear can't stalk effectively. Summer becomes a time of fasting, of living off stored fat reserves. Occasionally, however, a bear has been observed hunting in the water. He slips his immense body, headfirst or hindfirst, into an open lead without making the slightest splash. He stalks, paddling silently with huge forepaws or gliding like an unremarkable slab of white ice. Eyes, snout, and ears are all that show on the surface, trailed by the slight V of a ripple wake that barely disturbs the water. A bear can submerge for more than a minute and can swim considerable distances underwater with great accuracy, eyes open, nostrils pressed shut, and stubby ears flattened against his head.

Leaping from the water, the bear bursts in a splashing blur, a fluid extension of the sea he leaves behind. In one smooth motion he explodes from the water, charges onto the ice, and clubs the seal dead with a single paw swipe or repeated bites to the head and neck. Because he has approached from the water—from the seal's "safe" direction—the bear has a chance at grabbing the seal before it can escape. Even so, most of these attacks end in failure, and the seal drops into the sea, where it can outswim Nanook.

Bears also stalk basking seals from the ice. When a bear

spots a seal—or anything he thinks might be a seal—he freezes. He may drop his head and walk steadily forward or choose a lower profile. Dropping his chin flat, he slithers across the ice on neck and chest, pushing with his hind feet, rump high. This position blurs the bear's outline against the horizon and makes his approach less visible to the alert seal. The bear zigzags across the flat surface, taking advantage of every slab of ice, every hummock of snow for cover. He may, spread-eagled, push steadily along meltwater channels on the surface of the ice, looking like a child scooting headfirst down a waterslide. From the seal's low perspective, a bear in such a trough is all but invisible. Approaching with great patience, the bear freezes whenever the seal lifts its head to reconnoiter, then advances while the seal takes its brief naps. If the bear gets within fifty feet, the seal is doomed. A few great leaps, followed by a swat from the huge paw, and the hunt is over. The advantage in this deadly game is usually the seal's, however, and most stalks end with the splash of its escape.

In summer a bear may catch a seal in the open water, but this is apparently rare, for seals are excellent swimmers. Bears also hunt swimming ducks by coming up beneath them, or stalk lemmings and other small prey beneath the tufted grass or mounded snowbanks. Winter is the time of active hunting. Male bears and nonpregnant females hunt throughout the dark months. Seal aglus are drifted over with several feet of snow, often frozen into hard crusts that cover birthing chambers or haul-out shelves. Even if no sign shows on the snowy surface, a bear's nose can detect such dens, though the seals may have been absent for hours.

A bear's strategies at the aglu include incredible patience, stealthy approach, and lightning-quick attack. The surest approach, almost always fatal to a seal snug in its haul-out den, is from the water. The bear, having seen or smelled his quarry, dives beneath the ice and emerges in the seal's own breathing well, cutting off any possible escape. More commonly the bear detects the aglu while walking on top of the ice. Nanook's next actions depend on his nose's interpretation of the olfactory evidence: Is the aglu occupied? Has it been visited recently?

If the seal is present, hauled out in a birthing or resting den, the bear approaches slowly. The hair between his footpads muffles his steps. His shuffling, irregular gait further camouflages his approach. The bear may pause between steps to listen for seal sounds from beneath the snow. He must proceed carefully, for any creak of the ice or shifting of the snow cover will send the alarmed seal rolling to one side into the dark water. The final rush covers the last twenty feet and ends in a leap so high that the bear is truly airborne. All four of his feet smash down together on the roof of the aglu. Four hundred, a thousand, fifteen hundred pounds of white, slashing fury—death from above in a blinding avalanche of ice and snow, accompanied by a thundering crash, shattering the snug warmth of the seal's home. Then all that remains is the dark, and the cold, and the bear.

When Nanook comes across the scent of an empty winter aglu or summer haul-out, he displays his greatest patience. He may simply lie down and wait. On the downwind side of the hole, from an angle where he casts no betraying shadow, or in any position where he is out of the seal's line of sight, the bear will wait for hours. He may scrape away the snow and ice until only a thin crust remains and then cover the spot with his body so no sunlight will reveal his work to the seal cruising in darkness below. He may pile snow into a wall and wait behind it. He flattens himself against the snowy surface in mimicry of the rug that a hunter would make of him and presents an almost nonexistent silhouette. All his patience is rewarded by the sound of bubbles in the ice well. As a seal rises to breathe, it exhales. Effervescence in the aglu alerts Nanook. With explosive power his claws and teeth strike home, and once again there is blood on the snow.

"In the Alaskan Beaufort Sea," an Arctic veteran told me, "we watched a polar bear lie in wait beside a seal's breathing hole for hours. He lay on his belly with all four legs spreadeagled and didn't move a muscle. Finally the seal surfaced. The bear, with one swipe of his paw, threw the seal up onto the ice, away from the hole, and pounced on him."

The best hunting is during the six to seven weeks of midspring, before seal pups are weaned. These newborns rapidly increase their body weight from about ten pounds at birth to more than fifty pounds at six weeks, and most of the added weight is the fat that bears love. The bears snatch the helpless whitecoats from their birth lairs in an orgy of feasting reminiscent of shark feeding frenzies. Food is so plentiful during this time that the bears, no longer hungry, appear to kill for sport. Humans may not be the only creatures that kill for the killing and not out of need. Bears flip baby seals in the air like stuffed toys in a ghastly game. Mother bears with cubs also kill more seals than they can possibly need, either to teach the technique to their babies or for the sheer pleasure of the kill.

Biologists who have examined the caloric content of whole seals (by slicing them lengthwise and mincing them in meat grinders) speculate that the lack of fat on newborn seal pups explains why they are often left on the ice uneaten. Bears prefer the recently fattened suckling pup and its mother.

A hungry bear gulps down the entire seal—flippers, claws, bones, and all—without much chewing. If not starving, Nanook is a more finicky eater. Holding down the carcass with one paw, he peels the skin and blubber off the meat and bones. He then opens the body cavity and eats the steaming entrails. The remainder of the seal's carcass is left for foxes, ravens, and subadult bears who haven't yet perfected their hunting skills. A fast meal is essential, because the odor of the kill will soon draw other bears, who may be larger. Adult males, especially, will steal food from smaller bears.

On rare occasions bears have the opportunity to hunt where animals have been trapped in a fjord by ice that closed off escape to the open sea. In the remaining pool of open water, called a *savssat*, hundreds of narwhal and beluga whales may congregate, each, in turn, rising to breathe in the small opening. Bears have been seen at the edges of savssats, killing these 10- to 20-foot whales with a single blow and lifting them clear of the water. The whales thus killed and lifted may be five to seven times as heavy as the bears. Such slaughter may continue for days. One observer saw thirteen dead belugas on the ice next to a bear that kept killing more. Because one whale would make a meal and more, it again appears that bears may kill for sport.

Even with the advantages of surprise, size, strength, and

weaponry, Nanook is, under the very best conditions, successful in less than a quarter of his attacks. Typically a bear catches and eats a seal once every four or five days. This means that a bear encountered by chance is very likely hungry, and a hungry bear is a dangerous bear.

Polar bears are opportunists. They forage at garbage dumps. They pick dead birds from the tundra and spit out the feathers. They face herds of walrus, containing bulls that may outweigh them two to one—bulls that brandish three-foot tusks and powerful flippers—in the hope of isolating a walrus calf from its parents.

After feeding, a bear lumbers to the water's edge, where he washes and licks himself fastidiously, his black tongue cleaning between his toes, smoothing the fur on his forelegs. Like a cat, the bear washes his face with his newly cleaned paws. In winter, when open water is rare, a bear cleans his face by rubbing his muzzle in the snow.

How intelligent is a polar bear? There are numerous instances of bears learning to hide in snow caves from helicopters after one encounter with scientists shooting tranquilizer darts, or pacing back and forth outside two doorways, waiting for the unwary human who might become dinner. Bears plan for the future and lay traps for the unwary, as Mark Rosenthal, curator of mammals at Chicago's Lincoln Park Zoo, discovered about Mike, a resident polar bear. "We were feeding the bears a meat mixture. Mike would eat his food but would always leave a few scraps on the floor. Then he'd lie down with his paws forward like a dog, rest his chin on the ground, and pretend to be asleep. The food scraps were just inches in front of his nose. What he was doing was waiting for pigeons. When one would land to peck at the scraps, Mike would make a grab. Now and then he'd actually get one."

One of Chicago's bears cleverly took advantage of an opportunity that presented itself unexpectedly. "We were adding water to her pool from above, with a hose," Rosenthal told me, "during a cold winter. The splashing water built a tall ice sculpture in her enclosure. It wasn't long before she climbed the ice mound. We watched her do it, for about thirty minutes, but couldn't stop her. She managed to climb out of her pit and wandered around for some time in the vicinity—she wasn't a threat to people, because we'd cleared the area, but we had an exciting time of it before we tranquilized her and brought her back for a long sleep."

The white bear's intelligence is also evident in his prodigious ability as a navigator. On the hunt, or on his random wanderings, Nanook displays an innate sense of geography. In a world that appears at first both featureless and changeless, a wandering bear must actually contend with continually shifting patterns. The winds blow with varying intensity, though often from the same direction. Where yesterday there was smooth ice, today there is an open lead, with black water rising and falling heavily between the floes. Tomorrow at the same spot there may be a pressure ridge forty feet high. And around the horizon rolls the sun, casting shadows in every possible direction.

Scientists simply don't understand how bears store the mental maps required to travel in straight lines across the shifting icepack. Or how they walk against the circumpolar drift, staying in one area while the icy turntable of the polar pack rotates beneath their furry feet. Or how they devise shortcuts across points of land to avoid a long swim or a region of bad ice. Or how they find the coast by walking in straight lines from far offshore. Or how, once inland, they can head unerringly for the sea. Or why they climb mountains over 6,000 feet high.

Eskimos use the guideposts in the sky—including a constellation named Qilugtussat (Barking Dogs about a Bear)—to navigate across the mobile ice. Their knowledge of celestial constellations, winds, and currents is impressive. Without the benefit of formal mathematics, they perform complex vector analysis in their travels. Can Nanook do the same? Surely visual cues are limited for bears out of sight of land. Some researchers suggest that the constancy of the wind direction provides a steady scent trail or consistent snowdrifts.

That bears travel immense distances is well documented. One bear tagged on Svalbard, north of Norway, in 1966 was killed a year later in Nanortalik, Greenland, some 2,000 miles to the southwest. Most bears remain in one region, even though (as in northern Alaska) staying put may require a steady march toward the east to compensate for the westward ice drift. Others prefer to travel. Studies by the Norwegian Polar Institute have tracked bears walking 800 miles from east Greenland to Svalbard during one month, and from Greenland to Franz Josef Land (600 miles) in the same length of time. Bears walk from Russia to Alaska and ride the drift ice back home. One female, marked and recaptured, had traveled 205 miles (measured in a straight line) in two days.

Unlike many bears, Nanook is not a territorial creature. The only property worth owning in his frozen domain is a seal, and seals move. Polar bears do have definable ranges, but these vary from year to year as the seal population shifts and as the boundary of the icepack fluctuates. Bears stay where hunting is good, which means wherever ice and seals are found together. An individual bear may cover hundreds of miles each year in pursuit of food. Bears fitted with radio collars can be tracked using satellites; such research in western Alaska reveals bears with home ranges of almost 200,000 square miles—an area larger than the state of California.

When a polar bear walks, his feet turn in, leaving pigeon-toed tracks. The front feet move, even on land, in the rhythm of paddles. I learned as a boy that an oar or canoe paddle has a four-stroke rhythm—catch, pull, feather, recover—as it grabs the water, powers forward, "feathers" into the wind, parallel to the water, and swings forward for another bite. In exactly this way, a polar bear plants his foot in the snow (catch), treads with his full weight, muscles thrusting forward (pull), swings his leg out to the side and folds his paw inward toward his body (feather), and flicks it forward into position for the next step (recover). The rear foot steps neatly into the depression left by the forefoot. Nanook's forward motion is a shuffling, rolling gait, with its own curious grace.

The tracks Nanook leaves in the snow can be read like a book by native hunters. The depressions indicate the sex, age, and condition of the bear: male bears leave elongated tracks 13 inches long, showing a rim sculpted by long fringes of hair.

Tracks of female bears are smaller and more toed-in. The depth of the tracks shows how well fed or scrawny the bear is (and thus, perhaps, its mood).

Nanook's slow, meandering pace makes him appear aimless; it gives him an incongruously casual demeanor in his unforgiving world. But those who study these animals most closely report that there is nothing casual about them. Their slow pace is an energy-conserving device and should never be mistaken for lack of interest, especially if the bear is advancing slowly in your direction.

Bears whose wanderings are interrupted by humans, their dogs, their surface vehicles, or their aircraft may run in fear and become overheated. During the sunny summer months, bears have trouble staying cool. Their behavior in both instances reveals several strategies for coping with heat stress. Hot bears sit or lie down. They pant. They sprawl in the snow, resembling nothing so much as bearskin rugs. According to Ian Stirling, when a bear lies spread-eagled over ice blocks, it looks "more like a jellyfish than the ultimate Arctic carnivore." Bears roll, waving their legs and exposing their sparsely furred bellies. They dive in the water. They eat snow. To escape summertime heat, they dig into streambanks, often all the way to the permafrost. Here they pass lazy days, expending little energy, cool in their naturally air-conditioned dens. Some permafrost pits extend more than 20 feet underground and end in large rooms. Researchers speculate that as the ice in the permafrost melts, the bears dig deeper. Scientists believe some of these summer dens may have been in continuous use for hundreds of years. Seeking relief from the heat, bears also dig pits in summer snowbanks or in wet sand. They lie with great dignity, sphinxlike, forepaws outstretched and hind legs neatly folded. They loll in mounds of shore-strewn seaweed. They frequent windswept capes, or, in the southern part of their range, wander inland to the shade of coniferous forests. In the trees a white bear is easy to spot. Pilots laugh about bears that attempt to hide beneath the green spruce canopy as a helicopter passes overhead.

A gathering of bears is called a *sloth*. Surely whoever coined this term was thinking of summertime polar bears. Lolling on the beach or just hanging out with their buddies, polar bears excel at inaction. Summer is a time of segregation in this all-white community. Large adult males claim the choicest areas near the shoreline. Adult females with cubs move slightly inshore, where the young bears are at a safe distance from the troublesome males. Beyond them, farthest inland, are the young males and nonbearing females. Like human teenagers they seek their own and don't want to be bothered by their elders.

At the other extreme of their environment, bears must contend with temperatures well below zero and with winds that lash snow across the icecap at well over a hundred miles an hour. They curl up. They bury their heads in the fur on their chests, breathing warmed air, just as Eskimos snuggle deep in the fur ruffs of their parkas. They hunker down on their bellies. Turning their backs to the wind, they draw their hind legs tight against their stomachs, wrapping long forelegs around the resulting body bundle like schoolgirls clutching books. They let the blowing snow gently cover them with an insulating blanket. Hidden beneath snowbanks, they wait out the storm, dozing, snug in their drift dens. Their body temperatures drop a few degrees, and their hearts slow to 8 to 10 beats per minute (from perhaps 80 to 130 beats when active). This isn't true hibernation, just a mechanism for surviving the intense storms that sweep the polar regions. Arctic travelers report that they've sometimes spent hours near a snowbank only to have a bear burst suddenly from beneath it. Nanook was there all the time.

Polar bears dig winter dens, but only pregnant females stay in them for months. Observers differ on the denning habits of the other bears: some say that except for expectant mothers, bears use dens only to wait out storms. Others say that even mature males will stay in the same den for months at a time. Some bears, particularly the big males with thick reserves of blubber to nourish and insulate them through the long darkness, walk the ice, exposed to nature's worst, for the entire desolate winter, alone at the top of the world.

FIVE

Bear Behavior

Observing two half-grown polar bears playing in the glorious afternoon sun on an arctic beach, I was struck by the gentleness with which they cuffed and mouthed each other, careful to avoid causing injury. The killer bear of my icepack nightmares—all fang and claw—seemed far away. I might have been watching two puppies romping. The magnificent predator, when he chooses, can also be a gentle giant.

This bear of many personas leads a socially intricate life, which scientists have just begun to document from observations of bears playing, fighting, mating, and bringing forth cubs from winter dens, eager to face the snowy landscape. Such detailed reports are still rare, but they add dimension to bear behavior studies. Modern observers watch bears both in the wild and in captivity. The scenes that enliven their descriptions dispel old myths: bears are not solitary stalkers of the icepack but social animals that live by a complex code of behavior.

Polar bears are loners. They're not, however, as solitary as once believed. Before their social behavior was seriously studied, bears were presumed to have little interaction. In recent years, though, bear observers such as Ian Stirling and Fred

Bruemmer have watched hundreds of approaches, retreats, play fights, and genuine battles between polar bears. These bear watchers report that Nanook lives by a well-defined pattern of subtle signs that indicate status and intent, particularly when strange bears meet.

The simplest, most direct signal is running away. If, on rounding an ice wall, a female with cubs meets a male bear, she immediately flees, positioning her body between her cubs and the stranger. The alternative may be a violent fight. Those who have seen a mother defending her cubs report that she is dangerous, unpredictable, and utterly fearless. The big males are a real threat: they kill and eat cubs when they can, but such cannibalism is probably rare because the cubs and their mothers are faster and more agile than the heavier males.

Single bears that meet unexpectedly pass at a safe distance. If they approach each other, they follow a prescribed routine with the nervous tension of student actors trying to appear confident as they stumble through an unfamiliar script. Their anxiety is obvious. The smaller bear always moves downwind. He sniffs constantly, keeping track of the larger bear. Size connotes power, although, on occasion, a small, aggressive bear will chase a larger bear. Both bears may be particularly uneasy if they meet in the water, where it's difficult for them to assess each other's dimensions.

After gauging each other for several minutes, the two bears signal their intents. They circle each other at a distance, sniffing, looking for clues. Friendly bears show respect for each other and a desire for peace (or play) by keeping their heads low, their eyes averted. As among many other animals, a direct stare between polar bears is bad manners and often constitutes a threat. The bears are silent and keep their mouths closed. They continue circling, then move slowly together until their noses touch. They sit down facing each other.

This ritual dance takes only a few minutes, but its stylized steps have been rehearsed over thousands of years. The young actors continue the drama, whose script means survival of the species. No evolutionary advantage comes to a race that battles at every encounter. Even the victors might be mortally wounded, and a dying hero hasn't won anything: he'll have no chance to pass on his superior genes. In these meetings polar bears open their mouths and grasp jaws or chew tenderly on each other's necks. If they are the same size, this formal pas-de-deux can be the prelude to play. If the two are mismatched, the smaller bear may circle cautiously, then lie downwind and wait for a signal from the larger.

Sometimes bear-human interaction resembles the defined rituals of bear-bear behavior. In the Alaskan Beaufort Sea, an engineer was investigating a large pile of ice blocks. When he rounded the end of the pile and his helicopter came into view, he was dismayed to find a polar bear between him and the helicopter. Man and bear stood eyeing each other for what seemed an eternity. Then the engineer began edging his way to his right in a wide circle toward the helicopter. The bear, just as he might with a strange bear his own size, executed the same maneuver, circling to *his* right. Eventually, the two players in this drama had swapped places. The man jumped into the helicopter and took off, none the worse for his close-up encounter with Nanook.

During the late-spring mating season, genuine battles are common. The rest of the year bears conserve energy by avoiding confrontations. Play fighting happens at any time between equally matched bears (although large bears have been observed enticing smaller bears to play, being exceedingly careful not to hurt them—like human fathers, challenging young sons, they are also careful to let the little bears win most of the time). Although they could easily rip each other apart or knock each other senseless, the bears are cautious not to cause real damage: like greeting, play fighting is a ritual.

Bears that engage in play fighting are usually well-fed young males, four to eight years old. After the stylized greeting, one may raise a paw and push the other's shoulder. The two stand on their hind legs but keep their forepaws at their sides or folded inward against their bellies. The first contact may be in the form of gentle bites. Then the two slap, box, and shove, trying to knock each other off balance. When one falls, flailing his four legs in the air, his sparring partner pounces, and the two bears roll in the snow. Rising again, the two embrace—the classic bear hug. Like good friends savoring the happy weariness after a touch football game, the bears lean on each other. The hug ends; the moment passes.

The bears then resume their swaying dance, wrestling with abandon until, in sublime exhaustion, they sprawl panting in the snow. They kiss each other's feet and nibble on the fearsome claws. After a short rest they begin anew. Such mock battles may go on for hours. The charges, blows, and bites look serious—and they certainly could be. Some blood may be drawn, but seldom, if ever, is anger expressed. Quite the contrary: both bears appear to enjoy the contest immensely, and each seems reluctant to do anything that would cause the other to end the fun.

Other subadult males sometimes stand by watching the action. They don't join in, but, like would-be hustlers at a pool table, they may challenge the winner.

Play fighting gives young bears a safe taste of battle. It allows them to hone their strategies and skills without risk of serious injury and thus may be seen as yet another adaptation designed to ensure survival of the species. Viewed anthropomorphically, however, the bears are simply having a good time.

Real fights occur, particularly during the April breeding season, when mature males meet on the scent track of a female in estrus. What follows is a no-holds-barred duel, with slashing claws and snapping jaws. The huge canine teeth clash and sometimes even break, leaving bloody stumps. Violent and prolonged, these fights often leave both bears exhausted, bleeding, and scarred for life. The muzzle area, particularly, shows the dark scars worn as battle decorations by males old enough to join the fray. Other scars are prominent on the shoulders and rump, and at the base of the neck. Because these areas are protected by thick fur and blubber, little serious damage results. Still, there is always a winner, who heads off in pursuit of the female bear (she has remained unconcerned throughout the skirmish), and a loser, who retires to lick his wounds.

Just as bear etiquette dictates specific signals for nonviolent play, there is a bear code of war. Like boxers entering the ring, jabbing and swaggering but occasionally glancing across to size up their opponents, two bears prepare to do battle. They approach each other slowly, almost diffidently. They strut stiff legged. With lowered heads, they gaze fixedly at each other. They signal aggression from a distance by posture and by the threat of a direct, impolite stare.

The bears make a rumbling growl deep in their throats. Such sounds are unusual and are reserved to signal anger. When bears are agitated, they "chuff." This sound results from contractions of the chest and abdomen while the bear's mouth is open. Chuffing may progress to roaring if Nanook is sufficiently aroused. The roar of a polar bear, according to one witness, sounds exactly like the bellow of Chewbacca the Wookie in the movie *Star Wars*.

During the breeding season, male bears strut their stuff like senior boys at the high school prom, full of their own importance. They stand tall, recognizable at a distance, and challenge the world. Other bears stay clear. Freshmen and sophomores know their place.

Bears of similar size and age often gather congenially. A new bear approaching such a group walks uncertainly. He stops frequently and raises his head, sniffing expectantly from side to side. The other bears watch his approach and try to read some signal of intent from his posture, stride, size, and attitude. Like members of an elite club who recognize their fellows by their clothing and manner, they make a quick determination of the new bear's social standing. If he is large and seems aggressive, they may flee. If they don't like what they see but feel in control because the stranger is smaller or more timid, they may growl, hiss, or stand tall, defying the stranger to come closer. Facing such an unfriendly greeting, the newcomer almost invariably turns to leave.

The oldest, largest bears are frequently ill tempered and unpredictable. Fred Bruemmer, writing in the magazine *Natural History*, described the reception of these cantankerous giants by other bears. They "behave in his presence like people stuck in a subway car with a loud, obnoxious, and pushy drunk: they avoid eye contact, try to ease away, pretend to be oblivious, and hope he will pick on someone else."

Other confrontations involve immature bears who overstep their authority or contests over food. Neither incident is likely to result in injury. Rarely a youngster carries off a superb bluff:

most bears will defer to a cub, thinking its mother must be nearby as backup. Orphaned bears, even very small ones, have been seen posturing and posing, threatening bears far larger and getting away with it. This pretense can go on for some time, but sooner or later the young bear's bluff is called. In a few brief seconds the yearling is taught respect for his elders. A swat from a female or young male is better than a genuine attack from an old male—a painful lesson, perhaps, but necessary for survival in an icy world where the next confrontation may be deadly serious.

Bears use the same signals to communicate their intentions to humans. Norwegian researcher Erik Nyholm, who spent the winter of 1971–72 in a small cabin surrounded by polar bears on Svalbard, Norway's northern island outpost, learned to read the signals: "With friendly intention a polar bear approaches with raised head, slow, and heavy steps and with a long underlip as a sign of good humor." A friendly bear wants us to see and hear him coming. The extended lower lip gives him the appearance of a smile. "An attacking polar bear," wrote Nyholm, "approaches with lowered head, light and soundless steps and often with a long upper lip as a sign of anger."

Nyholm came as close as you can get to the white bear. He wrote in this passage about the day when man and bear were literally inches apart:

"The 12th of October was a big day for us, because at 9:30 P.M. a big polar bear came to the station. He was calm, had just come out of the sea, and the masses of fat on his round bottom and flanks shook with every step. The beautiful shimmering fur had no scar. The polar bear advanced towards the door to the south where I was standing. The dogs had already alarmed us, and now I received the big fellow, who in many ways showed that he was in a good mood. It looked as if he knew that there was seal blubber to be dished out.

"I let the polar bear come right up to a distance of four meters [13 feet]. Here he stopped on my command in their own language. [Nyholm used blowing sounds on several occasions— always successfully—to imitate the signals that he heard bears using with each other.] He showed time after time his peaceful intentions. I gave him some bits of seal blubber to taste. Since the bear was showing a composed behavior all the time, I decided to make an attempt to feed him by hand. Everything went well, and the same situation was photographed the next day. The bear had been lying in front of our steps all night.

"The bear was named Kalle, and his morning greeting was friendly. I was surprised to see him ask for food in the manner of bears by nodding his head. I gave him many kilograms with my hand, and he never made the slightest attempt to harm me. The distance between my fingers and the bear's nose was only 15 centimeters [6 inches], and when Kalle, with a bit of seal blubber between his teeth, sniffed my empty, calm hand, I was anxious about how much he wanted to sniff. I was not so sure that I would have the chance to jerk my hand back to me quickly enough if Kalle should try to nibble. Kalle did not smell how anxious I was, and he walked backwards to a snowdrift to enjoy the delicious fat."

Nyholm seems remarkably calm in reporting, matter-of-factly, that "the long winter passed without any really great difficulties in spite of the fact that the bears broke eight windowpanes and two doors. During the long winter night our 'friends' might lie behind any snowdrift. On the busiest days we had up to seven bears around the houses."

Nyholm's assistants were *karelske bjørnhunder*, Karelian bear dogs, used at the time by polar bear hunters in Svalbard. Nyholm valued them highly: "My Karelian bear dogs were our real life insurance. These dogs are used to big game, and were always prepared to go into a fight with a polar bear. Not one single polar bear could advance on us without our knowing it."

Nyholm's account reminds me of a warning common across the northern regions: When the watchdog growls at the door, someone's coming. When it hides under the table, look out for bears! This warning was brought to life for Hugh Miles and Mike Salisbury, cinematographers filming a BBC documentary on the Arctic. The two men befriended an arctic fox that they named Lief. The little animal usually played happily aboard their sledges: "Lief clambered about on the loads, receiving titbits for providing amusing photos, then suddenly fled, with tail between legs. We wondered what we had done to cause the alarm, then suddenly became aware of a large male bear marching purposefully into camp—too close for comfort. Mike grabbed a rifle whilst I dashed into the cabin for a thunderflash, but the sudden burst of activity frightened the bear and it lumbered off into the ice floes—we were relieved."

When an agitated bear confronts humans, he sends a clear message. He makes the same chuffing sound that he uses to warn other bears. He chomps his jaws loudly. He stares directly at the person, holding his head low, sometimes swinging it from side to side. His ears are pressed back flat against his head. Like a gunfighter in the Old West, he issues a challenge. "I'm here," he says, "and I won't back down." Anyone witnessing such a display had best consider it a very real warning. The bear's next action won't be for show.

Experts say every bear defends a "critical space." The size of this space varies from bear to bear, and from situation to situation. Whereas another bear may be able to read the signals and determine how close is too close, most humans cannot. This is an important distinction: intrusion within the critical space is a threat and may provoke an attack.

In the icepack a bear views anything unusual as a potential meal or a threat to be challenged. In the summer ice off Greenland, Nanook even challenged a large ship. Larry Brooks, arctic engineer and retired Coast Guard officer, recounts, "In the summer of 1970, I had a number of cadets from the Coast Guard Academy on board the icebreaker *Westwind*. We were cruising through broken ice on the west side of Baffin Bay, when we spotted a bear swimming in the distance. The entire crew, and my cadets, ran to the bow of the ship, hoping to get good pictures. We slowed the ship.

"As the breaker approached, the bear climbed up onto a floe. He reared up on his hind legs and waved his paws in the air. It was clearly a challenge: 'Come on, ship!'

"When we got within a hundred yards, he dove into the water, swam to another floe, and repeated the gesture. Without any apparent fear of a ship 269 feet long, the bear continued this behavior until we broke off the engagement out of concern that we'd exhaust him."

I asked whether the bear might simply have been trying to get a better view of this strange object that had entered his domain. Brooks responded, "No, he could see us quite clearly, and his paw gestures looked for all the world like the schoolyard bully, challenging all comers. He wanted to let us know who was the king of the ice."

Over food bears of the same size seem indifferent to each other—more than fifty bears have been seen feeding on a single dead whale. Smaller bears patrol the perimeter, meekly hoping for leftovers. Erik Nyholm has seen two-year-olds that had left their mother, begging food from more experienced hunters by nodding their heads up and down. The larger bear might rebuff them until he'd eaten his fill but would then let them have what remained.

In his role as an observer and forecaster of sea ice, arctic veteran Ken Vaudrey has seen many bears through the window of a helicopter. Some bears see him as a challenger: "Once when we flew over," Vaudrey told me, "a bear abandoned his kill and fled. After a few yards, he stopped in his tracks and seemed to be saying to himself, 'This is stupid.' He ran back to the seal carcass and stood with his body directly over it, with all four legs fencing it off. He was quite clearly communicating 'This one's mine.' "

Nanook perceives humans in any form as competition, as Walt Spring, an engineer who studies sea ice and icebergs for Mobil Oil Corporation observes: "In 1988 our ship had just entered the ice off Svalbard. The captain spotted a flock of birds in the distance. About the same time, we saw a mother bear and her two cubs walking purposefully across the ice toward the birds. Then we saw in the distance a male bear that had just killed a seal. He hadn't yet ripped into it, but there was enough blood to attract the birds, and the mother bear had scented the kill some distance away.

"The captain slowed our ship to a crawl. We watched the mother and her cubs walk toward the male, intending to share his meal—but he wanted no part of sharing. He stood over his kill, sending a very clear message: "This is mine. Don't touch it." The male and female stood about ten yards apart, glaring at each other in a fifteen-second face-off. The confrontation ended when the mother bear backed away.

"Throughout the encounter, our ship was still gliding closer.

The male bear walked over where the female had been standing and sniffed around. Then he looked up and saw the ship, perhaps for the first time. He started pawing at the ice as if he intended to bury the seal. Then he seemed to realize this wasn't going to work. He grabbed the seal by a hind flipper and dragged it backward, away from us. He lost his footing amid the broken ice floes but managed to scramble back aboard a floating slab. We were amazed at the strength in his head and neck: throughout his acrobatics he kept a firm grip with his teeth on the seal, which must have weighed almost 200 pounds."

When a polar bear defends his kill, he's not bluffing—his threats can be deadly serious. Ken Vaudrey once saw from the air a carcass on the ice. "We thought it was a seal until we flew closer," he told me. "It was the remains of a young bear, totally ripped open and eaten, except for the head. The legs were splayed as if the body had been dragged for some distance. A dead seal lay partly eaten nearby. I'm sure that we were looking at the aftermath of a battle over the seal. Whether the young bear was trying to defend his kill, or whether an older bear made the first kill and the younger bear challenged him, I don't know. All I do know is that it was a fatal mistake."

An area with good hunting and plentiful food draws bears from hundreds of square miles into social interaction on a scale that belies their solitary life-style. Although they're not eager to share their booty, they usually tolerate one another. As with every other activity, the bears don't waste energy in senseless fighting.

Occasionally, in a bonding pattern little understood, young males will form "friendships." Two or more males go off together on extended hunting trips. In summer and fall these friends are favored play-fighting companions and hang around together like teenagers out of school. As many as five males have been seen sleeping in a jumbled heap or feeding together.

Erik Nyholm wrote of two males that he named Kalle and Iso-Antti. They seemed such friends that Nyholm speculated they might be brothers, but no one knows if sibling bears continue to keep company after reaching maturity. These two had decidedly different personalities. One didn't even like to swim, a remarkable characteristic for a marine mammal: "Kalle was quick in his movements and decisions, but still had great patience when catching seals. Iso-Antti was slow, lazy and retiring, but very strong. Kalle liked to swim, but Iso-Antti walked nearly ten kilometers extra to avoid water. We never saw Iso-Antti take a swim.

"When the friends ate seaweed . . . Kalle made a hole in the ice and dived down to the depth of four to five meters [13 to 16 feet] and fetched up the food. Iso-Antti stood by the hole begging when Kalle came up with some in his mouth. Both ate of the algae. Kalle lay in the water with his forepaws on the edge of the ice. Then Kalle dived again for more. Kalle might do this for up to forty minutes. Then Kalle rose from the water, shook himself, and ate for a while lying on the ice. Iso-Antti had then had enough. What remained after such a seaweed meal was left for the other polar bears, especially Lulu and Lumu. All the polar bears ate algae.

"The friends Kalle and Iso-Antti hung about together a lot. The slower and water-shy Iso-Antti always came bouncing last. If anything happened, Iso-Antti was always there last."

The ultimate social interaction is finding a mate. Mating itself is a brief act. A female's estrus period lasts only three weeks, so the opportunity is limited and the competition furious. She marks her trail with frequent urine spots and soon has male bears following her scent. Frequent, serious, and decisive battles between males during the spring months guarantee that only the best genes will pass to the next generation.

Once paired the bears remain together, mating many times, for a week or longer. Ovulation, or egg release, doesn't occur until mating begins. This reproductive feat, termed *induced ovulation*, provides extra insurance in a world where the meeting of two partners at just the right moment in the midst of great emptiness cannot be left to chance. This time of intensity is followed by a curious biological slowdown: implantation of the impregnated egg in the uterine wall doesn't follow immediately. In fact, this essential step is delayed for months. The fertilized egg waits from April or May (rarely as late as July), when mating occurs, until August or September, when it finally implants and begins to grow. This strategy is shared by seals and some other members of the bear clan and is essential to surviving the cold winter. If mating were to occur in the fall, the bears would be in poor condition after their summer's starvation; their energies must be carefully focused on laying up fat reserves for the winter ahead. If the egg were to implant during the summer, the young bears would grow so large inside the mother that at birth their milk demand would be more than she could supply during her long fast. Some researchers speculate that a female makes a conscious decision to dig a den and that the egg doesn't implant until she's made that choice. This remains an unresolved cause-and-effect debate: does the egg implant and initiate a chemical signal that causes the bear to dig a den, or does the choice of a den site cause implantation?

During the fall freeze-up, when seal hunting from ice floes again becomes possible, a female bear must store a thick blubber layer in anticipation of the coming long period without food. Throughout her enforced fasting she'll burn off about two pounds of fat each day. Some females quadruple their body weight after mating, from about two hundred pounds to almost a thousand. In October these female bears dig deep into snowbanks, using their front paws as shovels, throwing the snow backward, like terriers in pursuit of burrowing prey.

Scientists and native hunters who have crawled inside polar bear dens almost invariably compare them with Eskimo snow houses. The proper type of snow is essential to a good igloo. A bear is very choosy about digging in the proper spot, with just the right kind of snow. She may walk many miles and dig many test pits during her search for the right home for her cubs. Then her engineering instincts take over as she begins to dig in earnest.

Beyond the entrance in a snowbank, an upward-sloping tunnel—often with a sill constructed at its inner end—serves as a cold trap. This is an exact parallel to the low igloo entrance and raised sleeping shelf that keep out the seeping cold and allow rising heat to warm the structure's interior. About ten feet up the den tunnel, its two-foot diameter expands into a room just big enough for a bear to turn around. Because the bear has selected a sheltered snowdrift in the lee of a ridge, and because snow is a superb insulator, the den is a snug home. Even with fierce arctic storms raging outside, the birthing den is seldom colder than 32° F. The female—known to the Eskimos as *Tayark*—scratches upward until she claws a vent hole several inches in diameter overhead. Claw marks on the interior walls and ceiling show that a mother bear continually adjusts her birthing chamber throughout her long confinement to supply fresh air and maintain a comfortable temperature for her cubs. Her body provides the only heat during the four to five months she remains in the den. After giving birth the mother may enlarge the den, digging side chambers where her cubs can play without having to face the terrors of the world outside.

In the den, Tayark dozes lightly and can awaken quickly if danger threatens. Her body temperature falls only slightly, in contrast to the dramatic cooling of true hibernators, who almost shut down their metabolic processes. Her respiration and heart rate do slow significantly, but they stay well above those of black and grizzly bears in hibernation. Occasionally, she wakes to swallow a mouthful of refreshing snow. Because she's living on fat reserves, and because fat breaks down completely, there are no body wastes to foul the den. Investigators report that the insides of birthing dens are very clean.

Pregnant females usually enter their dens in late October, urged on by insistent signals from their endocrine systems. They give birth, sheltered beneath the drifted snowbanks, between late November and early January. Four months after implantation—a very short gestation for a large mammal—two cubs, occasionally only one, rarely three or four, are born in the cozy den. Geneticists point out that these are fraternal, not identical, siblings. Each weighs about a pound and is the size of a guinea pig. The cubs are ill equipped to deal with their frozen world— the mother's den digging is now revealed as more than architectural skill: it's a basic act to ensure the survival of the species. The cubs are poorly insulated; their fur is only a quarter-inch long and covers slender bodies that wear no layer of blubber. The cubs are both senseless and defenseless. Three weeks will pass before they can hear, a month before they can see. At about six weeks the cubs develop tiny canine teeth and can smell their surroundings and walk a few hesitant steps. Throughout this time of total dependence on their mother, the cubs snuggle against her warm fur and suck rich milk from her four nipples. When nursing, she lies on her back, leaning against the walls of her snow cave like a human mother in a rocking chair, and cradles her newborn cubs in the shelter of her massive forelegs. She may even rock her children as she rolls gently from side to side. Outside, it may be 40 degrees below zero. In the den beneath the snow, all is peace, warmth, and contentment.

A mother bear must be vigilant, however. She keeps her cubs nearby while she teaches a two-year course in arctic survival: how to thrive in the most hostile environment on the face of the earth.

In March or early April (as early as February in southern locations, later farther north), the new family emerges. The cubs have grown fat on the rich milk, and they are chubby, twenty-five-pound fur balls in sleek new coats. It's time to break out of the den. They roll in the snow and slide, spread-eagled, down its slopes. The cubs, uncertain in their new world, stay close to their mother; they may climb on her back if danger threatens, or if they grow tired and cold. Air temperatures may still be well below zero. Once they have learned to swim, the cubs may also ride on their mother's back, or hold on to her tail, as she paddles through the sea.

Cubs begin to play almost at birth. When not nursing or sleeping, they seem always to be tumbling with each other, chasing each other, or biting each other. Like children heading home after a rain, they love to stomp in puddles and splash in meltwater ponds. Their mother is cautious and concerned: she licks and grooms them, or just touches them gently with her muzzle, many times a day. At first she keeps them within the newly opened den, but soon she leads them on brief jaunts to explore their new world. During this time the cubs are at great risk. Some are runts of the litter, known to Ian Stirling and his colleagues as the "underbears." Others fail to develop for a variety of physiological reasons. Still others fall prey to predators, including wolves and other polar bears. In mute testimony to this natural process, tiny claws of cubs are sometimes found in polar bear droppings. About one cub out of ten fails to survive the first few weeks out of the den. Some don't even make it that far: a malnourished mother bear may eat her own cubs to ensure that she will survive to mate again.

Although usually silent, cubs learn to make a variety of sounds. When frightened, they hiss loudly. When upset, they squall and whimper like human infants throwing temper tantrums. When uneasy, they chomp their teeth or make deep-throated rumblings and growlings. When contented, they purr. When petulant, they protrude their upper lips and blow wet, smacking bubbles. When lashing out with their claws, they make shrieking noises like cats in a fight.

Two weeks out of the den, the baby bear, known to Eskimos as *nanuark*, becomes *atertak*, one who goes to the sea. In another masterpiece of nature's intricate calendar, this trip is nicely timed to coincide with the birth of baby seals. Nursing whitecoat seals—*netiaks*—are a bear's greatest delicacy, and the new bear mothers haven't eaten for many months. They may have lost almost half their body weight during their long confinement in the den. The killing is fast and furious. A cub soon learns that the peace of the den has ended and the rough world begun: stalking, pouncing, and bloodshed.

Newborn cubs don't take part in the killing; they just watch. Yearling cubs may do some hunting on their own, but usually they stay within sight of their mother, walking when she walks, stopping when she stops, and learning by mimicking her behavior. At the tender age of one they face the icy blasts of the winter icepack alongside their mothers. Two-year-olds range more than a mile from their mother and may stalk seals in their aglus. When the snow has crusted over the seal dens, however, the cubs are too light, even at 150 to 250 pounds, to pounce and break through the way their mother does.

Sixty to 80 percent of cubs make it through their first year. Cubs that are weaned at age two have an excellent chance of survival. They go through a difficult adolescence, though, because they must learn to hunt on their own and to defend their kills from other bears.

The female may breed again after weaning her cubs and can give birth at three-year intervals. A female who is four to five years old can breed successfully although older females usually give birth to large litters. Males are sexually mature at age five or six but may not be big or bold enough to win a female until they reach eight or ten. Tag-and-release studies show that females may still be sexually active at age twenty-one. Two mothers eighteen years old had cubs with them when captured.

An adult bear is a hardy creature indeed. Perfectly adapted, at home in his world, he seems totally in command of the situation. For all his bulk, he moves with grace and dignity. In longevity, in mastery of a difficult setting, and in simple majesty, Nanook lives up to Ian Stirling's observation: "Once polar bears reach maturity, they seem virtually immortal."

The once-every-three-years breeding pattern means that although there are roughly the same number of male and female bears, in any given year all the males are competing for only one-third of the females. Put another way, there are three males for every breeding female. Competition is intense. Dominance of the large males is very real, a consequence of size and strength. Dominant males are two to three times as large as females. This disparity between the sexes—sexual dimorphism—is among the highest of all mammals. Stirling has observed: "In other species in which sexual dimorphism is prominent, there are usually far fewer males than females. The reverse is true of polar bears." The high male-to-available-female ratio, resulting from the long time cubs spend with their mothers, also ensures that only the hardiest genes are passed on to future generations. Dominant old polar bear males are among earth's most impressive creatures.

This continuing bear drama has repeated itself for thousands of years on the most featureless stage on earth. Cubs born and raised in the ice of the polar pack may live their entire lives without setting foot on land. In Hudson Bay, where food is plentiful, the statistics change slightly. Multiple births are common (triplets are born to 10 percent of the mothers). Yearling cubs strike off on their own, and two-year-olds are never seen with their mothers. Many Hudson Bay females give birth every second year. These short-term mothers chase off their grown cubs when it's time to dig a maternity den in the fall of the cubs' second year. This means that Hudson Bay mothers can bear 30 percent more litters during their lifetimes than bears at higher latitudes.

Scientists have yet to discover the young cubs' secrets for surviving the winter alone. They have, however, given them an endearing name: cubs of the year, abbreviated as *coys*. Coys are among the most appealing baby animals. With their shortened faces, lustrous black eyes, and shy but inquisitive natures, they are favorite subjects of wildlife photographers. Born far from human population centers, polar bear cubs nonetheless have a huge adoring public.

While her cubs are too small to face the world on their own, a mother bear rushes to defend them and may stand up to the largest male to protect her family. She is reluctant to abandon even a dead cub. Biologists have seen a mother bear killed and eaten by a large male while her yearling cubs watched, helpless. The scientists presume she died in their defense.

Females with cubs usually don't mate. Physiologists who study bear reproduction believe that hormones associated with milk production interfere with ovulation, offering a mechanism for natural birth control. When her cubs are old enough to hunt on their own, a mother bear may chase them away or allow them to be scared off by an amorous male.

Throughout their cubhood and into adolescence, bears continue to grow. Males reach their full size and weight during their eighth or ninth year. Females are full grown at only half the males' weight and grow little after their fourth year. The distinction between the sexes is evident at a distance: males are gangly and long legged, females compact, rounder, and less massive.

A bear learns as he grows. Nanook's greatest asset when learning the ways of the world is his curiosity. Many bear "attacks" may be simply the result of a curious bear checking out some new aspect of his environment. Two Canadian researchers, Susan Fleck and Steve Herrero, have described the scene: "The behaviour of a curious polar bear is similar to that of a curious black or grizzly bear or dog. . . . A polar bear investigating something different will stand usually on all fours and move slowly towards or around the object, stopping frequently to sniff the air and look around. The head will be held high with ears forward or sticking out and the bear will move its head around to try to catch a scent. Like other bear species or a dog, a polar bear will often circle downwind to catch the scent of the object of interest and approach from this direction."

When a bear gets curious, people get worried. To shoot or not to shoot—that is the question when the white bear comes close. "This is the dilemma of 'civilized' man in the north country," coastal engineer Craig Leidersdorf told me. In his many years of arctic experience, Leidersdorf and his colleagues have been careful to observe a modern wilderness ethic. "We consider ourselves guests in the Arctic. We have no intentions of injuring polar bears, or inflicting ourselves in any way on the environment, on the animals, or on the native people. But when you feel that your life is in danger and the adrenaline starts flowing, there's a point at which self-preservation instincts overwhelm logic and ethics."

Leidersdorf's story begins on an ice floe about seventy miles northwest of Alaska's Prudhoe Bay. He was working with a research party to describe the multiyear floe, a jumbled mass of ice about eight hundred feet across. "We knew a little about bears," Leidersdorf told me, "but we had no biologists or long-term arctic residents in our group. We were extremely careful the first year we were up there. We took one weapon for each person.

"The second year, we were a little more relaxed, because we hadn't had any bear trouble. Tracks in the snow showed that bears had been investigating our measuring instruments, but they hadn't appeared while we were working. We eventually became so complacent that we left the weapons near the helicopter when we moved away to service our instruments."

On the large floe Leidersdorf's crew was split into several teams. One group was drilling through the ice to measure its thickness; another was lowering oceanographic instruments into the water at the floe's edge. Leidersdorf was standing alone beside a tripod, using a radio direction finder to monitor ocean currents by tracking buoys drifting alongside the ice. He was listening intently through a pair of earphones, trying to pick up the faint beeping signals from the buoys. His concentration was totally focused on the work at hand. As Leidersdorf recalls,

"Suddenly the helicopter pilot was screaming, 'He's coming at you!' and gesturing wildly over my shoulder toward the water. I looked toward the edge of the floe where the oceanographic team had been working. Fortunately, they had completed their measurements and moved to another portion of the floe. A young bear had climbed out of the water right where they'd been standing, and he was heading for me at a fast trot. Quick steps, like a dog that's spotted something interesting.

"My first instinct—God knows why—was to turn off the radio. Then I bolted for the helicopter. When I took off, the bear bolted, too. The two of us were converging toward the helicopter, but it was clear that he was going to cut me off.

"I lost sight of the bear in the rough topography of the ice. Maybe he lost me, too, or maybe he just found the chase amusing. Anyway, he stood up on his hind legs for a better look. That gave me time to reach the helicopter.

About this time the pilot, who'd had bear adventures before, made preparations to start the aircraft's engine, hoping the noise might scare the bear away. His copilot grabbed a shotgun but was so excited that when he pumped it to chamber a shell, he just kept on pumping until he'd ejected all the shells into the snow. He dropped the gun on the ice and jumped into the helicopter.

Leidersdorf continues his story: "By now the others on the ice were streaming back to the copter. We crammed all seven of us, plus the two crew, into the aircraft, with two shotguns and an old buffalo rifle trained out the doors. It looked like the last stand at the Alamo, and everyone was yelling different instructions: 'Shoot!' 'No, don't shoot!' 'Wait till he charges!' There was so much adrenaline pumping, and so much sweat in a confined space, the helicopter smelled like the worst locker room you can imagine.

"I mentally marked a line of defense on a rise about forty feet away. If the bear approached any closer, I intended to fire a warning shot over his head. Like many animals, he seemed to sense the limit. At exactly the distance I was guarding, he stopped, reared, and regarded us with curiosity. He then ambled around the floe, sniffing and pawing at every single object we'd left on the ice. We had huge crosses made of cloth to mark our instrument sites. He toyed with these like a kitten clawing drapes. He snapped off our survey stakes. He stood like a circus bear with all four feet on top of our battery boxes. He even burned his nose on our propane generator.

"About this time, we got a little bolder and left the helicopter to test some of the deterrents we'd been advised to use. Our whistles and flares had absolutely no effect on the bear, who eventually just wandered away. We lifted off, none the worse for our adventure.

"The next day we returned to the floe to find that a bear—probably the same one, but we couldn't be sure—had ripped into everything again, had completely destroyed our equipment, and had strewn the wreckage all over the floe. We'd provided a great toy land for a growing bear."

The curiosity of polar bears can be entertaining—if you're safely out of reach. Walt Spring, arctic engineer, was on a ship in the icepack near Svalbard in 1988. "We'd shut down our activities at night, and the pack would freeze around the ship," Spring told me. "On alternate mornings, the cook would fix bacon for breakfast. On bacon days, we always awoke to find bears on the ice nearby. They'd follow the scent straight to us. We spent seven days in the pack ice, and counted fifty-seven bears.

"The bears would follow their noses until they saw the ship. Then they'd stop. They'd look us over a while and then sit down behind a ridge where we couldn't see them. Then they'd pop up again to see if anything had changed. Ducking down behind the ridge, they'd wait some more and then come up and check us out again. This might go on for hours. At least once the bears slept overnight behind a ridge, came out the next morning and looked us over again, and kept up the routine until we left the area."

Bears often seem annoyed or amused at the objects humans leave on the ice. They're fascinated by anything that might remotely be considered edible, but they also investigate everything else. A helicopter pilot reported watching helplessly from a distance as a bear spotted his own reflection in the dark Plexiglas bubble at the front of his aircraft. Apparently thinking he saw another bear, Nanook shattered the bubble with a single paw blow. Other bears have chewed on electrical cables, survey markers, inflatable boats, vehicle tires, oil drums, and grave markers. Just about any object left within a bear's reach will soon be wearing tooth marks.

Such curiosity, together with the constant quest for food, explain a bear's wide range and wandering tracks. Bears roam the ice, investigating every subtle odor or unusual lump of snow, without any apparent goal. They seem purposeful only when heading for open water, following an interesting scent, or choosing a place to dig a den.

Polar bear dens are not randomly distributed over the arctic region. Rather, they are concentrated in Canada (the Hudson Bay region, Ungava Bay, and Baffin Island), Greenland (along the northeastern coast), Norway's Svalbard Archipelago, and the northern margins of the Soviet Union (Wrangel Island and Franz Josef Land). Dens are also found on the ice near Barrow, Alaska, but these may have drifted from an area farther east.

These denning areas correspond to the major populations of polar bears. Nanook makes his home wherever ice, open water, and seals are found together. Canada's Arctic Islands are home to countless bears, scattered in about a dozen groups throughout the thousands of miles of shoreline. These subgroups occasionally intermingle and interbreed. So do the larger populations, but generally these remain isolated from one another. The East Greenland population is separated from the Canadian bears by the huge interior icecap, almost two miles thick, which sits in the center of Greenland like a mound of ice cream in a shallow dish. Svalbard's bear population outnumbers the human population: 4,000 to 5,000 bears, to include some trekkers that walk across the ice from the west (Greenland) and from the east (Franz Josef Land), to winter in the archipelago. In the summer months some 3,000 bears remain. (The permanent human population numbers 1,200 Norwegians and 2,100 Soviets, joined in the summer by 10,000 tourists.) Wrangel Island, north of Siberia, has a large bear population that intermingles with western Alaskan polar bears. A second Alaskan population ranges the North Slope eastward into Canada.

Den sites must be protected from human activity if polar bears are to survive. Biologist Steve Amstrup, a pioneer in polar bear research, monitors den sites in northern Alaska for the U.S. Fish and Wildlife Service. "Many of our maternity dens are at sea in the distant pack ice where human interference is at a minimum. Dens on land, however, produce about a third of our cubs. Just prior to parturition [birth] and for at least two months thereafter, the females can't abandon dens, or their cubs will be lost. Most cubs are born in early January, so the period of maximum vulnerability coincides, unfortunately, with the time of greatest over-ice and over-tundra human activity. Ironically, the period from January to March, the preferred time for human activities, was chosen to minimize environmental impact" [because the tundra is much less susceptible to damage by vehicles when it is frozen].

"One of our problems is that our dens are widely scattered. We don't have the high den concentration that characterizes Wrangel Island or Svalbard. We're trying to develop a base of information that would allow us to quantify the number of dens per square mile of various kinds of habitat. To do this, we put radio collars on bears that we think are pregnant and follow them to their dens. Aerial surveys in the spring augment these studies, but flights are limited by weather and darkness.

"I was the first to succeed at putting radio collars on polar bears," Amstrup told me. "The addition of radiotelemetry to polar bear studies has been a real boon. Prior to our radiotelemetry studies, locations of only thirty-five dens had been recovered in all of Alaska, in all the years since the whalers started coming here. In contrast, we've located over a hundred dens by radio tracking since 1981."

At one point, Amstrup tried a new technique. "We decided to mark maternity dens with radio-transmitter beacons that could be dropped out of airplanes. We intended to return on foot once the bears had left the area and it was safe to crawl inside the dens to take measurements. It was a great plan—on paper.

"We flew over the dens during the period in the spring when the cubs are getting acclimated to their new world, when they explore the area around the entrance but return to the den to rest. My partner was pretty accurate with the beacon drops, usually hitting within 50 feet of the den entrance, and we thought the transmitters would be easy to relocate, but the signals proved weak and confusing once we were on the ground. It turned out that four of our five beacons were picked up by the cubs and dragged into the dens. Once we figured it out, the beacons were exactly where we wanted them to be, but under several feet of snow. Our fifth beacon," Amstrup adds with a chuckle, "was picked up by an Eskimo from Barter Island, who just happened to see it in the snow and carried it back to the village. Not one of our radio beacons remained where we'd dropped it."

Tag-and-recapture studies reveal that most bears return to the same area year after year. Wildlife biologists refer to this behavior as "seasonal fidelity." This means that an individual bear is likely to reappear at the same time each year in the same denning area, the same seal-hunting area, the same summer sanctuary, and the same shoreline where the same bears wait every year for ice to form on the water.

The visible evidence of such studies—scientists' tags in bears' ears—bothers some observers. I've heard nature enthusiasts complain with anger and revulsion at the thought of live-trapping or tranquilizing even problem bears inside town limits. I'm not that adamant but the tags are somehow disturbing to me. I know many bears have been captured, weighed, measured, and released in the same spot, year after year. I know that the unobtrusive white-button tags don't harm the bears. Still, they diminish my sense of untrammeled wilderness, just as discovering a surveyor's benchmark atop an ice-scoured cliff shatters my illusions of being the first human to set foot on the precipice. The thrill of seeing a bear free to roam his icy world is magnified if he wears no indication that he's ever known human contact. I know, however, that the animals were tagged by researchers interested in the bears' welfare and ultimate protection. Perhaps a small piece of plastic in the ear isn't too great a premium to pay for insurance that the great white bears will continue to walk the ice forever.

SIX

From the Ice Age
to the Stone Age

At the blue-white foot of a Greenland glacier, I wandered aimlessly among boulders strewn across the gritty sand that the ice dropped as it melted. Gradually I became aware of a certain geometry in the rocks at my feet. Where moments earlier I'd seen only a random scatter of stones, I now recognized circular patterns ten to fifteen feet across. Rocks had been cleared from within the circles and set carefully around their perimeters.

I've encountered such mini-Stonehenges before, but they always amaze me. They bear messages from the past. The circles mark the former locations of sealskin tents, erected by hunters long departed. I like them for their mystery: to my untrained eye, there is no indication whether the campsite was occupied thirty years ago, or three hundred, or three thousand. Lichenometrists—scientists who can calculate the last time a rock was overturned by studying the patches of lichen growing on its exposed surfaces—might decipher the ancient story in detail, but to me the circles speak with an eloquent voice across uncounted centuries, as surely as any fossil.

I'm a geologist, and I delight in the record in the rocks, the evidence of ancient lands and seas and long-dead life revealed by inanimate objects. Polar bears, however, don't have much of a geological pedigree. Their fossil record tells an abbreviated tale.

Nanook is a recent arrival; his span on earth as a species has been brief. In fact, polar bears and humans have coevolved over roughly the same time interval. Polar bear ancestors moved into the arctic regions during the Ice Age, in the latter half of the Pleistocene Epoch (perhaps as far back as 300,000 years ago). Evolutionary biologists—including paleontologist Bjørn Kurtén, whose first name means "bear"—theorize that bears, including the European cave bear, *Ursus spelaeus*, thrived during warm interglacial periods. When the climate turned cold, the bears had to adapt to a changing world. About a million years ago, the bear that we know today as the grizzly or Alaskan brown bear evolved from the same line that produced cave bears. Brown bears spread widely across the Pleistocene landscape. Then, scientists speculate, an isolated population of Siberian brown bears found new opportunities as the temperature dropped still lower and sheets of ice began to cover the Arctic Ocean. The edge of the icepack drifted ever closer to the shoreline. Seals, hauled out on the ice floes, probably unwary and easy to catch because no predator had hunted them during the warm periods, offered an abundant food source.

No one knows just when the first bear ate the first seal (probably scavenging a dead one), nor when bears first hunted live seals, nor when the land dweller became primarily an aquatic bear, nor when the seal hunter's need for camouflage amid the snow-covered floes gave a reproductive advantage to bears with lighter coats. Certainly by the beginning of the last great glaciation (known as the Wisconsinian in North America and as the Würm in Europe)—about 70,000 years ago—polar bears were a distinct species, although recent DNA studies suggest that modern polar bears could have appeared as recently as 20,000 years ago. A fossil leg bone found in England confirms that Nanook, though a much larger and more wide-ranging variety than today's bear, had made his entrance before the last ice sheets plowed southward.

The story of this fossil shows how much information can be gleaned from a single fragment. The find, unearthed in a railroad cut near Kew Bridge in downtown London, was an incomplete right *ulna,* or forelimb bone. Its incompleteness is significant: missing was the distal end, the knobby ball joint that once connected the foreleg to the wrist below. In most juvenile animals these rotating joint surfaces are made of cartilage. As these creatures reach adulthood, the joint bearing surfaces ossify (turn into bone). If, in rambling through fields and forests, you stumble across the bleached skeleton of a lamb, a calf, or a fawn, look at the limb bones. They'll probably be missing their ends. Young bones leave only the central shaft to be preserved.

Because the Kew Bridge find's lower end is missing, the fossil leg bone probably belonged to a subadult animal. This is all the more reason to be astonished at its size. At 440 millimeters (17.3 inches), its length far exceeds the measurement of such bones in recent polar bears (the ulna of a very large subadult bear, similarly measured without the distal knob, was 387 millimeters [15.2 inches] long). At the minimum this Pleistocene bear was about 15 percent taller—and probably much heavier—than today's polar bear. That might make him almost thirteen feet tall when he stood on two legs. Tall enough to rest his chin on the top of a tractor-trailer or to peer over most one-story houses. More than a ruler of lands spread across much of northern Europe, this giant was potentially a fearsome tyrant. Thus his subspecies name: *Ursus maritimus tyrannus.*

The fossil leg bone was found near the remains of forest animals that thrived in the warm interglacial periods: bison, hippos, rhinos, and elephants. This seems an incongruous setting for the ultimate polar bear. However, in roughly the same rock layers, bones of another cold-climate animal, the reindeer, turn up from time to time. The record in the rocks tells of climatic change, of a shift from African-style grasslands and forests to a snowy landscape as the last great advance of the glaciers began. The polar bear probably never saw the hippos and rhinos, but his chilly world followed close on the heels of their warm one.

Many animals of the Pleistocene Epoch were giants by today's standards. Scientists pondering this size difference offer two possible explanations. The first relates body size and surface area to heat loss. Massive, chunky bodies conserve heat better than small or spindly frames. Biologists call this Bergmann's Rule: the colder the climate, the larger the body. The second cause of the apparent shrinking from huge Pleistocene animals to today's smaller forms may have been the spread of human hunters across the landscape. By killing both predators and their prey, early humans altered the population dynamics of animal communities at the end of the Pleistocene. Some beasts they hunted to extinction. Others were forced to adapt to conditions of sparser food or to increased pressure from hunters seeking the largest animals. (This last point is still an issue: in regions where sport hunting persisted longest, the average-sized polar bears are smaller than in other regions, perhaps because every hunter wants a trophy-sized bear.) Regardless of how it came about, those of us who have shared the ice with Nanook have reason to be grateful that he is a good deal smaller than his forebears.

Fossil polar bears have been unearthed at several locations across northern Europe, but they are rare. Nanook is not a creature whose bones are likely to be preserved. In the language of paleontology, polar bears have low *preservation potential.* They spend most of their lives on the shifting icepack, from which their remains would drop to the seafloor. Bears are scattered across an immense area. They frequent the beach, and their bones occasionally are found amid beach sediments, but most Ice Age beaches now lie submerged beneath the rising waters. In the arctic realm there are few fossil seekers digging through the postglacial layers of rock and dirt. Add to this list Nanook's brief duration as a separate species, a short time to leave much of a fossil record, and the paucity of polar bear fossil discoveries is easily explained. Enough evidence does exist, however, to suggest that by 100,000 years ago bears—presumably white—with teeth designed for tearing flesh were distributed throughout the arctic regions. Polar bears had made the leap, leaving the land behind, walking onto the frozen sea, and had become marine mammals.

When the continental ice sheets advanced again, they drove the remaining brown bears south, separating the two populations. In an isolated gene pool, and with the pressures of a new way of life, evolutionary change happened faster. The seal-hunting bears adapted to their new life-style. The trend accelerated toward lighter coats, longer necks and snouts, and the distinctive wedge-shaped body. Genetically, the two species are still very close, however, and polar bears and brown bears interbreed (in captivity) to produce fertile offspring with both brown and white fur. Some hybrid cubs are half and half. Others start out white but darken as they age. This reproductive closeness, together with the similarities of blood chemistry, skull dimensions, and teeth, is further evidence that the two species separated relatively recently. When the warm times returned, Nanook stayed on the ice and hunted seals; brown bears remained on the land. Although the two species theoretically might have recombined through interbreeding, their habitats had become so different that even chance meetings of the two were probably rare.

The white bear's closest living relative is probably the barren-ground grizzly bear of Canada's Northwest Territories. Canadian researcher Ian Stirling, noting that native bear watchers claim to have seen grizzlies hunting seals in their birthing lairs, wrote, "I would love to watch that myself, for I think it would give one the sense of watching the polar bear evolve."

Polar bears spread rapidly throughout the arctic regions, occupying a previously vacant environmental niche. No other large predator stalked the ice. Nanook was literally master of all he surveyed.

Some evolutionary changes are physical, others behavioral. Having adopted a carnivorous life-style, Nanook no longer shared the seasonal life patterns of other bears. Seasonal change governs the world of plants and thus the world of most bears, who depend on roots and berries for much of their diet. The polar bear's seasonality was now dictated by his ability to hunt seals, which requires an ice platform. The time of famine became not winter, when ice was abundant, but summer, when the floes were few and far from shore and from the seals that cavorted in inshore waters. Winter hibernation—a consequence of plants' being dormant—was no longer necessary. Snow caves were still dug; newborn cubs still needed dens for shelter against the cold, but other bears were free to wander the icepack throughout the long, dark winter. Summer, when the ice retreated northward, became the time to endure, to live off laid-up stores of fat until the ice returned and the bears could hunt again. Once again the ice bear changed his body to adapt. Scientists who have studied the blood chemistry of polar bears during the summer report that physiologically they resemble other species of bears that sleep away the winter. The researchers describe the bear's summer fasting condition as "walking hibernation." By far the most bear problems near human habitation are caused by summer and fall bears living off their fat reserves during the ice-free season. Anyone who's ever felt grouchy on a restricted diet understands Nanook's ill temper during his months of starvation.

The polar bear's changes, though recent, are profound. Not only has he gone from brown to white, from land to sea, and from omnivore to carnivore, but he has also completely reversed the seasons of the bear year. Winter is a time of activity; summer is for fasting, resting, and conserving energy.

During this time of change in the bear world, humans were evolving in more temperate regions. As they wandered from their African birthplace into Eurasia, early humans found themselves ill equipped—in a physical sense—for life in a cooler world. They were naked, gangly creatures, best suited for equable climates. Fortunately they were endowed with inventive, inquisitive minds. As temperatures dropped, these plains and forest dwellers moved into caves or built shelters. To cover their shivering, vulnerable bodies, they sewed garments from the warm furs of animals that shared their world. They adapted fire to their own uses and made tools from flakes of flint and obsidian, or from fragments of bone, tooth, and antler. They developed primitive religions.

Strongest among their spirits was the cave bear. They began a tradition of bear worship that continues into this century with the reverence of all the northern peoples, from the Lapps to the

Eskimos, for Nanook, the white bear. The bear, whether dwelling in the dark caves in central Europe or wandering the arctic ice pack, was clearly the most powerful element in the lives of such people. He determined the patterns of their lives and often the circumstances of their deaths. Awesome and awful, he possessed a majesty innately worthy of worship.

Moving slowly northward whenever the climate warmed, small groups of early humans spread across the continents, established footholds on the steppes of Asia, and eventually reached the forests and tundra plains of Siberia. They found large areas free of ice, where they could hunt abundant game: lions, hyenas, rhinos, mammoths, bison, horses, foxes, wolves, and many kinds of deer thrived on the Siberian mainland. There some of the people stayed and founded a culture that would eventually flourish in the arctic setting. These tiny bands of nomads would one day conquer the top of the world and become the polar Eskimos, the Inuit: People of the North. They would eventually occupy more territory, and for a longer time, than any other racial or linguistic group on earth.

Others, perhaps initially more adventurous, turned toward the east. To view the path ahead through their eyes is to see an untamed world. . . .

Through the dry valleys they trudged, their fur-wrapped feet kicking aside the tall grasses. The small band of hunters pursued the bison, woolly mammoth, and caribou: four-legged sources of meat for nourishment; sources of bone, tusks, antlers, and sinew for implements; and sources of furry hides to shelter the nomads against the cold. Facing the rising sun, chanting ritual prayers to their bear gods, the hunters walked eastward into a land that had never felt the tread of human feet. Leaving the world of their ancestors, they became the first Americans.

The land they crossed had only recently emerged from beneath the salt waters. Before humans walked these broad plains, plants had arrived, their seeds scattered by the winds or dropped by birds. Golden grasslands and forests of dark conifers edged onto the drying seabed, but harsh winds from the north swept most of the emergent land, and few plants gained footholds, even when the ocean's salts were leached from the soil by summer rains. Animals, large and small, foraged across the chilly plain. Now, pursuing them, came the hunters.

The seascape turned landscape looked to these people like other territory they'd hunted. Crisscrossed by game trails, it was otherwise unremarkable. The hunters had no way of knowing that its very existence bespoke changes on a global scale. Not for tens of thousands of years, not until the grass-tufted plain had disappeared as mysteriously as it had emerged, would scientists determine why this land bridge between Siberia and Alaska existed.

Over the million years leading up to the hunters' journey, the earth's climate had turned cooler—not once but at least four times. Just a few degrees cooler, but the chill was enough to shift the climate zones that encircle the earth. The polar world expanded. Warming trends shifted the same zones back toward the poles. Then the cold came again. Cycles: cold, warm, cold. During the most frigid times, immense ice sheets covered the northern landmasses and spread across the plains. Snow fell in the cold continental interiors, building the great glaciers to thicknesses of two or more miles. For water, rising by evaporation from the sea and settling as snow on the great ice sheets, the voyage was a one-way trip. The glaciers held on to their snowy prize. The oceans lost their water. Sea level fell. Coastal areas once submerged now lay naked, exposed, glistening beneath the Pleistocene sky. The thicker the glaciers, the lower the sea. More ice, more seafloor revealed. At the peak of each glacial episode, the ocean surface dropped hundreds of feet below its present position.

During such lowstands, migrations across the exposed seafloor populated the Americas with animals previously unknown in these lands. From the massive grazing herds of musk-oxen, moose, bison, caribou, and the predators that fed on them to small rodents such as beavers and chipmunks, they walked, hopped, stampeded, or swam eastward into a new world. Some went the other way: horses and camels that had evolved in North America crossed the land bridge westward into the Eurasian steppes.

The first humans across the land bridge—a piece of vanished territory called, in modern times, Beringia, after today's Bering Strait—headed south. Anthropologists call them Paleo-Indians. In search of warmer, gentler climates, they kept moving, because the ice was advancing again. Conditions that we would call arctic (geologists term such environments *periglacial*—literally "near ice") extended as far south as Kansas and Ohio. The first Americans found a chilly reception, a continent with a cold heart.

As the ice sheets alternately advanced and melted (we often speak of the glaciers retreating, but they don't back up; rather they melt in place), successive waves of two-legged creatures migrated eastward from Siberia. The timing of their first arrival is still a matter of vigorous debate. Everyone seems to agree, however, that the land bridge was passable for 14,000 years, from the time the sea drained off about 25,000 years ago until the ice melted and the seas once again covered Beringia, about 11,000 years ago. During most of this time, however, advancing ice sheets choked off the passage southward to the new world. A Paleolithic pilgrim might have walked from Siberia to present-day Alaska throughout most of this period but could have continued on to the central plains of North America only during the relatively short time between 25,000 and 23,000 years ago when the passage was ice free. For the remainder of the land-bridge time, he would have been forced northward, into the cold. Into the Arctic.

During relatively warm periods, when the waters were high, new waves of migration began. Siberian coastal peoples built small boats from the stretched skins of seals and walrus, and paddled their sturdy craft across the icy waters. Two warmings produced significant migrations across the North American Arctic, about 3,500 to 4,500 years ago and 900 to 1,100 years ago. During these intervals Eskimolike hunters walked, paddled, and dogsledded their way eastward, leaving settlements scattered across Alaska and the Canadian Arctic and eventually reaching as far as Greenland. Their numbers were small, their villages tiny, but their adaptations to the arctic world are legendary.

The first to make this prodigious trek arrived in Alaska from Siberia about 5,000 years ago. They are known, by the artifacts they left behind, as the people of the Arctic Small Tool Tradition. They crafted useful objects: small arrowheads for hunting birds, stone knives and scrapers, lamps for burning seal oil, bone fishhooks, and ivory needles. They were followed by a sled-building culture, known as Pre-Dorset, and, about 2,800 years ago, by the Dorset people (so named because their campsites were first excavated near Cape Dorset on Canada's Foxe Peninsula). The Dorset culture imbued ivory or bone carvings with powerful magic. Their most common carving was of Nanook, the white bear. They also crafted bear masks to represent Nanook's spirit. The Dorset people arose during a climatic cooling; their world must have been harsh, their lives grim. Those who study their stylized art invariably describe the carvings as dark, brutal, intense, powerful, bizarre, provocative, or grotesque. Against fearsome odds, the Dorset persisted for more than two millennia in the arctic and subarctic regions. Isolated bands of Dorset people were still eking out a feeble existence around A.D. 1400 in northern Quebec and Labrador, but Dorset culture had been largely displaced or absorbed around A.D. 900 to 1100 by the Thule culture.

The Thule people, named for archaeological sites near Thule, Greenland, were direct ancestors of the modern Eskimos. Their culture arose in the vicinity of the Bering Strait and surged across the North American Arctic with amazing vigor. Anthropologists believe they may have spread from Point Barrow, Alaska, some 2,600 miles eastward to northern Greenland in only two or three generations. The Thule people were whalers and superb hunters. They perfected the stretching of skins to form kayaks, the lashing of bone and ivory components into sturdy, dog-drawn sleds, and the carving of sophisticated toggle-headed harpoons. They built rock and turf homes, roofed with sod laid over skins stretched on the ribs and jawbones of whales. Above all else, they met Nanook on his own terms. Polar bear skulls lie buried in the ruins of Thule dwellings. The white bear was a central focus of Thule life.

The Thule culture thrived during a climatic warming. When the air once again turned cold, about A.D. 1100, the Thule people had to leave the high Arctic. They splintered into isolated bands in northwestern Greenland, on Baffin Island, and on the Canadian mainland. From these three small tribes arose the present Eskimo, or Inuit, culture. These people are still few in number: there are three times more babies born each day on earth than there are living Eskimos.

Throughout this evolution the northern people were adapting to their world. Physiologically, the Inuit are well equipped for their harsh environment. They are short and stocky, with flat Asiatic faces. Their cheekbones—which underlie the only flesh exposed to the arctic winds when a parka hood is drawn tight—are padded with fatty tissue as defense against the cold. Their tiny, low-bridged noses and small hands and feet minimize their exposure to frostbite. Their limbs are shortened disproportionately: the arm below the elbow, the leg below the knee. Compared with other peoples of the world, their limbs are the shortest in relation to other body proportions. This stubbiness reduces the distance life-giving blood must travel to warm fingers and toes. The Inuit have a slightly higher metabolic rate than more southerly peoples, another defense against the cold.

As anthropologists have pointed out, however, the Inuit are a recent people. There simply hasn't been time for a truly arctic, furry, compact human to evolve. Instead, an arctic *culture* has been the adaptation that allowed humankind to survive in the frozen kingdom of the white bear. Superbly tailored garments—some for insulation, others for waterproofing—keep the hunter warm and dry as he waits beside the aglu. A diet high in saturated fats provides internal energy and gives the hunter his own fatty insulation. The snow house, constructed entirely of the natural materials literally underfoot, gives shelter from the wind. The hunter's daring, his wife's skill, their courage, and their trust in the world of spirits give protection from Nanook.

Coming into the new lands, the early wanderers found an experienced teacher already at home in this challenging setting. Human hunters learned many of their seal-hunting techniques by watching bears. An Eskimo hunter mimics the white bear's stalk across the ice on all fours, sliding forward concealed behind a patch of white bearskin stretched over a bone frame. Nanook's still hunt, the patient wait beside the aglu, became the characteristic stiff-legged Eskimo pose beside the seal's breathing hole. Bent at the waist, his upper body parallel with the frozen surface and forming a right angle with his legs, the hunter minimizes contact with the cold ice and waits for the telltale whoosh of a seal rising in the ice well. Crossing new ice not yet blanketed with snow, the hunter straps bearskin muffles to his mukluks. These pads soften his footfalls and make him as silent as the white bear in his approach. He may also, like the bear, avoid scraping away the snow cover from older ice: if sunlight shines through from above, a seal may become wary and choose another spot to rise and breathe.

The patience Eskimos learned from the bears became the basis of legend: the tale is told of a group of Eskimos who traveled up a fjord seeking grass to dry for hay. When they arrived at the meadow, they found the grass too short to cut. They simply sat down and waited for it to grow.

The women, too, copied Nanook. Like the bears Inuit mothers nursed their children until they were able to function on their own in a harsh world. According to Sam Hall, author of *The Fourth World*, "It was common for a mother to continue to nurse a son until he was thirteen or fourteen years old, when he could drive a dog team with all the expertise of his father, and had probably caught his first seal."

Just as a bear conserves his precious energy in a world that continually seeps it away, the northern people learned to guard against nonessential actions or emotions. War, revenge, and quarreling were unknown in the Inuit world. It was absolutely necessary to live for today and be cheerful, for any day might be their last. As Pierre Berton has written in *The Arctic Grail*, "When food was available, they ate it all; when there was none, they went without, uncomplaining." Berton also noted that in the midst of a watery world, the Inuit were always thirsty: eating snow was taboo, for the resulting loss of body heat could be fatal.

The Eskimos learned Nanook's steady pace across the ice, a precaution against overheating. White explorers struggled against the Arctic, exhausting themselves. They cursed the natives for their "laziness," but in reality that pace was a strategy that allowed the nomads to arrive at their destinations, in Berton's words, "with minds and bodies unimpaired—able to move forward, day by day, without collapsing."

The Arctic ecosystem is the youngest on earth. As the ice sheets melted, they exposed the bare rock and tundra soil now supporting the abundant life that springs anew with each summer's thaw. Fewer than 10,000 years separate the Arctic's present inhabitants from the Pleistocene Epoch. In the high Arctic, and in Greenland's interior, the Ice Ages haven't gone away. In a sense the Pleistocene never truly ended. Rather it was displaced northward on the warming globe.

There the ice waits. If the present warming trend continues (or even accelerates as a result of the much publicized greenhouse effect), the ice may disappear altogether, and meltwater streams will rush in tumbling torrents toward the sea. The oceans will rise to cover more of the land, and the Ice Ages will at last have come to an end. If the average temperature of the earth should drop by even one degree, however—perhaps because we'd passed through a dusty corner of the galaxy and less sunlight reached the planet—the great grinding glaciers might advance again. Straining against the walls of their valleys, they would obliterate everything that blocks their paths and spread far across the plains that other ice scraped smooth not so long ago. The cold could come again.

With this icy prologue, the curtain lowers on the Arctic's opening act. The stage is set; the white bear and humans are in their places. The drama about to unfold will reveal a story paralleled the world over and all too familiar: natives coexisting with the natural world, their discovery and subjugation by European adventurers, followed by exploration and exploitation of the land. What makes this script unique is that throughout the various acts, Nanook waits in the wings. He is there behind the ice ridge, watching, as the Eskimo builds his snow house. He lurks beneath the overhanging stern of the explorer's brigantine. He waits outside the mission church for an unwary child to finish her prayers. He creeps silently past the fence guarding a military installation. He hides beneath the steel steps of an oil-drilling rig. Always, it seems, the bear is waiting. Throughout the centuries there have been only three constants in the Arctic: the white and the cold and the bears.

SEVEN

People of the Bear

I WATCHED, FASCINATED, as two sealskin kayaks—their sleek sides painted white for camouflage among the floes—glided up the ice-choked fjord. Two sturdy hunters clenched pipes in their jaws; when they paddled with short, choppy strokes, they puffed like tugboats, leaving a wake of small clouds. The men were pursuing narwhal, small, spotted whales known for their spiraled ivory tusks as unicorns of the sea. The whales swam near, oblivious. The kayakers paddled their boats up onto the animals' backs when they rose to breathe, then struck with short harpoons. As line payed out, the hunters heaved overboard large buoys made from black, inflated sealskin (swathed in white cloth to complete the disguise) that had been strapped to the kayaks' afterdecks. Eventually, the whales—exhausted from dragging the buoys—resurfaced, gasping for air. The hunters drew rifles from leather scabbards on their foredecks, and the chase was soon finished. Pulling knives, the men cut the glistening black dorsal fins from their whales, then chewed the fresh meat as a delicacy before it cooled. This *muktuk*, or narwhal skin with the blubber still attached to its undersurface, is considered a treat in the northern community. I looked on in amazement. I had encountered my first polar Inuit.

A man of the Arctic is an *Inuk*. Two or more are *Inuit*, literally "the people." (The word *Eskimo*, derived from an Algonquin word for "eaters of raw meat," is used primarily in Alaska. Elsewhere in the Arctic, it is considered offensive.) Isolated for thousands of years from the rest of the world, the Inuit—particularly those living in northwestern Greenland—believed themselves to be the *only* people on Earth. And well they might, for they knew of no others. Their entire world encompassed coastal settlements numbering only a few hundred inhabitants. Everyone knew everyone there was to know. Beyond lay nothing but ice, snow, sea, and mountains. It was a world they understood. It was *their* world, prowled by familiar animals, governed by familiar spirits. Every prominent rock, every island, every mountain had a name; every kind of snow had its uses. The world of the Inuit, hostile as it seems to us, was to them both comforting and comfortable.

Into this circumscribed setting, with the same impact that an extraterrestrial spacecraft might have on us today, sailed the British ships *Isabella* and *Alexander*, under the direction of Commander John Ross of the Royal Navy. Ross, seeking a Northwest Passage in 1818, explored the rocky straits and inlets in the vicinity of Etah and Thule, Greenland. The local Inuit had never encountered men with pale skin, wearing garments of cloth. They marveled at such wonders as coffee, bread, mirrors, and firewood. Working through an interpreter from southern Greenland who had stowed away two years earlier to England, Ross presented these northernmost people in the world with such improbable gifts as forty umbrellas. Even more miraculous than Ross's gifts to the natives were the ships that carried the commander and his men. These northernmost Inuit had never seen a vessel propelled by sails: they thought the sheets of canvas were the wings of a large bird. Believing the ships to be living creatures, they attempted to speak with them: "Who are you? What are you? Where do you come from? Is it from the sun or the moon?"

To indicate their peaceful intent, the Englishmen sent a

white flag ashore, bearing a painted picture of an olive branch. The natives, of course, had no idea what an olive branch—or any branch for that matter—meant. Commander Ross made a more practical gesture: to the flagpole he tied a bag of presents. This instantly had the desired effect.

The Inuit community Ross discovered—he named them Arctic Highlanders—was typical of a people spread broadly across the top of the world. Unique in their isolation from one another and from the rest of mankind (one Inuit community in East Greenland had virtually no contact with the outside world before World War II), they nonetheless shared a remarkably cohesive culture. Although the people of each region had their own beliefs, taboos, customs, and dialects, the cultural unity of this scattered handful of small bands was—and is—remarkable. In 1977 Greenland natives met with Alaskan Eskimos who lived three thousand miles away. The two groups were overjoyed to be able to carry on conversations in their native language, although their tribes had had virtually no contact for four thousand years. This astounding continuity of the spoken word is unsurpassed.

Like most New World cultures, the Inuit lacked a written language. The glue that held their culture together over such immense time spans was their oral tradition. Their history was embodied in tales told beneath the flickering light of seal-oil lamps in skin tents and snow houses. Faithful retelling preserved details intact: when explorer C. F. Hall landed on Baffin Island—well south of the Ross discoveries—in the middle of the nineteenth century, local Inuit gave him an accurate account of Martin Frobisher's visit some three hundred years earlier! Their story even provided the answer to a mystery three centuries old—the fate of five men who deserted the tyrannical Frobisher. As the natives told the tale, the men had sought shelter among the Inuit, but later, homesick, had built a small boat and set sail for England, never to be seen again. The story of these men, carefully nurtured and passed down over ten generations, indicates the strength and cohesiveness of the Inuit character.

As journalist John Dyson wrote in *The Hot Arctic*: "One of the most remarkable features of the Eskimo culture has been its continuity. When ancient Egyptians first smelted lead . . . small bands of Eskimos were already moving seasonally across the tundra-top, wresting a meagre living from the most hostile physical environment Man has ever mastered. When Jesus Christ was born the Eskimo culture had been established many centuries and was to change only in detail through the entire span of Christianity. During the rise and fall of successive European powers, and the discovery of the New World, the Eskimo hunter stood with rock-like patience and poised spear beside seal-holes on the Arctic ice as he had always done, and as he continued to do long after the sky above him became striped by the jet contrails of Boeing 707s carrying passengers over the Pole."

This cultural unity developed only because cooperation meant survival—an Inuk continually suppressed his own thoughts, aspirations, and actions for the good of the community. Inuit life was the purest form of communism, demanding that all property be shared, that the group be everything and the individual nothing. Against the elements, or against Nanook, an Inuk was the ultimate individualist, but his life in camp was something he shared intimately with everyone present, whether member of his family or complete strangers. At all costs an Inuk avoided standing out from the crowd. Instead of saying, "I am going hunting," he might say, "Someone goes to hunt for seals." Instead of using the self-centered "I," his wife might say, "This woman will sew the skins."

An Inuk's possessions were few, because he was constantly on the move. A knife, a few skins, and a dog whip might be his only material goods. All else belonged to the community. This sharing meant that whatever the Inuk saw, he was likely to pick up and walk away with—an action interpreted by arctic explorers as thievery.

When two totally foreign cultures intersect, such misunderstandings are common. The Inuit were happy with their lot, their men handsome and their women beautiful in each other's sight, and they kept their own beliefs and taboos with almost puritanical zeal. Yet the Norsemen called these happy people, cheerfully at home in their world, *skraelings*, "wretched ones," and viewed them with loathing and pity. Other outsiders from the south invariably described the Inuit as dirty, unkempt, lazy, heathen, wanton, and inferior.

Ignorant of the white man's ways, the Inuit were easily cheated. Peter Freuchen wrote of Ukujag, a famous hunter who one day killed a fine bear and offered its skin for sale to a ship's captain. According to Inuit custom, Ukujag began the bartering with a very modest request: he'd like some ammunition for his gun. The captain, seeing a fantastic bargain, leapt at the chance and called off the negotiations, which otherwise would have rapidly escalated. He quickly gave the hunter fourteen cartridges and disappeared with the skin. As an old man, Ukujag loved to tell the story of the ignorant white man. Everyone would laugh at the tale. To think that the white master of a large ship wouldn't know that a fine bearskin was worth much more than fourteen cartridges!

In the Inuit camp, food was shared. Only in the hunting of meat was prestige conferred on individuals. Prowess in hunting was prized above all else. To be a hunter was to be a man. A skilled hunter might be elected leader. A lazy or dishonest man would be held up to public ridicule, and shame before the group could be as potent as a sentence of death. Shunning, or isolation from the group, *was* a death sentence, because no man or woman could survive long in the Arctic apart from family and friends.

Tales of the white bear were passed down from generation to generation and served to reinforce the group's expectations:

A man named Angutdligamaq never hunted but would murder successful hunters and steal their seals. Others lived in fear of him but finally agreed that something must be done. They decided to show him how to hunt, but Angutdligamaq proved exceedingly clumsy and had to be shown how to do everything, including how to sleep in a snow house. The others told him he'd sleep best if he left one leg out of his trousers.

When his companions saw Angutdligamaq's bare backside exposed, they buried a spear in it. Angutdligamaq jumped up, bellowing with pain and rage, but this agitation forced the spear farther in, and the murderer died. His mother, Anoritoq, mourned for her son and asked the hunters to give her a bear embryo, that she might raise it as her child.

When the hunters took a pregnant bear, they presented the unborn cub to Anoritoq, and she raised it as her son, so it could catch seals for her. All went well until winter came. Unable to see seals in the darkness, the bear began stealing other families' meat. Soon the bear's cousins, the village dogs, surrounded him and held him until the people killed him. Anoritoq sobbed a song to her dead bear-son until the tears froze on her cheeks and her body turned to stone.

In the 1920s the great Greenlandic chronicler Knud Rasmussen reported that Anoritoq's stone body was still visible on a headland near Etah, Greenland: "Her mouth is covered with a layer of hardened blubber, for they say that it brings luck to the bear-hunter if, before he goes out, he tries to feed the bear-mother with blubber. And in the quiet winter nights, when the northern light sends its ghostly rays across the heavens, one sees old hunters going toward the mountain under some plausible pretext. The next day fresh tracks in the snow show that the bear-mother has had visitors, and her face glistens with blubber."

The theme of a bear raised as a child is common in Inuit legends. . . .

An elderly couple, beyond the years of childbearing, yearned for a son. One day the man killed a bear and sang to its blood, begging it to come alive again. The blood became a little bear. The old couple cared for the baby bear as they would their own child. They fed it, nurtured it, and took it inside their own sleeping skins at night.

The little bear grew bigger, until it was able to hunt. The old couple rejoiced, for the bear brought much meat. He hunted harbor seals, ringed seals, even walrus. One day the old man asked for the meat of an ice bear. The young bear balked, for he did not wish to kill his relatives, but his adoptive father was insistent. The young bear went hunting and returned with a big she-bear. As the couple ate of the bear meat, the little bear-son walked away, never to return. Eventually, without their bear-son to hunt meat, the old couple died.

The bear-child tale is also told with the roles reversed:

Once a she-bear killed and ate a pregnant woman but kept the boy she ripped from the woman's womb. The bear raised the boy as her cub and taught him how to hunt. She taught him to fear the creatures that walk on two legs.

One day the boy discovered his mother's skull in the bear's den. His bear-mother pretended not to know how it got there. The skull became his favorite plaything, and he carried it wherever he went. Eventually the skull began to talk to him. It begged for help. It pleaded that it was his true mother.

The boy went out one morning to hunt seals. He took the skull with him. Against his bear-mother's warning, he came near a party of hunters who walked upright. The shaman of the group looked in amazement at the naked boy holding his mother's skull. Using his magic, the old man brought flesh to the skull and made it grow arms and legs. The reborn mother cradled her son for the first time. She lived with her boy for many years, but the bear-mother mourned her boy-cub for the rest of her life.

The best-known symbols of Inuit life are the kayak and the igloo. Both are admired for their elegant simplicity of design. Each is a utilitarian tool suited to the hunters' life-style. The kayak (or *baidar*, as it is known in Eurasia) is still widely used in Greenland. It is without doubt the finest one-man craft ever made. Sealskin stretched over a frame of wood or bone, it is so well fitted to its owner that the Greenlanders speak of "wearing" it and refer to their boats as extra sets of trousers.

Bears might be hunted from kayaks, but the Inuit would try to force Nanook onto the ice before striking. The bear's body is so densely muscled that even attached to an air-filled buoy the carcass would sink if harpooned in the water.

Compared with the kayak, the igloo hasn't fared so well as a traditional symbol of the North. Few Inuit today can build a snow house, and, anyway, the popular image of Eskimos living in snow houses is wrong. An *iglu* was actually a low hut constructed of turf and stone. The Inuit lived most of their lives in such houses, or in skin tents. On extended journeys, however, they built a temporary shelter of snow blocks called an *illuliaq*. Such a house might have been constructed in about an hour from hard-packed snow, which contains enough entrapped air to be a superb insulator. A ventilation hole allowed excess heat and moisture to escape. If a storm were brewing, all exits would be closed and a seal-oil fire started so that the interior walls would begin to melt. Then cold air was allowed back in, freezing the entire structure into a solid wall that could withstand nature's worst.

I have never been inside a snow house, but I've talked to women who accompany their Inuit husbands on bear hunts, crossing the sea ice on dogsleds. They sleep in caribou furs, snug within a translucent dome constructed by their husbands in about an hour from white blocks of crusty snow. The women describe the pallid enclosure—the original White House—as cozy, humid, quiet, and light. Photographs of such dwellings at night are stunning but can't do justice to reality: snow houses illuminated from the inside glow like cabochon jewels set in black mountings—they gleam as beacons in the night-bound snowscape.

Rifles would be left outside—I have seen them today outside Inuit houses, lying, as I thought, discarded in the dirt—for good reason. Moisture is the enemy of gunmetal, and outside in the dirt or snow a gun is drier than in the steamy interior of a wood house, skin tent, or illuliaq. Many are the tales of hunters who heard Nanook approach during the sleeping hours and leaped naked from their snow houses to search for their rifles. Such men find little unusual about killing a charging, 1,000-pound polar bear while standing barefoot in the snow.

Nanook was both predator and prey. Nanook was also a spirit. Always he was a daily part of an Inuk's life. The spirit realm was as real to the Inuit as their physical realm. Believing their tribes to be the earth's only inhabitants, they knew the spirits that watched over them must surely outnumber their small bands.

Inuit life was governed by strict taboos and by a religion that divided a person into three parts: soul, body, and name. The soul existed outside the body and followed it like a shadow. At death it joined the souls of the fathers in the arching heavens or in the depths of the sea—both very good places. The body died, and all evil remained with it. Thus great care must be taken when handling the bodies of the dead, lest the living be contaminated. An Inuk's name was his spirit and had attached to it all his power and skill. A person named after someone deceased inherited all his or her qualities. A mother in labor called out many names: if one name caused the birthing to speed up, she assumed that the name spirit had entered the infant's body.

Everything, living and nonliving, in the Inuit world—rocks, bears, sledges, ocean waves, harpoons—was considered to have an *innua*, a soul. The innua of a polar bear was thought to reside in the bladder. After a bear was killed, its bladder would be inflated, dried, and sometimes painted, and hung indoors. Then a "bladder feast," during which the inflated organ was offered food and water, would be held to honor the bear. Knives, scrapers, needle cases, and other tools were given as gifts to the innua of the dead bear. Bears were believed to be so wise that they'd never be killed unless they willingly let themselves be taken by great and generous hunters so they might obtain the tools they needed for life in the next world.

Nanook's body was treated with reverence by all the people scattered across the Arctic. Failure to pay homage to the bear might turn its innua into a crooked spirit, a terrifying monster. Bear souls were especially dangerous. They lived on the tip of the hunter's spear for several days and watched the exacting post-hunt rituals. Often after the killing of a bear, ceremonial dances and gift giving might last a week or more. The dancers' hope was that the bear's soul would return to the village of spirits and tell of Inuit generosity so other bears would be eager to be killed by hunters of such prowess and concern for proper tradition.

In Siberia the Nenets people extended this reverence to worship of bears at ceremonial altars or mounds constructed of polar bear and reindeer skulls. Soviet researchers report finding such mounds as high as ten feet, containing the skulls of many bears. In Nenets culture an oath of great seriousness might be sworn while holding the snout of a polar bear skull or the paw of a bearskin.

The white bear was a powerful shaman who communed with the spirit world. Coming silently, leaving silently, he stalked the ice as a spirit himself. He was not feared so much as respected. An old person who had become a burden on the family was left alone to die and patiently awaited Nanook's coming. With all the dangers of Inuit life (Inuit continually faced, among other calamities, drowning or attack by walrus or whales, death by starvation or exposure to the cold wind, death from their extraordinary sensitivity to the whites' many diseases), being eaten by a polar bear was considered a "good" way to die. Such a death liberated the spirit so it could be reborn in a new body.

Nanook was flesh, fur, tooth, and claw. Nanook was a spirit who walked the ice. He was also larger than life: he controlled the workings of nature. Siberian natives believed that ocean whirlpools were caused by a giant polar bear who lived at the bottom of the sea and sucked water through its nostrils. Other myth bears included Nanorluk, giant bears that swallowed men whole, and Kokogiak, an immense ten-legged bear who ruled the polar icepack. Few Inuit spoke of meeting him: to look on Kokogiak was to foresee your own death. Many more Inuit claimed to have seen Kinik, a bear too big to haul himself out of the water onto the ice.

Inuit stories often involve such bears of exaggerated dimensions.

Once a hunter named Papik returned from a seal hunt without his companion. He told the man's mother that her son had fallen out of his kayak and drowned. The mother, claiming that Papik had killed her son, swore she would avenge his death. She went to the seashore and covered herself with a bearskin. As the tide came in, it swept her out to sea.

Years later hunters on an ice floe saw a huge creature approaching them. A she-bear of monstrous size, it dwarfed even a snow house. Its eyes were like burning coals, its claws like sharp knives. As the hunters ran in fear, the bear followed them to their village. It went straight to Papik's house, where it found the old hunter cowering under his sleeping skins. The she-bear ripped Papik's eyes, ears, and nose from his face and then dragged him by his intestines through the village.

After eating Papik, the bear fell asleep. The villagers approached cautiously. When they got close enough to see clearly, the people found the bear was nothing more than the old woman's bearskin, draped over a pile of bones covered with sea snails.

Intervening with the spirits was the *angakok*, a sort of medicine man and spirit doctor, who could move at will between the world of humans and the spirit world. Through rituals and particularly through self-induced trances, the angakok spoke with spirits and interpreted the spirit world to his people. Together with the best hunter, the angakok was the leader of the Inuit community. He was also a performer and used the only musical instrument of the Inuit, a skin drum, to accompany his magical dancing. His songs were both soporific and electrifying.

In the warmth of a skin tent or snow house, packed with the members of the tribe, their bellies full after a major feast, the angakok raises a thin drum in his left hand, a heavy stick in his right and begins to beat a hypnotic rhythm. His body, a moment earlier gnarled and bent low with the burdens of his people, comes alive with intense power. He evokes in exquisite pantomime a male bear, lusting after females. The shaman chants his magic song and begins to dance, slowly at first and then faster and faster, until it seems that the old man must soon drop with exhaustion. The steady drumbeat, the rhythm and intensity of the song, and the mesmerizing power of the angakok combine to induce a kind of mass trance in his listeners. The old man, again made young, dances for hours, *becoming* the amorous bear, whipping his watchers into an erotic frenzy. The angakok might—in the midst of such a ceremony—enter a trance and awaken later to relay instructions from the spirits. This person has broken a taboo; that person must make restitution; such-and-such must be done to cure so-and-so's illness, or to bring back the seals, or to call Nanook. The angakok might order a temporary exchange of wives, shuffling couples in differing combinations until game once again becomes plentiful.

Wife trading was a normal activity, dictated by the nomadic Inuit life-style. A man hunting seals needed a woman to keep him supplied with dry, supple clothing and to stretch and scrape the hides. If his own wife was sick, pregnant, or busy with babies, he'd take his neighbor's wife on the trek. A woman was expected to acquiesce—all decisions in the Inuit society were made by men. The angakok was always a man, although women were also magic makers and might call forth Nanook with a bear song. Women hoped to curry favor with the shaman, for his powers were great. The angakok might, through his magic, render one woman barren at the sly request of another. He might enable another woman to conceive (it was a great honor in many tribes for a woman to lie with the angakok).

The angakok shared a special relationship with Nanook: he communed with bears and was expected to dominate by force of will any that he encountered. The spirit of an animal might become the *tornak*, or spiritual guardian, of an Inuk. The angakok usually had the white bear as his tornak, for Nanook was a powerful spirit. The angakok might easily make the transition from his human body to become Nanook, given the similarities of man and bear—the upright stance, the arrangement of muscles beneath the skin, and the fondness of both for seal meat. In Inuit legends bears live in houses like people, walk upright like people, and *are* people. When they step outside, they put on their fur coats and become bears again.

Tales of the ice bear were often told to teach a lesson or reinforce taboos.

When the men of a family were hunting for seals, the ice shifted suddenly and left them stranded, adrift on a small floe. As the ice began to melt, the hunters called on the eldest, who was their angakok. By interceding with a spirit bear, the angakok turned all the men into bears, and they slipped into the water and swam with great ease.

When they found some seals, the angakok warned them

that they must not kill any until they became men again. But one of the men was too hungry. Ignoring the angakok's warning, he killed and ate a seal. While he was doing this, the other bears swam ashore and were transformed into sea-birds. They flew back to their village and became men again, but the one who had killed the seal against the warning of the angakok could not change back. He remained an ice bear for the rest of his life. Such is the way of men who misuse the magic of the spirit world.

Early arctic explorers ridiculed Inuit beliefs or tried to turn them to their advantage. Seeking the North Pole, Cook and Peary had to overcome the objections of their Inuit companions that the world is flat. (Certainly the Inuit world is flat—ignoring pressure ridges, no plain on earth is flatter than frozen sea ice.) To the Inuit, the quest was a mystery. The natives were convinced that the white men had driven a gigantic nail into the earth somewhere farther north and that this peg had become lost. Thus the Inuit called the Pole *Tigieha*, "The Big Nail." They found this nail a worthy object to seek. As explorer Frederick Cook wrote, "Since iron is more valuable to them than gold, they were interested in the search."

Other Inuit beliefs were affronts to the Christian missionaries who followed the explorers. Determined to stamp out "heathen" ways, missionaries from the early 1700s on fought to overcome the power of the angakok and refused to teach Inuit children in Inuktitut, the native language. They demanded that all the old ways be cast aside and often enforced their message with beatings and humiliations. Thus the gentle teachings of Christ were pummeled into some of the gentlest of the earth's inhabitants. In their attempts to Christianize the Inuit, the missionaries broke their spirit and began the destruction of their way of life, a process that continues today.

Teaching the Inuit was difficult not only because of language barriers but primarily because the gulf between the cultures was so wide. The Lord's Prayer, for example, pleads "Give us this day our daily bread." For an Inuk who had never seen, smelled, or tasted bread, this was an empty phrase, one of many that must have puzzled him during a Lutheran or Catholic service imported in its entirety from Europe. Eventually the churchmen learned the art of compromise: the translation became "Give us this day the seal meat we need."

Frederick Cook wrote, "The myth world to the Eskimo is to them more real than the Bible is to us." Inuit myths and legends were recited night after night by seal-oil lamplight in the coziness of the snow house or skin tent. The tales featured both humans and animals, including ravens, foxes, walrus, and many other daily companions. Most prominent in the Inuit mythology, however, was Nanook. According to Richard C. Davids, author of *Lords of the Arctic*, the northern peoples believed that while the men of the arctic told stories of great bear hunts, the bears themselves were busy telling of hunting Man, a creature they knew as "the one who staggers."

Bear legends often had the human outsmarting Nanook.

One day an ice bear wandered into the camp of Nakasungnak, a large but foolish man. The bear wasn't hunted, because it was thought to be an evil spirit in disguise. All the Inuit ran in fear, for a hunter who killed such a bear would surely die. Not Nakasungnak. He ran toward the bear, brandishing his knife. The bear opened its huge mouth and swallowed Nakasungnak whole, knife and all. The villagers gave the man up for dead, but soon the bear staggered and fell. A knife emerged from beneath the bear's fur, carving an opening between his ribs. Out jumped Nakasungnak, unharmed. Nakasungnak the fool proved a worthy hunter. His bear fed the village for a long time.

At the beginning of this century, Knud Rasmussen asked an elderly Greenland Inuk to define the greatest happiness of life. The man replied: "To run across fresh bear tracks and be ahead of all other sledges."

A bear hunt might take several months and cover hundreds of miles. It was a journey of great deprivation and hardship, of trials that residents of a warmer world cannot even begin to understand. Even so, it was an Inuk's single greatest pleasure.

Rasmussen captured some of the Inuit enthusiasm for the chase: "One has seen on these bear-hunts old men with white hair, men who during their life of hunting good and bad have experienced everything nature could offer them, hunters who have long ago forgotten the tally of their deeds; and young men, half-grown lads—all of them go crazy with the hunting-fever as soon as there is a chance of challenging the white king of the Polar waste. And for one single harpoon duel all the resultless and evil toil which preceded this supreme moment is forgotten."

Even today this emotion persists, and killing a bear is still a rite of passage from boy to man. In northwestern Greenland a young man isn't worthy of the daughter of a great hunter until he has killed his first bear. Because ammunition must be purchased with money, and because both bullets and dollars are often in short supply, some men still face Nanook with only a spear or knife. Before rifles, which the Inuit acquired from traders in the late 1700s to defend themselves against Indian raiders from central Canada, the only way to hunt a bear was to use a stone trap or to encircle Nanook with dogs and then attack with a spear. Arrows or small-caliber rifles were ineffective, because water sometimes freezes in the bear's fur, making a tough outer shell.

Many tales are told in the snow house of a single Inuk on the ice with a bear. Tracks in the snow tell the age-old story: the hunter stalked the bear; the bear doubled back to stalk the hunter. Again the hunter doubled back. This cycle might repeat itself many times during the hunt. A man with dogs, however, could keep up the pace for hours; the bear, growing overheated, would soon tire.

The traditional hunter used a spear five or six feet long, tipped with jade or copper pried out of surrounding hillsides or even with a sharp flake of iron chipped from a meteorite. (Iron from a meteorite that fell in the vicinity of Cape York is the only known human use of an extraterrestrial resource.) A special harpoon head, reserved exclusively for hunting bears, could be attached to a sealing harpoon, especially if a longer spear—used for hunting musk-oxen—was unavailable. In more recent times a ten- to fourteen-inch knife was lashed to the end of a walking stick. When the bear reared up on its hind legs, the Inuk would strike. Or the hunter might stand like a matador, stolidly facing a charging bear. At the last possible moment, the Inuk would thrust his spear into the bear's neck and leap to one side. Another hunter, using a slightly longer spear, might calmly face Nanook's headlong rush or rearing fighter's stance, plant the butt of his weapon in the snow, and impale the bear as it charged. Although this incredible one-on-one with a creature standing ten feet tall on its hind legs is a mark of Inuit manhood, no Inuk would claim it as unusual bravery—it is simply the way you hunt bears. Even if he intends to use a high-powered rifle, a skilled Inuk hunter may creep within five feet of a bear before firing.

Inuit hunters are hired today as bear monitors by construction and exploration teams working in the Arctic. During fieldwork in the Canadian Beaufort Sea, engineer Larry Brooks landed on a gravel island two days after an oil-rig worker had been killed and eaten by a bear. "We were all nervous," he told me, "and only the natives were permitted to carry firearms.

"We hired a young native hunter, Peter Silastiak, to be our polar bear monitor. Peter was only eighteen or nineteen years old, but he was a phenomenal marksman. Every morning when we arrived at the work site, Peter would tilt up a small piece of ice, walk back about fifty yards, lie down in a shooter's prone position, and level his grandfather's 1906, single-shot, bolt-action .30-06. He'd squeeze off one round, the ice would disintegrate, and we'd work safely all day. We never saw a bear.

"We spent the day bent over our surveying instruments. Peter would walk in a slow circle around us, perhaps a quarter-mile away, looking for tracks or bears.

"I don't know whether his morning shot was intended to reassure us, to scare away bears, to sight in his rifle, or to restore his own confidence, but it was impressive, and it worked."

A traditional Inuit bear hunt would have men on the ice, riding sledges pulled by sturdy dog teams. The dogs catch the familiar bear scent. Tails curl high over muscled backs. The sledges surge forward as the lead dogs increase the pace. Drivers bellow one long, drawn-out, joyous word: "Nanooook!"

Kicked up by the dogs' frantic paw scrabbles, snow whirls in dense clouds about the sledges, obscuring the chase. When the men can see the bear, it is ambling forward at a relaxed trot, stopping every hundred yards or so to stare back at them. The dogs grow increasingly tense. Now they can see Nanook as well as smell him. They strain at the taut harness leather, cut from strips of thick walrus hide. Bounding on the sledges, drivers lean forward to loose the leather traces. In an instant the dogs leap free and are gone, chasing after the bear. The sledges coast to a stop. The dogs catch up to their quarry and encircle Nanook, snapping and snarling in a frenzy of excitement.

The bear, overheated, stands with head low, chuffing and growling. When a dog nips his hind legs, he whirls, massive teeth and claws flashing. Grabbing a dog by the heavy ruff collar, the bear flings it fifty feet away. The dog, who has played this deadly game before, goes limp in the bear's grasp and allows himself to be thrown without a struggle. Landing with a thump, the dog reassembles his dignity and renews the attack.

Although the dogs continue yapping, snapping, and harassing the bear, they can do him no real damage. Their quarry, by contrast, is an angered half-ton predator. He lashes out with massive paws, and soon there is blood on the snow. Dogs limp away or lie on the frozen surface, licking their wounds.

Approaching the whirling melee, the hunters, armed with spears or rifles, must take care not to hit the dogs, who are in constant motion. Finally, the mighty creature goes down. As magnificent in death as in life, the white bear lies silent in the snow as the dogs close in. The hunters must act quickly, or their trophy will be ripped to shreds by their canine partners.

The bear is laid on the ice with his head pointing toward the Inuit village. This shows Nanook's departing spirit the way to carry home word of the successful hunt to the rest of the family. When it is time to skin the carcass and divide the meat, tradition dictates that the bear's body be turned so the head faces eastward.

Whoever first spotted the bear has claim to the skin. As the thick pelt is stripped from the yellow fat that lies beneath and then the insulating bear blubber is peeled off the huge muscles, the form that emerges is disconcertingly human in shape and structure. The bearskin will make three fine pairs of men's trousers, worn with the fur on the outside. These will bring much prestige to the hunter's family, and to the wife who sews the fur. The meat, fat, and skin will be loaded on the sledges. The guts, still steaming in the cold air, are thrown to the dogs as their reward. A few dogs still limp or nurse their wounds, but most carry themselves like victorious soldiers, strutting their pride for all to see.

Most Inuit scorned bear meat, eating it only in time of famine. Because it was consumed raw, and because bears are often infected with trichinosis, the meat could cause debilitating sickness. In Greenland over a quarter of the bears carry the *Trichinella* larvae, which form cysts in the muscle tissue. When the meat is eaten, the cysts dissolve in the small intestine, and the larvae invade their new host. They soon burrow into the human muscle, causing a wide variety of symptoms that mimic other diseases. If untreated, trichinosis may cause death within four to eight weeks.

Even so, some Inuit relished the stringy, greasy meat of the polar bear. The Inuit of Canada's Prince Albert Sound lived on bear meat through long winter hunts and were very fond of it. Vilhjalmur Stefansson, whose book *The Friendly Arctic* opened many southern eyes to the world of the Far North, described a meal of bear: "Chewing half-frozen meat is like chewing hard ice cream, while eating unfrozen raw meat cut in small pieces is like eating raw oysters." Filmmaker Doug Wilkinson, who lived among the Inuit and ate often of their bear kills, wrote of his fear of trichinosis in *Land of the Long Day*: "I ate cooked bear meat with gusto, although I still cannot eat bear meat raw without murmuring a short, silent prayer."

Despite the danger, raw bear meat was often consumed in time of need. The liver, however, was treated with greater respect, for it carried the potentially serious threat of vitamin A toxicity. The normal adult intake of vitamin A should be around 5,000 units a day. In a single gram of polar bear liver, there are 13,000 to 30,000 units. A typical 8-ounce serving would contain about 3.6 million units, or at least 800 times the daily adult dosage. Vitamin A overdose produces nausea, vomiting, abdominal pain, diarrhea, vertigo, headache, and sleepiness. These symptoms result primarily from increased pressure in the spinal fluid. Another symptom, loss of hair, was also reported to early explorers by the Inuit, who cautioned them not to feed bear liver to dogs, lest they lose their fur.

Two men of Stefansson's party who ate dinner of fried bear liver awoke during the early morning hours with excruciating headaches. They vomited throughout the next day, and were so weak that they could barely travel. Their leader then resolved to experiment further. He fed cooked liver to his five companions, all of whom developed headaches and some of whom became nauseated. Stefansson came through the experience without suffering any symptoms and eventually ate six to eight bear livers without ill effect. He believed the organ meat to be relatively innocuous. His companions seem to have been unusually long suffering. It is not surprising, though, that he found "this was the last occasion when I was able to get any member of the party to make experiments with me."

Nanook has many uses. The fur holds just enough water, and releases it just smoothly enough, to be used in icing the runners of the *komatik*, or sledge. This vehicle of universal arctic transport might be made from a whole polar bear skin, rolled and frozen, its slippery hairs providing low-friction runners. More often, the sledge is hand built from many components, often over several months. The Inuit are skilled improvisers: a komatik is built of whatever materials are at hand. The preferred material in their woodless world is ivory or bone, fashioned in intricate jigsaw pieces lashed together by sealskin thongs. Uprights and crosspieces are made from walrus bone and caribou antlers. In an emergency, frozen walrus meat can be used for runners and frozen salmon lashed across to form the load-supporting frame. Thus the sledge becomes, in time of famine, both transport and traveling frozen-food locker.

The Volkswagen of the Arctic, the komatik is the ultimate in basic transportation. Split fish can be glued together with frozen blood to make the runners. Caribou hides can be rolled wet and allowed to freeze in runner shape. Bones and tusks already have the right curvature; they can be lashed in place. All of these, however, need to have a glass-smooth bearing surface to glide effortlessly across the ice. Mud is often packed on the undersurface, allowed to freeze, and then shaved with a knife to the ideal smooth shape. Then a piece of polar bear fur emerges from the seemingly random collection of skins that follows the Inuit encampment. This patch is dipped in boiling water, urinated on, or sprayed with a mouthful of melted snow. Stroking the wet fur along the komatik runner, the sledge builder leaves a thin film of ice to harden and smooth the undersurface and thus speed his travel.

Nanook's fur also might be tied on the end of a long caribou bone to make a *kumak-sheun*, a louse mop. When drawn through the hair of the family as they sat in the snow house, the fur would attract the little pests, which quickly disappeared into the mouths of the grinning Inuit, much to the dismay of proper Victorian explorers.

The bear's hide also makes fine boot covers that muffle the sound of hunters' feet as they stalk across the shifting floes. Pieces might be cut from the skin to make sitting pads or foot mats to warm the hunter who waits long hours beside the aglu, or to make elbow pads to ease the stalk across the ice. Bear hide is also stretched over bones to make the collapsible, umbrella-like white camouflage shield that the Inuk slides in front of him when hunting seals on the ice.

Nanook's bones, stripped of their meat (the bare-bones bear bones) are useful wherever a dense material of great strength is required. They can be sharpened or rounded for digging or pounding. The skull itself, embodiment of Nanook's power, is used in ritual magic. The long canine teeth become amulets, assuring protection against the spirits of the dead.

With such a variety of uses, Nanook is an essential part of Inuit life. As author Richard Davids noted, other animals in the arctic domain can provide food, light, heat, clothing, tents, and other daily necessities, but more than any other single element of the frozen North, Nanook confers *prestige*.

Most descriptions of the Inuit in this chapter should have been written in the past tense. The way of life I have described has largely disappeared. There are living members of the Inuit community who were literally born into the Stone Age. In the space of a single lifetime they have been yanked, willing or not, into the Space Age. Television-watching natives now tune in transmissions of IBC, the Inuit Broadcasting Corporation. Skin tents and turf *igloos* have been replaced by prefabricated buildings, designed by people well to the south, who have little knowledge of Inuit needs. The art of building snow houses has been almost forgotten as the monthlong nomadic bear hunts have been abandoned. The people that, Peter Freuchen wrote, "believe themselves to be the happiest people on earth living in the most beautiful country there is" have more recently been described in an appeal to the United Nations as "the most socio-economically depressed population in the world." First tuberculosis, then alcoholism and venereal disease ruined lives already pushed to the bottom rung on the economic ladder. Decades of governmental neglect and unwise social directives have turned the once proud, fiercely independent Inuk into a permanent welfare case.

Such terrible changes are consequences of the policies of the white men who "discovered" the arctic world. It is poignant to note that modern arctic development began at the very site where John Ross and his Royal Navy crews first encountered the polar Inuit, at Thule, Greenland. The culture that the explorers found there exists no longer. The setting has been forever altered. Man has marked the Arctic with his visible castoffs and polluted even the ice of glaciers with unseen contaminants. The only aspect of arctic life that remains as it was in 1818 is Nanook, still hunting, unchallenged, in the polar pack.

EIGHT

Enter the Kabloona

My childhood heroes were explorers. I loved their books, set in exotic locales. I thrilled to their tales of discovery on the flanks of icy mountains, in the heat of oppressive jungles, and deep beneath the sea. When I set out for college, I pursued a career in geology, full of expectation, planning to live my adventurous fantasies. Most of my subsequent geological travels were tame by comparison with the yarns spun by my idols, but when I headed north I found what I'd been seeking. The northern world fulfilled promises that I'd heard the earth whisper when I chose it for my field of study. Romance and reality merged.

Yet when I wear warm clothing sewn from nylon and stuffed with synthetic insulation, or when I drag a lightweight sled made of fiberglass, or when I ride a snowmobile or crunch boldly through the ice in a steel-hulled ship guided by satellite signals, it's difficult for me to understand the world arctic explorers faced. To appreciate the dangers and deprivations that men like Peary and Amundsen conquered, I must remember that their equipment was handcrafted from wool, leather, canvas, and wood; their wooden sledges incredibly heavy; their wood-hulled ships vulnerable to being crushed by moving ice; and their navigation dependent on clear skies for celestial observations. It's easy today to look back and laugh at Gilbert-and-Sullivan scenes, like the members of the C. F. Hall Expedition launching a canvas boat from northwestern Greenland singing, "We are going to the Pole." But if that is my only view of these men, I slight their bravery, their dogged determination, and the inner fires that drove them to seek, as they often described it, their Destiny.

If such men were to enter *my* arctic world, they'd recognize very little. They'd be claustrophobic in huge northern bases where workers don't step outside for weeks at a time. They'd marvel at steel icebreaking vessels powered by 60,000-horsepower jet turbines, and at the hourly radio messages the ships receive reporting the latest news and sports scores. My work on the ice, however, would seem familiar to them. They'd recognize the tasks involved in surveying pressure ridges or sounding the ocean depths. And they'd understand my daily worry that over the next ridge, behind the fogbank, or hidden beneath the drifted snow, lies Nanook, the white bear.

The white man, or *kabloona* (also *qallunaat*), was a rare visitor to the North well into this century. The arctic regions, described as "trackless frozen wastes," were largely unexplored. Other than the Inuit, no one went there, for there was no reason to go. For centuries the North remained a place of forbidding mysteries, a land beyond comprehension.

Well before the time of Christ, the northern lands were rumored to be regions of unrelenting cold and darkness. About 330 B.C. the noted Greek astronomer and geographer Pytheas sailed northward from Marseilles to a land he named *Thule* (probably Iceland or Norway). His label stuck, but the area remained a mystery—a blank on early maps. The north country continued to be an elusive myth, a source of exotic stories (based on truths too fantastic to believe) for centuries to come. The Romans, who marched their legions overland but sailed few ships out of sight of land, referred to the distant northern lands as *Ultima Thule*, the farthest reaches of the earth. Marco Polo, the intrepid thirteenth-century explorer whose descriptions of the riches of the Orient were ultimately responsible for the exploration of the Arctic in the search for a Northwest Passage, didn't venture far north himself but reported tales of a "Region of Darkness" where the sun disappeared for most of the winter, a place inhabited by "bears of a white color, and of prodigious size."

The one group that did venture into the icy waters were the hardy Norsemen, living up to their name: *north* men. These Vikings were great seafarers who explored farther north than any Europeans had yet traveled. Norse colonists from Iceland settled in A.D. 984 on the rocky, treeless shores of a huge gray and brown island. They wanted their new home to appear attractive to prospective tenants, so they named it *Greenland*. Their small villages imported many necessities from Europe through a well-established trade network; by 1100 the settlers were paying for these materials by exporting arctic souvenirs of great value, including the white bear. The skins of polar bears were treasured decorations in many a European castle and cathedral. Live bears were even more valuable; the owner of a single healthy white bear could command a price equivalent to a ship and all its cargo. In addition to the bears, white gyrfalcons from Greenland were traded at fantastic prices to European princes and Arab potentates. Narwhal-tusk "unicorn horns" brought several times their weight in gold, because they were believed to have magical powers. This trade persisted until the Little Ice Age (1550–1850), during which the northern lands were largely forgotten because they were almost totally isolated from the rest of the world by the southward advance of the pack ice as the earth's climate turned cooler. The last ship left Greenland in 1408, carrying a few survivors of colonies decimated by scurvy, tuberculosis, and inbreeding. This closing of supply routes made polar bears even more rare and valuable.

In fact, such exotic relics of the frozen lands had found their way south even earlier, reaching surprising distances from their origins. Ptolemy II, king of Egypt from 285 to 246 B.C., kept a polar bear in his private zoo in Alexandria, and an Egyptian funerary chamber contains hieroglyphics depicting plans for a burial vault for a white bear. By circuitous routes polar bears found their way to the Romans, who pitted them against seals in flooded arenas, and to the emperor of Japan, who received two bears as a gift in A.D. 858. Little geographic knowledge about the Arctic accompanied the bears south, though, primarily because traders were a secretive lot, guarding with the utmost caution any information about their routes.

Nanook, king of the arctic realm, mingled easily with the crowned heads of Europe. His innate majesty and haughty demeanor served him well. Aloof but appealing, the ice bear seemed a dignified companion for a monarch, and a fitting symbol of sovereignty. No court was complete without its white bear, no cathedral whole without a bearskin rug to warm the feet of its priests.

The appearance of white bears in European courts began with the reign of Harald the Fairhaired, the first king of Norway, who was presented about A.D. 880 with a mother bear and two cubs, captured on the northern coast of Iceland after having traveled aboard a drifting ice floe. The beautiful bears proved docile when well fed and were immensely popular as mascots at court. Kings vied to outrank neighboring monarchs in the keeping of bears. The king of England displayed a polar bear in the Tower of London. The emperor of Germany soon had his own bear. Royal decrees were posted, particularly in Iceland, where polar bears were most often encountered, announcing that they were the exclusive property of the Crown. Royal bears were traded as far as the Middle East. They were presented as gifts of state from one ruler to another. As author Richard C. Davids put it, "Polar bears moved around Europe like chess pieces in a game of international diplomacy."

Explorers of the fifteenth and sixteenth centuries probed gingerly at the margins of the arctic icepack. Superstitious sailors, they feared sea monsters and unnamed terrors beyond familiar horizons. They weren't disappointed. Their logs record shock and surprise at the size, number, and ferocity of polar bears. In these encounters, before the development of accurate firearms, the home-ice advantage was all the bears'. The explorers

The polar bear's body is a wedge, tapered toward the black nose. This shape cuts through the water as the bear—truly a marine mammal—swims tirelessly for miles.

The polar bear's neck is long and snakelike, allowing his sensitive nose to swing from side to side so he can home in on a faint scent in the icepack. The elongate face can get the bear's teeth deep into a seal's breathing hole.

A young bear has a face still unscarred by battle.

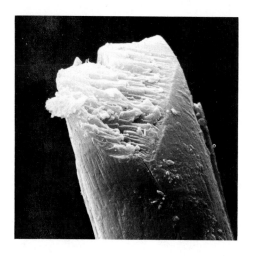 

Seen under the high magnification of an electron microscope, polar bear hair reveals one secret of a bear's strategy for keeping warm. The soft under-fur *(left)* consists of solid fibers. The longer outer guard hairs *(right)* are hollow. This construction traps insulating air and also conducts sunlight down the central tube of the guard hair to warm the black skin beneath the snowy coat. *Ben Powell*

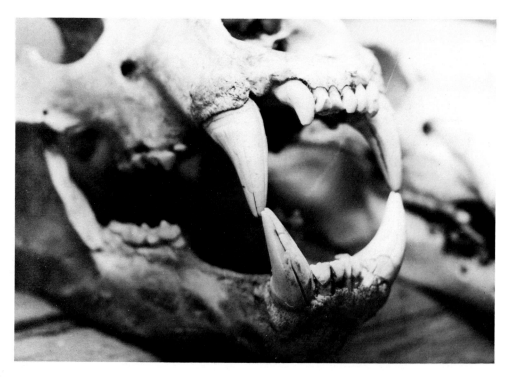

A polar bear skull shows—a lot closer than most people would ever want to see them—the huge canine teeth that can grab a 200-pound seal and lift it from its deep snow-covered den.

Standing on two legs to get a better view or scent, a polar bear (who may
be more than ten feet tall) is impressive. *Mel Woods/Point Defiance Zoo
and Aquarium*

When polar bears run, they pace, moving the legs on one side of the body together *(top)*. When they lift their feet, the paws fold inward with each step *(bottom)*.

When you're hiking through the tundra at the edge of Hudson Bay, this can be a disconcerting sight.

Play fighting is a ritual that prepares young bears for the real battles of adulthood. *Mike Beedell*

A mother bear must prepare her cubs for life in an unforgiving world. For two years they remain at her side, learning techniques of hunting and defending their kills from other bears. *Mike Beedell*

Even at the end of the ice-free season during which a bear fasts for months at a time, a sizable mound of fat covers a bear's backside.

A young bear catches an unfamiliar scent. His head comes up immediately to investigate.

Ancient enemies, a bear and a dog argue over a scrap of food. The meeting begins peacefully enough *(top)* but the action swiftly changes to a frenzy of snapping jaws and throaty growls *(bottom).* *Ben Powell*

This bear was unusually submissive to a sled dog, and seemed to enjoy its company. It played with the dog, hugged it, and slept beside it. *Mike Beedell*

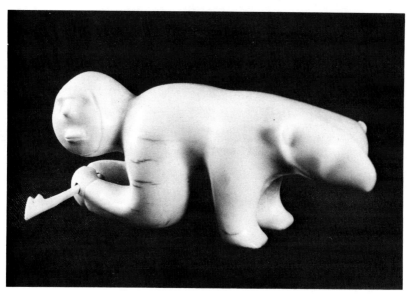

The polar bear is the dominant theme in much Eskimo art. Nanook the bear and Nanook the spirit are embodied in carvings in soapstone *(top)* or walrus ivory *(bottom)*. The lower carving depicts a shaman or angakok who transforms himself magically into a bear shape.

Traditional Eskimo bear hunters used a dog team, arrows, and spears to pursue their quarry.   *Frederick Lewis Co.*

Churchill, Manitoba, has the world's only polar bear jail. Officers of the Polar Bear Alert staff catch a problem bear in the two steel culvert traps shown at top, then the bears are locked in the metal building until fall freeze-up, when they're released onto the Hudson Bay ice.

When you live in polar bear country, your quarters may resemble a prison. Bears often peer into these windows to watch scientists at work.

A scientist weighs a tranquilized bear. *Mike Beedell*

This bear has been tagged in both ears with discreet white disks. Such marking has replaced an older method that involved painting the sides of bears with large numbers that might have interfered with the bears' ability to sneak up on seals.

Outside Churchill, tourists can see the white bear up close from the safety of a tundra buggy. Riding on immense tires, these vehicles creep across the spongy soil and splash through shallow ponds. *Ben Powell*

Continued hunting in Canada results in the sale of polar bear hides at prices in the thousands of dollars. These skins cannot, however, be legally imported into the United States.

Polar bears are among the most popular animals in zoos—especially when they can be viewed both above and below the water. *Mel Woods/Point Defiance Zoo and Aquarium*

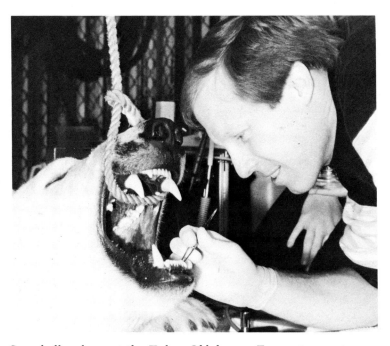

Snowball, a bear at the Tulsa, Oklahoma, Zoo, gets a root canal from a dentist who normally works on human teeth. A missing tooth is common in zoo animals, because they gnaw on the bars of their enclosures or roughhouse with other bears. *Jim Wolfe/Tulsa World*

Basking in the last warm rays of sunlight, a bear waits near Churchill for the November ice to form on Hudson Bay.

were out of their element and stubbornly refused to adapt to their new surroundings. All about them lay displays of superb adaptation to the North—in the clothing, hunting styles, eating habits, and survival skills of the Inuit—yet the European adventurers viewed the native peoples of the Arctic as dirty, ignorant savages, incapable of knowing anything of value. All the traits and taboos of the local people—earned at terrible cost and evolved through thousands of years for very specific reasons— the explorers deemed worthless and beneath the dignity of civilized gentlemen. Thus the explorers froze in their navy-issue woolens while nearby natives worked happily in furs. The newcomers starved or sickened with scurvy, while the Inuit thrived on a vitamin-rich diet consisting of nothing but seal meat. Europeans were handicapped by an attitude that permeated their every arctic thought, extending even to the bears. The northern peoples respected and revered Nanook; the explorers feared him.

Their fears were based on incidents like one on the day in 1595 when, on the island of Novaya Zemlya, north of Russia, a crewman in William Barents's expedition was seized from behind by a bear. The man had bent over to collect rocks when the bear crept up behind him, grabbed him suddenly, pulled him to the ground, and bit off his head. The man's companions rushed the bear, brandishing guns and lances, but the angered animal turned on them, killing another crewman. The rest of the men scattered. On their return to warmer climes, they no doubt told dramatically embellished tales of the tragedy and their lucky escape. A 1597 account of Barents's voyages includes descriptions of bears that "desired to taste a piece of some of us." Nanook's role as villain was firmly cast in the unfolding drama of arctic exploration, and he continues to play this role in the minds of some arctic travelers today.

The white bear was a ghostly creature who appeared suddenly out of the fog or darkness. He attacked without warning. He ate his victims. He tore open graves and toyed with the corpses. He walked boldly among men, and had no fear of their weapons. Nanook was an enemy to be shot on sight.

As European and North American explorers ventured into the Arctic, bear encounters punctuated their otherwise matter-of-fact reports, in which every other adventure—including frostbitten toes, the deaths of companions, and the crushing of ships in the ice—was described in the calm terms of everyday experience. Meeting a polar bear was different. Today these tales seem unusually bloodthirsty. Descriptions of most early encounters end with the death of the bear. Especially heartrending are tales of mothers shot as they defended their young, or cubs killed at their mother's side, so that she called out to the little white bodies, sniffing, pawing, and licking them "with signs of inexpressible fondness," as one explorer wrote. At the time these accounts were written, though, attitudes were different. A polar bear was fresh meat, valuable fur, and a very real danger to men and dogs on the ice. It was a daring hunter who challenged the white bear alone.

In the middle of the nineteenth century, more and more whalers moved into arctic waters, pursuing the great leviathan. Demand for whale oil, to light the lamps and lubricate the machines of the Industrial Age, was at its peak. Great numbers of men went to sea in search of the mighty whale. Following the whales' migration routes, the whalers ventured from the familiar Atlantic northward to probe the recesses of Davis Strait and Baffin Bay. From the west they rounded Point Barrow to explore the southern margins of the Beaufort Sea.

The whalers found abundant bears. When a whale carcass washed up on the beach, as many as a hundred bears would gather to feed. Growled threats and arguments could be heard at a surprising distance as the bears disputed claim to the blubber banquet. The whalemen ignored the bears until the annual take of whale and walrus began to decline; then the bears acquired economic importance, and demand for polar bear skins back home in the United States escalated dramatically. The whaler-hunters found it easy to shoot the bears: without fear of man, they would follow their noses to camps that smelled of seal or whale oil.

This threat to the bears wasn't restricted to the western Arctic: in northern Baffin Bay, between Greenland and Canada, in 1864 the whaler *Constantia* encountered a large number of polar bears feeding on a single whale carcass. In a profligate day of easy shooting, the whalemen killed sixty bears.

Soon a substitute for whale oil was discovered beneath the earth's surface. The petroleum business was born—an industry that has done more to save the whales than any group of environmental activists. Whales are no longer killed for their lubricating oil, nor for their baleen, or whalebone, which has been replaced by plastics. It is ironic that the first oil well, drilled in Titusville, Pennsylvania, in 1859, both began the demise of the whaling industry and spawned a new era of exploration that eventually reached Nanook's world. Equally ironic is the origin of the Alaskan oil exploration boom of the twentieth century in the seashore wanderings of nineteenth-century whalemen: it was a whaler who discovered the tarry surface seepage in the tundra that led, one hundred years later, to the discovery of a giant oil field at Prudhoe Bay.

The men who explored the Arctic were a breed apart. First they sought the Northwest Passage to the riches of Cathay—a path beyond the reach of the Spanish and Portuguese, who controlled access to the Pacific Ocean. Then the explorers became obsessed with the North Pole itself. *Obsession* is the proper word, for these were men with missionary zeal.

I've worked in the Arctic, and I can appreciate what it was that drew these men northward again and again, and caused them to forsake families and friends in their quest. The very emptiness of the land lures adventurers. No one else walks these shores. Outside of a few settlements, I can travel miles of coastline, mountains, and glaciers and find not a sign of other humans—no footprints, no beer cans, no telephone poles, no fences. I am the master of all I survey, and it is through my own skill that I will survive. The explorers of the nineteenth century were domineering men, convinced of, and absorbed by, their destiny. The Victorian era provided the perfect stage for such men to act out their dramatic roles. The Arctic is the ultimate scene for an egocentric actor, and it fixes itself so firmly in the mind that it becomes an irresistible lure. I know, because I've felt the pull. Before venturing north I marveled at this compulsion, so visible in the explorers' writings, and at the overbearing, driven personalities that dominated the world of arctic discovery. Now I've succumbed. I want to go back, despite pressure ridges, darkness, snow, and cold. A thrall in his service, I'm eager to return to Nanook's kingdom.

Early explorers feared the polar winter and made their northern forays during the summer months. Robert E. Peary changed the nature of arctic exploration by daring to challenge the icepack in its coldest months, on the theory that a completely frozen sea surface would be easier to cross than a field of jostling floes with open water between. During his attempts to reach the Pole in the winter of 1894–95—a goal that would elude him for another fourteen years—Peary encountered numerous polar bears. He shot most of them from distances of only five or six yards. One came much closer: "I could feel his warm breath upon my face, could see the gleam of his teeth and the shape of his long gray tongue, and the furious glare in his savage eyes. I had just time to remove the rifle from my shoulder . . . and to thrust the barrel with all my force into his open jaws, and then drew it back for another thrust. This was a trifle too much for him, apparently, as he whipped short round and took to the water. . . . My left hand which entered his mouth up to the wrist, as shown by the teeth-marks on it, bled a good deal, although the wounds were little more than deep scratches."

Dr. Frederick Cook, whose claim to the Pole was aggressively denied by Peary, was nonetheless an experienced arctic explorer. Much of his long time in the North was marked by near starvation. Nanook the source of meat promised salvation. Nanook the meat thief condemned Cook and his party to death. The delicate balance could shift from moment to moment.

"At the end of about fifteen hours, a stir about our camp suddenly awakened us. We saw a huge bear nosing about our fireplace. We had left there a walrus joint, weighing about one hundred pounds, for our next meal. We jumped up, all of us, at once, shouting and making a pretended rush. The bear took up the meat in his forepaws and walked off, man-like, on two legs, with a threatening grunt. His movement was slow and cautious, and his grip on the meat was secure. Occasionally he veered about, with a beckoning turn of the head, and a challenging call. But we did not accept the challenge. After moving away about three hundred yards on the sea ice, he calmly sat down and devoured our prospective meal."

Cook and his companions had almost no ammunition remaining for their rifles. They were forced into a traditional confrontation with the white bear.

"With lances, bows, arrows, and stones in hand, we next crossed a low hill, beyond which was located our previous cache of meat. Here, to our chagrin, we saw two other bears, with heads down and paws busily digging about the cache. We were not fitted for a hand-to-hand encounter. Still, our lives were equally at stake, whether we attacked or failed to attack. Some defense must be made. With a shout and a fiendish rush, we attracted the busy brutes' attention. They raised their heads, turned, and to our delight and relief, grudgingly walked off seaward on the moving ice. Each had a big piece of meat with him.

"Advancing to the cache, we found it absolutely depleted. Many other bears had been there. The snow and the sand was tramped down with innumerable bear tracks. Our splendid cache of the day previous was entirely lost. We could have wept with rage and disappointment. One thing we were made to realize, and that was that life here was now to be a struggle with the bears for supremacy. With little ammunition we were not at all able to engage in bear fights. So, baffled, and unable to resent our robbery, starvation again confronted us."

Some time later, as Cook's small party staggered in gaunt resignation toward their certain doom, they came across the fresh tracks of a bear. They resolved to end their starvation: "A snowhouse was built, somewhat stronger than usual; before it a shelf was arranged with blocks of snow, and on this shelf attractive bits of skin were arranged to imitate the dark outline of a recumbent seal. Over this was placed a looped line, through which the head and neck must go in order to get the bait. Other loops were arranged to entangle the feet. All the lines were securely fastened to solid ice. Peepholes were cut in all sides of the house, and a rear port was cut, from which we might escape or make an attack. Our lances and knives were now carefully sharpened. When all was ready, one of us remained on watch while the others sought a needed sleep. We had not long to wait. Soon a crackling sound on the snows gave the battle call, and with a little black nose extended from a long neck, a vicious creature advanced.

"Through our little eye-opening he appeared gigantic. Apparently as hungry as we were, he came in straight rushes for the bait. The run port was opened. Wela and Etuq emerged, one with a lance, the other with a spiked harpoon shaft. Our lance, our looped line, our bow and arrow, I knew, however, would be futile.

"During the previous summer, when I foresaw a time of famine, I had taken my last four cartridges and hid them in my clothing. . . . These were to be used at the last stage of hunger to kill something—or ourselves. That desperate time had not arrived till now.

"The bear approached in slow, measured steps, smelling the ground where the skin lay.

"I jerked the line. The loop tightened about the bear's neck. At the same moment the lance and the spike were driven into the growling creature.

"A fierce struggle ensued. I withdrew one of the precious cartridges from my pocket, placed it in my gun, and gave the gun to Wela, who took aim and fired. When the smoke cleared, the bleeding bear lay on the ground.

"We skinned the animal, and devoured the warm, steaming flesh. Strength revived. Here were food and fuel in abundance. We were saved!"

Vilhjalmur Stefansson, an American anthropologist of Icelandic ancestry who spent almost six years living with Eskimos, foraging with them for seals and exploring the arctic regions, was traveling by sledge across the frozen Beaufort Sea in 1914 when his dogs began barking wildly. A bear appeared on the sheet of ice opposite a stretch of open water about five yards across. Stefansson had two immediate worries: that the bear might swim across to his side and that the dogs might leap after the bear and drag their sledges into the deep water. The bear was clearly not intimidated by the dogs. Stefansson wrote, "He bore no hostility towards them, nor had he any fear of their barking, or of the shouting of the six men who ran back and forth telling each other what to do."

As the men fumbled for their rifles amid the equipment lashed to the sledges, Stefansson noticed that he was directly between the bear and S. T. Storkerson, the first man to raise his weapon. He later wrote, in words doubtless more refined than those shouted across the ice, "I requested him to be careful to get the bear and not me."

Storkerson fired, so close behind Stefansson's ear that the expedition leader was partially deafened for some time. The bullet struck the bear, who spun around and fell backward into the open water. Stefansson peered over the edge of the ice and watched the bear sink deep into the clear water. He was soon startled to see the animal turn over, swim back to the surface, and haul himself out on the ice. Storkerson fired his .30-30 twice more. The bear, wounded, ran off. Although bleeding severely, he showed no sign of slowing.

Stefansson fired his powerful 6.5-mm Mannlicher-Schoenauer rifle. The bear rolled over, and the men breathed sighs of relief—too soon. Just as Stefansson returned his rifle to its case, the bear struggled to its feet and stumbled off again. It took several more shots to dispatch the sturdy creature. Stefansson chastened his companions for their wild aim during the fracas: "An exciting bear hunt may be interesting to read about, but it is a poor hunt. One properly located Mannlicher bullet is all that should be necessary. . . . In a party used to bears the men stand with guns ready, while the one who is to do the killing sits quietly and waits until in his natural zigzag approach the bear exposes one side or the other so as to give a chance for the shot near the heart."

Stefansson described a bear's approach to a camp that smells of seal meat: from downwind, he walks boldly into camp, knowing that he smells a dead seal incapable of escape. If he spots a dog, particularly one that moves in its sleep, the bear, thinking he sees a live seal, freezes. "He then instantly makes himself unbelievably flat on the ice, and with neck and snout touching the snow advances almost toboggan-fashion toward the dogs, stopping dead if one of them moves, and advancing again when they become quiet. If there is any unevenness in the ice . . . he will take cover behind a hummock and advance in its shelter." If a dog should bark, the bear realizes it's not a seal after all and loses interest in the stalk. Getting up from his prone position, he resumes his leisurely walk into camp.

Stefansson tied his dogs apart, so they wouldn't fight, and spread them so one or more would be likely to catch the scent of a bear approaching from any direction. He tethered them on the windward side of the camp, so a bear following his nose would discover the seal smell and follow it to its source, not to his dogs.

Stefansson once saw a bear stalking his dog team, presumably thinking they were seals. He shot the bear but then foolishly positioned himself in the ten-yard path between the wounded beast and the open water. "Suddenly and without any preparation he launched himself directly towards me. I had my rifle pointed and it must have been almost automatically that I pulled the trigger. Had not the bullet pierced the brain I am afraid it would have gone badly with me, for as it was he covered about three and a half of the five yards between us, and collapsed so near that blood spattered my boots."

Donald MacMillan, an explorer and popular author, traveling in 1916 with Eskimo companions across the Canadian Arctic by dogsled, spotted a bear and gave chase. It soon proved to be a female with two small cubs. The mother bear stopped running twice and turned back to face her attackers, but she turned again to flee when she saw forty dogs rushing toward her. One of the drivers, Nookapingwa, cut the sled traces and let his dogs run free. Bolting forward eagerly, they overtook the bears and encircled them in a frenzy of barking, howling, and snapping of teeth.

MacMillan heard, ,id the pandemonium of rifle shots and

yelping dogs, the cries of a baby bear. Seeing the mother bear safely surrounded to one side, he dove into a second fray. Shoving snarling dogs aside, he grabbed a yowling ball of white fur, pulled it free, and lifted it high overhead, out of reach of the leaping dogs. Safe on his perch, the cub thanked MacMillan by sinking his sharp teeth into the explorer's wrist. Eventually, as the dogs were restrained, the bear calmed, perhaps soothed by the familiar scent of MacMillan's bearskin pants.

By this time one of the hunters, Arklio, had shot the mother bear; Nookapingwa had picked up the other cub. As feisty as the first baby bear, this one chomped on Nookapingwa's lip, which bled profusely. Both cubs cried loudly until they were placed on their dead mother's body, where they suckled contentedly. MacMillan wrote, "Interesting to note, they were now no longer afraid of us, knowing that if their mother did not protest it must be all right."

Later, the cubs and their mother's carcass were hauled by sledge to MacMillan's camp, renamed Cub Camp in their honor. Several days later, a large male bear wandered in. MacMillan's diary records the scene: "We arrived here after a long march of nine hours, to find our igloo smashed in and our things left here considerably scattered. Papa bear has been home. Not finding the cubs, as I had them well hidden, and not getting any response from his spouse, he grabbed her by the hair of the head, dragged her out of the igloo, ate off both her hind legs and her belly, and left her a complete wreck behind an ice hummock, the cannibal!"

MacMillan eventually took his cub, which he named Bowdoin, back to Etah, the northernmost community in the world (now in ruins, it lies north of Thule, Greenland). He led the little bear through his house and tied the rope around his neck to the bench in his workshop. Less than three minutes later MacMillan was startled by a cry from his companion: "For God's sake come in! He's tearing hell out of the house!"

Running into the back room, MacMillan found a chaotic scene. The cast-iron stove had been turned around, and the stovepipe lay on the floor. Cans, boxes, clothing, and sledge runners were strewn about wildly. Everything was in total disarray, except the top of the workbench, which had been swept clean. On top of the bench stood Bowdoin, tearing madly at the back window. In a rage, the little cub charged MacMillan, who was, fortunately, dressed in his thick outdoor skins. Bowdoin's bites and scratches couldn't penetrate his arctic armor. MacMillan recalled, "When he discovered that his attacks were always met with a laugh and were not resisted, he would drop his head, protrude his upper lip, blow, and cry for all the world like a baby with the croup."

Soon the cub was following MacMillan about like a puppy, getting underfoot, and tripping him by rubbing his head against the explorer's legs. He proved to be a great source of amusement in the little village. MacMillan even harnessed him to pull a sledge but noted, "We went to ride very often, always going where he wanted, never where I did."

But, MacMillan went on, "One morning he was gone. Once before I had found him free, sitting on top of his cage, looking wistfully out over the harbor ice to the blue stretch of open water beyond. Here shelter, comfort, and food, a life of indolence and ease; but out there that for which he was born— troubled waters, drifting pans, flying spray, a matching of his wits and his strength against the elements. I was glad the pen was empty."

Macmillan had numerous other bear encounters but none that brought him so close to Nanook's jaws as the incident of April 3, 1916. His field journal records the day's events:

"If I live to be a hundred, I shall never see a better scrap with a bear than we had to-day. About an hour after turning into Eureka Sound, we saw a bear sitting at a seal-hole . . . she did not see us coming until we were about 150 yards away. The dogs were then at full gallop, and every Eskimo shouting at the top of his voice.

"She jumped to her feet, turned her black muzzle toward us, stretched out her neck, and sniffed the air. Then she decided to leave, which she did in jumps . . . a small pup of Nookapingwa's was right at her hindquarters, taking a nip whenever she touched the ice.

"I was second in the chase, my dogs going at full speed. I

turned to get my camera out of the case, and when I looked again I had passed Nookapingwa and was within ten yards of the bear. Just then she turned. My dogs split, some going one side of her and some the other, with the result that I scooped her up with my sledge. When I realized that she was 'coming aboard' I deserted my ship and ran out to one side. In a few seconds she was fighting for her life against ninety dogs. What a moving picture that would have made! They fairly buried her.

"I was running everywhere, trying to focus my camera and yelling at the Eskimos to shoot to save the dogs, which we could hear howling with pain. To my surprise, there was not a rifle in sight. I yelled for Arklio to get his revolver, a .45. By this time the circus had started south, with me hanging to the back of my sledge and threatening my dogs in all kinds of language if they didn't stop; but that was the last thing they thought of doing.

"In the mean time the Eskimos were spending their time yelling and snapping their whips. Nookapingwa was brandishing a sealing-iron, and finally threw it into the body. Seeing Akkommodingwa hopping around with a Winchester .35, full-cocked, I grabbed it out of his hand, thrust the muzzle down between the dogs, and pulled the trigger. This ended the scrap."

The great polar explorer Roald Amundsen, best known for his later conquest of the South Pole, began his explorations in the Arctic. He was living aboard his ship *Maud*, frozen into the November 1918 icepack, when suddenly his dog Jacob perked up his ears and dashed off the vessel and onto the ice. Amundsen, curious, followed. He walked on the frozen surface to the ship's bow, where a faint sound caused him to pause. The sound grew louder and was soon recognizable as heavy breathing.

Suddenly Amundsen saw Jacob ripping across the ice and snow as fast as his four short legs could carry him. Immediately behind the dog charged a huge polar bear. A moment later a cub came running down the same path. Amundsen quickly surmised that Jacob had teased the cub, provoking the mother's fury.

The bear saw Amundsen, and immediately sat down, staring hard at this strange, two-legged beast. Explorer and Nanook faced each other across the white silence. They remained motionless, each the same distance from the ship's gangway. Amundsen was alone, and his right arm was in a sling. (During an earlier mishap his shoulder had been broken when he'd tripped over Jacob and fallen down the gangway.) Amundsen slowly turned toward the ship as he tried to clear his thoughts.

He decided to make a dash to safety. When he broke into a run, so did the bear. Amundsen described the effort as "a race between a healthy, furious bear and an invalid."

They arrived at the gangway at the same moment. Amundsen turned to run on board but was knocked sprawling by the force of a huge paw slapping his back. He fell heavily on his broken shoulder. Face down on the snow-covered boards, he awaited the killing blow, certain that his time had come.

At this dramatic moment, like cavalry to the rescue, Jacob returned—not with any sense of loyalty to his master but, as Amundsen later wrote laconically, "probably to play with the cub." (Had it not been for his timely arrival, Jacob was probably in danger of becoming Amundsen's least favorite best friend.) The mother bear jumped high and resumed the chase. Amundsen, in understated summary, concluded, "It did not take me long to get up and disappear into safety. It was one of the narrowest escapes of my life."

Despite this encounter, Amundsen had a fondness for the white bear. For a short while he kept a polar bear cub named Marie, but in a sad entry in his diary, he recorded: "Put Marie down with chloroform. I had given up hope of training her. After I had cared for her and fed her for a month, she . . . went for me in a fury. Under the care of an experienced animal trainer, perhaps she could have learned to behave herself, but I had to give up."

In 1912 the *Titanic* disaster focused international attention on the waters of the North Atlantic and on floating bits of Greenland ice that imperil the shipping lanes. In the wake of the tragedy, a great public outcry prompted the formation of the International Ice Patrol. In addition to tracking icebergs, the ships of the patrol, operated by the United States Coast Guard, began to explore the northwesternmost reaches of the Atlantic Ocean, where the ice-laden waters of Davis Strait and Baffin Bay separate the land masses of Greenland and North America. In 1928, the Coast Guard cutter *Marion* steamed into these remote waters, usually visited only by whalers, sealers, and polar expeditions. *Marion*'s primary mission was a survey of ocean depths, currents, and ice conditions, but the expedition also encountered polar bears.

On August 15 the ship's lookout spotted a large female bear with two cubs eating a seal on a floating cake of ice. The bears tried to escape as *Marion* approached, but the crew shot two of them. The third, a 200-pound cub, remained near the body of her mother. As she roared her anguish and confusion, *Marion*'s crew lowered a boat and rowed alongside the ice floe. The cub was quickly lassoed. The two dead bears were trussed and hoisted aboard the cutter, to be eaten by the crew. Fresh meat of any sort was a treat aboard ship, and the bear steaks were pronounced "as sweet and tender as veal."

The live cub, growling and snarling, was lifted onto the ship by lines slipped over her head, body, and legs. Once on the wooden deck, she was overpowered by the crew, dragged forward, and thrown into the forehold, a dank, dark storeroom containing coiled lines, bags of coal, and cans of paint.

The following day the hatch was opened to allow the bear some light and fresh air. But the sailors' concern for their visitor proved too generous. The crew believed that the heavy steel hatch, located high above the bear's head, would be escape-proof. One of *Marion*'s officers described the ensuing melee.

"In a short time, however, the officer of the deck saw from the bridge that the bear's head and paws were prying the hatch cover farther open. An instant later the bear squirmed its way free and began running about the forward deck. The alarm was given and officers and men rushed madly forward to keep their prize from getting away. Four times the bear tried to leap over the rail into the sea, but each time it was pulled back by the hair on its hind legs. On one of these occasions it turned and severely bit the hand of its restrainer before he could let go. An attempt was made to throw a blanket over the bear's head, but the big cub was too fierce and quick. It tore the blanket aside, knocking down the man who was holding it and ripping the back out of his coat. A lively fight ensued until many men closed in on the bear and by force of numbers held it helpless until it could be dragged to the hatch and thrown into the forehold once more.

"A little later the bear was securely noosed by several lines and lifted from the hold. It was dragged to a strong cage that had been constructed of lumber and wedged in among the oil drums on the deck aft. Here the bear, which was soon named Marion, was kept until shipped from New London, Conn., over one month later, to the National Zoo at Washington, D.C.

"She ate very little during this period, practically refusing to touch any food except slices of her dead mother and brother, of which she would eat sparingly from time to time. She was always trying to scratch and gnaw her way out, so the cage frequently had to be repaired with new boards and reinforced with more wire. Marion was extremely sly and vicious and would make sudden rushes to surprise and bite those working about her cage. The only time she seemed to like her captivity was when the washdeck hose was turned on her to give her a daily bath. Her bad temper at all other times was well understood by everyone, and many anxious hours were spent by light sleepers who had visions of her escaping at night and seeking vengeance upon her abductors by means of tooth and claw."

Marion was shipped in a strengthened version of her deck cage to Washington, where for the next twenty years she delighted visitors to the National Zoo. She died in captivity, far from her birthplace but adored by her adopted country.

The frozen world Marion had left behind was about to change forever. During World War II and its attendant buildup of military bases in the remote northern parts of the globe, the first encroachments of arctic "development" began. Like scouts in advance of a huge, unstoppable army, engineers moved north with their bulldozers and Quonset huts. Scientists established research stations, first to serve wartime meteorology, later out of curiosity about the glaciers that tell so many tales of the earth's past. Traders introduced the Inuit to all the supposed benefits of southern civilization. And, like snow geese, tourists began flocking northward during the warmer months.

During the interval between the postwar years and the present, the face of the Arctic was irreversibly altered. This era of arctic history began a new chapter in the story of the delicate balance between Nanook and kabloona. There is one modern tale, however, that belongs with the descriptions of the early explorers. Like their adventures, it is the story of one man against the ice, and against Nanook. It is the story of Naomi Uemura.

Uemura was a young Japanese adventurer who made a solo dogsled trek to the North Pole in March of 1978. With resupply by aircraft and radio communication to a support team, he had a high-tech approach to the Arctic, but the struggles and deprivations he endured were every bit as taxing as those that had faced Peary decades earlier. Far outweighing the threat of frostbite, hypothermia, exhaustion, or a thousand other perils was the danger from the white bear.

"Shortly before dawn the polar bear attacks. From the great surrounding ridges of ice he emerges like a wraith, padding silently toward the camp.

"From my sleeping bag inside the tent I hear the sudden yammer of the dogs and sense a note of alarm. In the Arctic there are few creatures a sled dog fears: One is man, another is the polar bear.

"As I reach for the zipper of my sleeping bag, the barking trails off, and I realize that the dogs have broken loose and scattered. Seconds later I hear the footfalls.

"Unlike those of a dog, they are heavy and shuffling, with a weight that sends tremors through my pillow. The sound of breathing follows, and I feel the presence of the bear, inches away on the other side of the nylon tent wall.

" 'It's all over,' I think, 'I'm going to be killed.' "

As the bear rummaged through his supplies, Uemura lay as quietly as he could in his sleeping bag, even trying not to breathe. The bear returned.

"Turning to the tent, he begins ripping at the flimsy nylon with his great claws and grunting loudly as I literally hold my breath. A new terror seizes me as the tent wall bulges inward and I feel the bear's nose thrust against my back.

" 'Now it is surely over,' I think, 'Live human meat is tastier than pemmican or frozen seal. He's found my scent. I'm finished.'

"And suddenly, unaccountably, the bear leaves. With a final sniff at the tent he pads off, the sound of his heavy footsteps slowly receding. Silence at last."

Uemura thought during those harrowing few moments of his wife, far away in Tokyo, and of his rifle, much closer but unloaded. The next day he awaited the bear's return, this time with a loaded weapon. Uemura took the additional precaution of soaking the firing mechanism in kerosene so it wouldn't freeze in the −40° F air. The bear approached his camp again. The explorer fired when the bear was fifty yards away and dropped him in the snow. Uemura reported his kill to Canadian authorities, who agreed that he'd acted prudently.

Throughout this litany of encounters, the common thread has been the sheer physical and emotional threat posed by meeting a bear in his own element. It is clear that except for the Inuit, who have adapted to arctic life, humankind are interlopers. We are, at best, temporary visitors in Nanook's world. Increasingly, we are the stewards of his wealth, the guardians of his resources. Like faithful attendants at court, who often wield the power behind the throne, we would do well to remember that the white bear, not man, rules the top of the world.

NINE

The Cold War
Heats Up the Arctic

Two of my arctic summers required travel through the military installation at Thule, Greenland. Wandering around the huge base, I took some time to realize that every face I encountered appeared to have come from Europe or the United States: there were no natives to be found. Where had Commander Ross's Arctic Highlanders gone?

The tiny Greenlandic village of Thule was for centuries the focus of life for the world's most northerly inhabitants. Then, by vote of its citizens, the village was uprooted. The ancestral home of the polar Inuit was relocated to Qaanaaq, some one hundred miles farther north. Its former site, on the ice-scoured strip of brown land that separates the waters of Inglefield Fjord from Greenland's huge interior icecap, was overrun in 1949 by men and equipment from the United States. Out of the gritty glacial debris teams of construction workers bulldozed the foundations of Thule Air Base. They raised the kabloona's version of igloos: huge white radar domes. Immense bombers and cargo aircraft lumbered down the new runways. Man's military might had come to the pristine arctic world.

It was an inauspicious beginning. Throughout the conflicts

that humans use to mark our "progress," the northern lands and seas had remained aloof, unreachable and uninvolved. The U.S. Civil War passed the Arctic by (with one historical footnote: the Confederate raider *Shenandoah* ventured northward into Alaskan waters to decimate the Yankee whaling fleet). The Spanish-American War was fought in warmer climes. World War I largely ignored the Arctic. In World War II, except for scattered weather stations and Russia's involvement as an ally of the United States and Canada, the northern lands escaped again. Concern of these northern allies for German-overrun Norway and Denmark (and the resulting threat to Greenland) caused a flurry of interest in the Arctic. Even so, the northernmost territories avoided the devastation that pockmarked Europe and horrified North America. The buildup at Thule, however, augured change.

The former inhabitants of Thule fled to a cluster of twenty-seven one-room wooden shacks, to a semblance of their former way of life. The Inuit moved largely out of disgust. At Thule they saw more material goods wasted in a single day than they had owned in their entire lives. They saw what the white men did to the landscape, and they left.

The change was not without a sense of loss. Relocating their homes was hard on the community of the People, but beyond sadness lay another, more profound loss. Arctic adventurer Peter Freuchen, who lived among the Inuit of Inglefield Fjord, wrote poignantly, "Polar bears no longer come to Pitufik across the bay from Thule; instead there are seven thousand soldiers."

What had been a small weather station during World War II grew almost overnight into a massive air base and radar installation. Gigantic white domes and metallic screens peered northward, over the Pole, toward the Soviet Union. One author described the result: hordes of workers—20,000 in two years—had built on one of earth's most severely beautiful shores "the listening post for Armageddon."

Before long many such ugly electronic flowers blossomed across the northern landscape. Along the imaginary line of 70° north latitude, buildings, towers, and antennae sprouted not only in Greenland but also in northern Canada and Alaska.

Known as the Distant Early Warning System, or more commonly as the DEW Line, this chain of radar stations was the coldest consequence of the Cold War. Its construction marked the first real "development" of arctic North America. Until this time Nanook had had no enemies other than the hunter with his team of sled dogs. There had, of course, been whalers cruising the coast, isolated mining operations, and fur trapping and lumbering to the south, but the northern regions remained largely untouched through the first half of this century. Inuit nomads, an occasional missionary or Hudson's Bay Company trader, and a rare anthropologist, geologist, or wildlife biologist were widely scattered across Nanook's kingdom. The bears outnumbered the humans.

The abrupt arrival of uninvited thousands of military men and electrical engineers shifted the balance of power in the Arctic, and not just in North America. On the other side of the grinding icepack, the Soviet giant, most often portrayed in the Western press as a bear, was also awakening to the possibilities of northern development. Because the USSR contains so many frozen regions, the Soviets were initially more adept at establishing arctic outpots. It is ironic that their infamous gulags in Siberia gave them a head start in the technology needed to develop their cold territory.

The DEW Line was supplanted a decade after its construction by the three-station Ballistic Missile Early Warning System (BMEWS), which cast its electronic net over the polar regions from installations in Alaska, Greenland, and Britain. Today's world of cruise missiles, satellites, and Star Wars technology has rendered the BMEWS radar obsolete as well. A new chain of unmanned robot stations that can track low-flying cruise missiles has been discussed for the 1990s. Perhaps with the current thaw in East-West relations, they won't be needed.

All this northward encroachment brought surprisingly little contact with the white bear. Most workers at such listening posts spend their months of isolation indoors, tending the blinking lights and gently glowing screens of the silent electronics world. They seldom venture outside. If they do, they must be on guard, for Nanook may lie in ambush near buildings, knowing that a meal walking on two feet could emerge from any doorway.

At such north country installations I've encountered men who were hired as bear monitors only because they had experience hunting in the hills of west Texas. With no special knowledge of polar bears, they are motivated primarily by fear, with not a little of the trophy-hunter mentality thrown in.

At the other end of the spectrum, these sites serve as operational bases for specialists in bear management, who find it all in a day's work to reach inside Nanook's mouth to pull a tooth or tattoo his gums. To these researchers bears are dangerous animals, deserving respect, but they're also beautiful creatures, deserving protection. Polar bear biologists don't enter Nanook's kingdom without firearms, but they are reluctant to use them. They're concerned, in their efforts to minimize human–polar bear interactions, as much with the safety of the bears as with human safety.

Poles apart in a polar world, one group sees Nanook as a threat, a terrifying nightmare vision, all tooth and claw; the other sees the white bear as the one who belongs here unmolested, the majestic lord of the arctic realm. In between are the arctic natives: Eskimos, Inuit, and Greenlanders, who in recent years have shifted their views toward Nanook's protection because they see polar bears as valuable resources in a growing tourism industry.

Men who came north to work at the burgeoning military installations of the 1950s increased the demand for polar bear skins as souvenirs of their time in the Far North. In his book *Land of the Long Day*, filmmaker Doug Wilkinson wrote of the trade imbalances that this desire spawned during the 1950s: "Jacko [a native hunter] sold the bear skin he had shot on our trip to one of the Americans. Having no money, the American offered other items, starting with a cigarette lighter and cigarettes, which Jacko declined, and ending up with the offer of a winter parka plus two cartons of cigarettes, which Jacko accepted. Now the cash value of these items was roughly fifty dollars. On the surface, this was a good bargain, and Jacko could not refuse it, for it was probably three times the cash value he would have received from the Hudson's Bay Company post manager for the skin. But he did not really need the parka, whereas he was short of kerosene and flour, items he could only purchase at the Bay store with money or skins to trade. By trading with the American he and his family did without some of the necessities of life in his land."

Following the polar quests that opened this century, Americans largely ignored the Arctic, with one major exception: the film *Nanook of the North*. When I was about ten my father took me to a showing of this movie in the public library; it was already a classic. Today everyone seems to recognize the name of the film, but few have seen it; fewer still recognize the polar bear's name in the title. Television viewers shivered with vicarious chills as they watched the occasional arctic documentary but thought little about the cold lands and seas at the top of the world.

Except for workers at remote installations, no one thought much about the northern lands during this period until two nonmilitary events returned the Arctic to public consciousness in the United States. In 1959 Alaska entered the Union as the forty-ninth state. Overnight the nation had inside its boundaries a new, largest state, miles of arctic shoreline, and thousands of polar bears. Then in 1968, an icebreaking oil tanker, SS *Manhattan*, shouldered its broad-beamed way through the Northwest Passage, demonstrating a route to transport oil from Alaska's North Slope to markets along the eastern seaboard. The rapidly developing Prudhoe Bay oil fields awakened public interest in the cold lands. Impressive in scale and arrayed against a hostile environment, northern engineering projects assumed heroic dimensions as workers struggled against incredible odds.

Following the launch of *Sputnik* in 1957, explorers focused their attention skyward. If we thought about the Arctic at all, we stared upward, ignoring the flat, frozen world. We craned our necks to ponder the mysteries of the aurora but hypothesized more about magnetic fields and solar particles than about the polar environment where the Northern Lights decorate the heavens. We plotted the polar trajectories of satellites and manned spacecraft high overhead without a thought of the frozen polar sea below.

Discovery of large accumulations of metallic minerals and

petroleum beneath the surface of the arctic regions brought a new kind of "civilization" to the northern lands at the hands of roughnecks, miners, and construction laborers. Like the electronics technicians, however, these burly workers—although they may be outdoorsmen interested in fishing or moose hunting during their off-hours—live sheltered, privileged lives in the high Arctic. Workers at Prudhoe Bay, for example, often remain indoors during their entire stay at the immense complex. Inside are all the amenities of a southern city: snack bars, swimming pools, gymnasiums, television, and, occasionally, real trees. Boredom and loneliness have replaced starvation and frostbite as daily concerns. And, in contrast to arctic workers of the past, these employees of major international corporations are very well paid.

Insidious in its approach, and outwardly attractive, a wage economy has thrust its way into the Inuit world. The natives weren't prepared for its arrival. The material goods appealed to them, but the white man's world didn't provide jobs or training, and a welfare state evolved. The hunter whose greatest pleasure was going out on the ice to pursue seals and bears was lured into the modern era by the appeal of television sets, snowmobiles, alcohol, and drugs. In the words of journalist John Dyson, "The Eskimo asked for nothing and was given everything."

Nanook, too, suffered from this development: polar bear hunting escalated. By the 1960s the white bear's future looked bleak. Hunters in aircraft, on snowmobiles, and aboard northern cruise ships were taking an appalling toll. Native hunters complained that killing a bear no longer conferred any honor. A Soviet researcher reported that there were more hunters than bears in the Arctic. On Svalbard, a group of islands north of Norway where the white bear was considered a "nuisance predator," trappers used the set gun, a baited trigger with a high-powered rifle pointed at it. Set guns killed or wounded bears indiscriminately, male and female, adult and cub. One Norwegian hunter claimed to have killed more than 700 bears over the years.

At the height of unrestricted hunting, over 300 bears a year were slain on Svalbard, almost 400 in Alaska, and over 700 in Canada.

With rifles, hunting was easy. With snowmobiles and aircraft, it was absurdly easy. Even before such modern contrivances, explorer Robert Peary shot more than sixty bears during his first year on Franz Josef Island. The second year, he shot twenty-five; the third, twelve. Given a few years, he wrote, he could exterminate the species entirely.

The first response to this burgeoning problem occurred in 1955, when the Soviet Union banned all polar bear hunting. The second came in 1968, when the Canadian Northwest Territories imposed a polar bear quota on its native villages. Each settlement's kill for the previous three years was totaled, and the villagers were allocated a number slightly below the average for those years. No reliable figures on polar bear populations were then available, so no one knew whether such a quota might do further damage, just break even, or allow the stock of bears to increase. Inuit hunters were told that their quota might need adjustment in future years. Today, about 680 permits—each valid for one bear—are issued to Inuit hunters each year in Canada, so the total kill remains close to prequota levels. Some bear permits are transferable, so an Inuk can guide nonresident hunters. Mechanized vehicles are prohibited in the hunt, and dogsleds are returning to the Northwest Territories.

An encouraging sign is the acceptance of the quota system by the Inuit people. They, too, are concerned about the size of the bear population. Increasingly, they appreciate the economic value of living bears as a draw for tourists. Today some of the most ardent polar bear conservationists are the Inuit of northern Canada. Too much tourism, however, might also be a bad thing. Inuit tour leaders have been reported using snowmobiles to chase bears to near exhaustion and then steering the docile, panting bears toward strategically positioned camera tripods, obliging their paying customers.

Occasionally, however, the native reaction to polar bears and the visitors they draw from the south is laconic, as Lieutenant Tom Johnson discovered when he took a break from his

scientific duties aboard a Coast Guard icebreaker. His ship-
mates suggested a trip ashore, at Barrow, Alaska. The local
highlight, they assured him, was the chance to see a pair of
polar bear cubs at the United States Navy's Arctic Research
Laboratory. The ship's captain, they said, had recently visited
the cubs and had been bitten in the crotch, to the amusement
of everyone else aboard.

Johnson and a graduate student located a Quonset hut with
signs proclaiming it the laboratory and opened the door. Inside,
an Eskimo sat behind a desk. He looked up and grinned.

"We heard you have some bear cubs," they said. Still the
Eskimo grinned. Without saying a word, he nodded toward a
side door. Cautiously they opened the door a few inches. Two
black snouts surrounded by white faces appeared in the gap and
wedged the door open wider. "Two of the largest bear 'cubs'
I'd ever seen in my life," Johnson says, "nosed their way into
the open doorway. They were the size of full-grown St. Ber-
nards, and wanted to *play*!"

Still the Eskimo gazed at the scene and grinned, apparently
both amused and disgusted with these interlopers who threatened to ruin a perfectly peaceful afternoon.

The two men managed, with considerable difficulty, to
shepherd the cubs back inside. "We followed," says Johnson,
"closed the door, and backed unsteadily against the wall. The
bears moved close, snorted, pushed, and sniffed. (Why do they
always sniff *there*?) Memories of the captain's fate leaped into
our minds."

The cubs were becoming increasingly aggressive. The student raised his arm to chest level to fend off the furry creatures.
This seemed to be a signal for playtime: one of the cubs took
the forearm in his mouth. The other stood up on his hind legs
to get an eye-to-eye perspective on his new playmate. As the
first bear tugged happily on his forearm sandwich, Johnson
moved in, holding his arms close to his sides. A gaping hole
appeared in the student's new Eddie Bauer down parka. Rip-
stop nylon doesn't thwart polar bear teeth.

The student realized that Johnson had the right approach.
He lowered his arms to his sides. The two adventurers shuffled

anxiously toward the doorway, back to back. They kept the cubs at bay, buffeting them with their knees and hips. Somehow, the men managed to open the door, back through it, and slam it shut before the cubs could join in the escape. Johnson and his colleague stood panting in the main Quonset hut, staring at the door. Except for his ripped clothing and some minor scratches, the young man was unhurt. To this day he remains one of the few people on earth to have had polar bears slobber all over them and live to tell the tale.

As the two beat a hasty retreat from the research laboratory, the Eskimo still sat at his desk, grinning.

Tom Johnson clearly learned from his experience with the cubs, as I discovered when he shared my Canadian campsite. One night a black bear climbed a tree near our tents in an effort to reach our food pack. I suggested a strategy that had worked for me in the past: a yelling, screaming, pot-banging charge directly toward the bear. Johnson pondered this for a minute and then turned slowly toward me. The look on his face suggested that he thought I might be certifiably insane. Very thoughtfully he said, "You know, my specialty has always been *watching* bears."

In 1971 the state government of Alaska followed Canada's lead by restricting hunters to an annual limit of three bears per person. Previously no limits had existed. Sport hunting permits were issued to nonnatives for an additional 300 bears, or 75 percent of the preregulation sport kill. These state regulations were superseded in 1972 by the federal Marine Mammal Protection Act, which permits Alaskan Eskimos to hunt polar bears but prohibits all other hunting of the white bears in the United States.

Norway acted in 1970 to reduce the number of bears taken on Svalbard to 300, including all kills by residents, trappers, weather observers, seal hunters, and tourists. In 1973 even these permits were revoked, and a moratorium was established on polar bear killing (originally for five years but still in effect).

These pioneering protection and preservation attempts

paved the way for a mid-1970s international accord that protects polar bears and their fragile environment. Safeguarding
the bears is only part of the story, however. Restricting hunting
may prove easier than protecting arctic ecosystems from the far-
flung poisons spewed by the industrialized nations.

Development of the Arctic proceeds fitfully, in bursts of
enthusiasm alternating with dormant stupors. Such cycles are
dictated by outside forces: the price of oil, demand for (or rejec-
tion of) fur coats, or spot-metal markets in far-off exchanges.
The white man's role in the Arctic is still evolving, with continued probing, mapping, and exploring. Contrasts between old
and new, Stone Age and Space Age, are seen every day. You
don't sail very far in the Arctic before you run aground on such
conflicts.

I was once aboard an icebreaking ship slowly working its
way northward through Kennedy Channel, the narrow defile
that separates northwestern Greenland from Canada's Ellesmere island. The gray walls of rock—northernmost land in the
world—closed in, causing a certain degree of claustrophobia
among the blue-water sailors. The navigator's charts were the
product of nineteenth-century explorers: they'd been updated
somewhat by aerial surveys during World War II, but much of
the coastline was drawn as it had first been mapped by the
Charles F. Hall and Elisha K. Kane expeditions shortly after
the U.S. Civil War. Our ship was equipped with the latest
satellite-positioning devices, so we knew exactly where we were
on the globe in coordinates from the satellite. When we plotted
the satellite fix on the old charts, however, we appeared to be
perched atop a 2,500-foot mountain. The navigator reluctantly
accepted the accuracy of the modern equipment but had to rely
on the old charts for nearshore piloting. It was far easier to steer
between the rocky bluffs than to insist on the satellite's precision. Once again, common sense triumphed over technology.

In another striking juxtaposition, I knew the modern era
had reached Greenland when, in 1970, a shipmate commented
in a small tavern in Jakobshavn, "If only they took American
Express cards, I'd buy the whole crew a beer." The proprietor
beamed: "Ah, yes, American Express!" At the lieutenant's ex-

pense—almost a hundred dollars—we all enjoyed our beer while icebergs drifted leisurely past the inn's balcony.

Though modern times have wrought many changes, the face of the land is as barren as it was when the ice first melted, and as empty as it was when explorers first ventured north. The open space can be daunting. Meeting an unexpected fellow human being in the midst of emptiness is an occasion for rejoicing. High on a rocky ridge in northwestern Greenland, I was in charge of a survey party aiming instruments at a distant glacier. I turned the telescope toward the bay and was fascinated by a pair of natives paddling across the dark waters far below the foot of our outcrop. We could see the kayakers, and, as it developed, they could see us as well. Our survey crew, clad in bright orange high-visibility suits—originally the uniforms of street sweepers in Washington, D.C.—must have been easily visible from the water, silhouetted against the pale sky.

A short while later the two natives appeared on top of the ridge. A study in old and new, they wore modern cloth sweatshirts above trousers sewn from polar bear fur. The pants looked huge and made the hunters' lower bodies appear twice as massive as their torsos. The shaggy white fur gleamed as orange as our coveralls in the warmth of the afternoon sun.

Our visitors spoke no English but smiled and eyed a pile of cheese sandwiches that we'd just laid out for dinner. We couldn't resist sharing our food, respecting the common bond of humanity but breaking the laws that forbade any unauthorized exchange with the Greenlanders.

Vittus, age twenty-six, wrinkled with the lines of middle age (the average lifetime in Qaanaaq, his home, was about forty-five), was accompanied by Jakob, age twelve. I was eager to break the language barrier. I began pointing to objects, or sketching them in my fieldbook, and having the two men speak the words in their language. Boat = *umiaq*. This was a word I recognized. I knew we were on common ground. We grinned in agreement. Ship = *umiarssuit*. I dutifully wrote the word, spelling it as best I could. Seal = *puisse*. This I had trouble spelling. Vittus, looking over my shoulder, laughed. He took the pencil from my hand and wrote the word next to my crude drawing of a seal. This man that I had foolishly assumed to be unschooled because he didn't speak my language proved quite literate in his own. I was abashed at my patronizing thoughts. Wanting the word for walrus, I pointed two fingers down from my lips, in crude pantomime of ivory tusks. "Ah," Vittus roared, "*Valrus!*" Our two worlds were closer than I'd ever dreamed.

Beside me the radio squawked to life. Our support ship, enveloped in a fogbank ten miles away, was calling to make certain we were safe. I responded: "*Westwind*, we have visitors."

"What kind of visitors?" The icebreaker's executive officer was clearly concerned. For all he knew, we had a bear in camp. I looked at our new colleagues, happily sharing our meal. I smiled and picked up the microphone. Only one word seemed appropriate, or needed: "Friends."

Although this period of recent arctic history saw the greatest incursion into Nanook's world, it also began efforts to afford the polar bear protection. In all his encounters with humans, the great northern bear seems to wish primarily to be left alone. While the forces of Armageddon carry their nuclear bombs high above arctic clouds and their missiles and torpedoes deep beneath the polar ice, the white bear walks in majesty across the snow-covered floes, his dignity unruffled by the posturing and saber rattling of mere mortals. Conflicts and treaties concern him not in the least, with one significant exception: a remarkable international agreement that guarantees his freedom to walk the frozen sea with impunity.

TEN

Bear Attack!

My FIELD PROJECTS in the Arctic—geology, glaciology, oceanography, and sea-ice studies—all led me to the same conclusion about the white bears: that they are life-threatening menaces. All the old hands "reassured" me with frightening tales. On the ice we carried weapons or went out with armed guards. Polar bears were enemies to be feared.

Hugh Miles, BBC filmmaker, wrote in *Kingdom of the Ice Bear*, a book about the Arctic coauthored in 1985 with Mike Salisbury: "Like everyone else who takes an interest in the Arctic I had been indoctrinated by all the stories of people being killed and eaten by bears, about bears terrorizing towns, stalking scientists, chasing explorers, tearing down camps and cabins, in fact causing mayhem throughout the north. I suspect some of the polar bear's reputation for being dangerous has been created purely to enhance the 'macho' image of some of those who have worked in the Arctic, and there are certainly some appalling recent examples in the media of the bear's false image as a 'man-eater' being perpetrated for personal and monetary gain. . . . They are gentle giants, playful and inquisitive, not the aggressive killers that their reputation demands."

Both impressions are accurate. Like humans, bears are gentle, expressive, and playful. Like humans, they can be aggressive killers. They're not malicious or evil, but they are dangerous predators, and deserve respect.

How real is the danger? The answer depends on the bear's mood, his condition, and his intention. I asked an expert how many bear incidents have resulted from humans feeling threatened when no threat was intended. "I've been on the ground with bears," biologist Chris Davies responded. "The threat isn't just perceived; it's real.

"However," Davies continued, "bear researchers often say there's no such thing as problem bears—only problem people. The bears are just behaving naturally. Unfortunately, most 'problem' incidents end with the bear being shot.

"I've worked in Churchill eight years," he said, "and in Polar Bear Provincial Park for three. I've probably seen more than five thousand polar bears. I've lived in the center of a major bear gathering area. I've been tracked by polar bears, I've been scared by polar bears, I've been run out of camp by polar bears, but I've never shot one. I've had bears follow me around, I've had bears hunt me, but I've never even shot *at* a polar bear."

Polar bears *do* attack people. Fortunately, they do so rarely. Some polar bears attack people to eat them. Others attack in campsites and towns to which they were lured by the scent of meat or garbage. Mother bears attack people anywhere they perceive a danger to their cubs. Polar bears in zoos attack people who enter their cages. In fact, over the past fifteen years more people have been killed by polar bears in zoos than have been killed by wild polar bears throughout the North American Arctic.

The danger, however rare, is real. When it comes to humans, Nanook is curious but not easily amused. He does not suffer fools, or even the unwary, graciously.

Problem encounters often involve a bear that hasn't eaten for several days. A hungry bear is a very dangerous bear. As Ian Stirling has written, "The common thread in problem incidents is that hungry, sometimes starving, animals have nothing to lose by trying something different. After all, investigating new possibilities is the hallmark of success for carnivores."

In January 1975, on an artificially constructed island that supported an oil-drilling rig in the Canadian Beaufort Sea, an eighteen-year-old worker was killed by a bear. The animal was a five-year-old male in poor condition, with so little fat on his body that he was literally starving. In midmorning the man was bending over some steps, chopping ice away from a doorway. Without warning the bear attacked. The blow was so sudden, and so silent, that co-workers less than twenty-five feet away inside the building were unaware of any trouble.

The bear dragged the man almost a mile and stopped to eat him. Eventually the other workers at the drilling camp discovered that their colleague was missing and gave chase. They found the bear guarding the partly consumed body. They approached the bear with vehicles and fired a flare pistol at it, but the animal only dragged his victim's body farther away. The men finally managed to kill the bear, but it was too late to save their companion.

In this incident it seems likely that the bear intentionally attacked the man. Other attacks, however, may have been cases of mistaken identity. In some instances the victims may have resembled seals. At Magdalena Fjord, north of Spitsbergen, Svalbard, an Austrian tourist was attacked in 1977 as he popped his head out of his tent. The camper was apparently peeking out to check on a sound that he'd heard. To the bear he must have looked very much like a seal emerging from its breathing hole. Nanook devoured his victim while the other campers watched helplessly.

I've always found it ironic that after I've pulled on a drab, insulated full-body suit, zipping the hood around my face, and realized how totally seal-like I must look from a distance, the bear experts would say, "All you have to do is avoid looking like a seal."

Over the past ten years arctic tourism has grown at an ever-increasing rate. The burgeoning number of tourists seeking arctic adventures means more encounters with Nanook. Visitors to Churchill, Manitoba, where much of this tourism is focused, watch bears from the safety of tundra buggies high off the ground. In at least one instance, however, they were not high enough. Fred Treul, a Wisconsin businessman, was in Churchill on Thanksgiving Day 1983, intent on photographing wildlife. His group had been observing polar bears for some time and had counted more than forty in the area. "I'd been to Churchill four or five times before," Treul told me, "but this was the greatest number of bears I'd seen in one spot." The group spotted a lean male bear, apparently in poor condition, but lost sight of him in their enthusiasm for other animals.

A rare gull flew by and landed on the ice. Treul was on the back deck of the vehicle. "I opened the door and said to the people inside, 'There's a bird on the ice.' One of my companions, Fred Bruemmer, moved across the aisle to the driver's seat and opened the sliding window. I'd just finished a roll of film. I set my camera down and slid over to Fred's seat. Trying to maneuver the lens barrel around the large outside rearview mirror, I leaned out the window."

At this moment the scrawny bear seen earlier reared from a concealed position directly beneath the vehicle. He chomped down hard on Treul's arm. He began tugging, trying to pull the man out the window.

With amazing presence of mind, Treul said to Bruemmer, " 'Take my camera. I've got a bear on my arm.' Roy Bukowsky, a biologist who understands bear behavior, reached over me and punched the bear repeatedly in the nose with his fist. I think he broke one or two bones in his right hand as he hit the bear.

"The bear had my left elbow in his mouth," Treul told me, "and was jerking me hard against the window frame. It was like having your arm caught in an elevator door and trying to pull it free." The bear finally let go.

"I was wearing a down-filled shirt over a fairly heavy cotton sweater. The bear tore the nylon but didn't actually get his teeth into me. Nonetheless, my arm was ripped open in a spiral from the middle of my upper arm, around the elbow to the top of my lower arm, ending at my wrist on the little-finger side."

Treul's arm was badly mangled, with skin and muscles dangling loose. On later reflection, he said, "I turned out to be extremely lucky: there was no major nerve damage, no major tendon damage, and no major blood-vessel damage. I did tear some cartilage in my rib cage where I was pulled against the windowsill."

It took more than fourteen hours to drive back to Churchill in zero-visibility weather (60-mile-an-hour winds and blowing snow). Dan Guravich radioed Churchill for assistance, but the response wasn't encouraging. The town was engulfed in a raging storm. The voice crackling on the receiver warned, "And if you're not in the middle of a blizzard, you will be shortly."

Treul nearly bled to death during the long drive. His companions rigged a platform for him to lie on. He told me, "Roy Bukowsky drove the tundra buggy. He had to pick his way from the cape to the road in a virtual whiteout. There were little high-tide streams or sloughs in the tundra, hidden by the blowing snow. Roy hit one at a right angle and couldn't get the machine unstuck. We left the tundra buggy and transferred to a snow-track machine. They laid a piece of plywood across the engine cover box for me to lie on."

At this point Treul's adventure was only half over. The tough ex-marine remained calm despite the jolting that continually reopened his wounds. "I was conscious during the entire trip, and felt no pain. I'm sure I was in shock. I was more concerned about my companions than I was about myself. Fred Bruemmer had come off heart surgery to make this trip. The others had enough to worry about, too. The wind ripped off the windshield wipers and tore a hatch off the roof. Len Smith had to stand in the open hatch to try to see where we were going and shout commands to Roy at the controls. Those people really suffered up there. Anne Fadiman stayed at my side and talked to me the entire fourteen hours. The timing of the whole episode was extremely lucky: a few seconds more at any stage of this incident, and I would have died. Every one of these people was heroic."

Meanwhile, back in Churchill, Dr. Harry "Pat" Brown readied the small but well-equipped hospital for which he'd given up a medical practice in Vancouver. He said he wanted to get away from the rat race and get back to the excitement of medicine. Excitement was about to descend on him in the form of Fred Treul. Treul said, "About midnight we pulled up at his surgery. I walked to the building, then up a few stairs. I'd lost a lot of blood but was still in no pain. One of the bear's teeth had chipped my funny bone, and the nerves just weren't sending signals."

Dr. Brown worked on Treul's arm for more than an hour. The weather cleared sufficiently that an evacuation flight was scheduled for 3:00 A.M. "We arrived in Winnipeg about 6:00 A.M. They took me by ambulance to the Health Science Centre. A team was waiting for me. Dr. Strank, a reconstructive surgeon, looked me over and said, " 'Well, you got a love bite. Can you move your fingers?' It took him only a couple of minutes to say, 'There will be some permanent damage, but we will be able to save your arm.' "

Treul was in the Winnipeg hospital for more than a week. The medical staff was under increasing pressure to put him on public display. It didn't help matters that only two days after his encounter, a man in Churchill had been killed by a bear. Local residents wanted to kill Treul's bear (*a* bear, perhaps any bear). He demurred, saying that the bear deserved to live.

"My wife, Ruth, flew up. We spent long hours talking, and she took careful notes. We discussed the situation and finally agreed to meet with reporters. They set up a news conference— the place was packed with reporters. There were three TV camera crews. I read my wife's notes and asked if there were any questions.

"One asked, 'What were you thinking at the time?' I didn't satisfy the reporters, because I didn't really know—the only thing I was sure about was that I wanted to get my arm out of the bear's mouth."

Dr. Strank found a flap of skin that could be used in a graft to bridge the spiral wound. Treul was transferred to the hospital's burn ward, and eventually flew back to Milwaukee, where the local hospital continued monitoring his condition. "It was four to five months before all the skin openings were fully healed. I'd begun therapy immediately, and I now have almost full use of my arm back. I had to relearn a number of things, but the right arm 'taught' the left how to do most of them.

"During recovery, the pain was severe. I'm told this is typical with skin grafts, and with so much muscle tissue gone. The tissue death was probably a function of time: if I'd gotten back to Churchill in a few hours, I wouldn't have lost so much muscle. Dr. Brown had prepared cultures from my torn tissues but found no septicemia [blood poisoning]. That was a mystery until I looked at my down shirt later and realized that the bear had never really touched me."

Treul concluded his amazing story: "I went back to Churchill the following year. I didn't have any strange feelings with respect to the bears. Several people in the group apparently joined just to find out what kind of a guy I really am. It was like 'What's this crazy American doing up here getting bitten by a bear, anyway?' "

To evaluate a potential danger you have to analyze the hazards involved. Two Canadian researchers did just that, compiling an extensive collection of information about polar bear attacks. Susan Fleck and Steve Herrero studied incidents that occurred in Manitoba and the Northwest Territories between 1965 and 1985. During this time five men and one teenage boy died; thirteen men, two boys, and one woman were injured; and at least 230 bears were killed because they were perceived as threats to life and property. Although aggressive bears, curious bears, and bears protecting their young were reported in a number of settings, the greatest incidence of human injury by bears was in mining and oil exploration camps during winter operations.

The researchers divided polar bear incidents into two categories: depending on the outcome for the humans involved, encounters were classed as injurious or noninjurious aggressive interactions. The authors tried to document what behavior by the bear caused it to be perceived as threatening, as well as the results of a typical polar bear attack. Their study was designed to provide information from which park managers and arctic travelers might make safety decisions. Although they concluded that "most polar bears appear to be very tolerant of humans and will steer clear of them," they also added a warning: "What one bear will do, another may not. The Boy Scout motto is good advice. Always be prepared. Even if visitors take all the necessary precautions," Fleck and Herrero wrote, "aggressive interactions may be unavoidable when humans are active in the vicinity of polar bears."

The behavior that most people find threatening—a polar bear advancing in their direction—might mean that the bear is curious, that the bear perceives the humans as a threat, or that the bear is hunting two-legged prey. There is no doubt, however, that polar bears *are* curious. Several biologists interviewed by Fleck and Herrero "felt that the reason for such curiosity was linked to a polar bear's constant search for food. Thus anything that was out of the ordinary could potentially be a food item and needed to be investigated. Polar bear tracks followed from a helicopter sometimes veered off where a bear had spotted a dirty piece of snow or an abandoned fuel barrel and then returned back to their original course after the object was investigated."

Another author, Richard Davids, showed how Nanook's curiosity governs human impressions of the white bear: "The trouble with being a polar bear . . . is that everyone takes you seriously. When you're big and powerful and your paws are studded with claws like medieval instruments of torture, people flee, assuming you're out to eat them, even though at the moment you may be nothing more than curious. And curious is what you are always, for good reason. After roaming the ice for days of nothing but blinding white snow, the slightest change in color or form is bound to be exciting. So you move toward it, nose held high to catch the scent. You stop and lift yourself to your full height to get a better look. Then you drop down and move forward, sometimes at a run. So men fear you and from the beginning of time have fought you with dogs and spears and knives, and later, in their igloos, whiled away the long hours of night with stories of your strength, your wisdom, and your ferocity."

Subadult males, according to Fleck and Herrero, were at least twice as likely as any other sex or age grouping of bears to be involved in aggressive interactions. Cubs stayed out of the fray, but mother bears behaved aggressively. In all classes of bears, poor physical condition increased the likelihood of aggressive interaction. As the authors pointed out, however, all these observations from the dry world of statistics are of little practical value, "because it is rarely possible to determine the sex, age, or condition of a polar bear without killing the bear."

The data these researchers examined indicate that male polar bears appear to prey on humans, a statement supported by a variety of observations. First is the nature of their victims' injuries. Just as he kills seals, a polar bear attacks humans with bites or paw blows to the head and neck. Nine out of ten male bears that attacked humans caused head and neck wounds. Second is the behavior of the bears involved in human attacks. Polar bears have many ways of signaling their agitation, but they rarely show these before attacking humans. They don't telegraph their intentions to prospective prey.

Out of twenty interactions in which humans were killed or injured, two-thirds were probably predatory (because the people had no warning). Only male bears were involved in such encounters. Incidents in which female bears were surprised with cubs are not considered "predation" encounters: the mother bear usually breaks off the conflict and leaves without killing the human involved. Fleck and Herrero did concede one point to the white bear: "Lack of warning is not always related to predatory intentions. Female polar bears will act aggressively to protect their offspring and, during sudden encounters, productive female polar bears are likely to injure a human. The data suggest," they wrote in their report to the government, "that the intent of a male polar bear during an injurious interaction is to kill the person. Single adult female bears have not been involved in attacks on people. To date only adult female bears accompanied by young have attacked people. It is most likely that they viewed the human as a direct threat to their cubs."

This contrast between male and female behavior is also apparent in the actions of grizzly and black bears. The females generally want only a chance to escape with their cubs. A hunting male bear, however, clearly doesn't want his intended target to be alerted. In only two of nineteen incidents in which a person was injured were the victims aware of the bear's presence before the attack began. Nanook uses both his seal-hunting strategies—the still hunt and the stalk—on humans as well. He makes no sound; he gives no warning.

Finally, and most vivid, is the direct evidence: in the incidents studied five bears ate parts of their victims, and two other bears were shot before they could consume their victims' flesh.

Attractants such as food, garbage, animal carcasses, or live animals were present in almost all the noninjurious situations and in almost half the injurious attacks. People themselves may have been the attractant in many situations. Various attempts were made to repel the attacks, including firing warning shots, chasing the bear with a vehicle, shouting, firing small explosive devices, dogs barking or chasing the bear, setting off bird-scaring bombs, shooting flares, or firing rubber baton bullets from a shotgun. Other impromptu deterrent methods reported would be comical if the problem were not so deadly serious: chasing the bear with a road grader, flashing lights, banging on pots and pans, slamming doors, throwing objects, and so on. (Except for the doors and the road grader, this list recalls my own experiences with black bears in Canadian wilderness campsites. All I usually managed to accomplish was to get a confused bear up a tree in the middle of camp.)

In 96 percent of the noninjurious encounters Fleck and Herrero studied, the deterrents worked. Chasing the bear with a vehicle (truck, heavy equipment, or snow machine) was the most effective. Other deterrents (trip wires, electrified barbed-wire fences, sirens, and loud recorded noises) have been tested outside the town of Churchill with varying degrees of success. The trip wires and sirens worked well occasionally, but the most consistently effective deterrent was a rubber projectile fired from a gun. In a sobering comment on such attempts to dissuade Nanook, the researchers wrote: "Until such time as [deterrents] of proven efficiency are readily available, the ability to shoot to kill should always be present as a last resort."

The strongest recommendation for carrying weapons in the north country is that "no one died when a firearm was available to a witness of a mauling." In addition, three out of six deaths might have been prevented if a firearm had been available, and, according to the authors of the government report, the presence of firearms definitely prevented an additional nine people from being killed. All the Inuit hunters, biologists, and others interviewed always carry a firearm when they travel in polar bear country. Fleck and Herrero summarized the observations of these veterans: "Carrying a firearm will not always prevent a bear from attacking a person. It could, however, prevent the death of someone who is being mauled by a bear. In addition, if the firearm is a shotgun, it can first be used to deploy deterrents such as cracker shells, plastic bullets or warning shots in the hopes of scaring the bear away before it or a person is injured or killed."

Firearms are, however, a wise choice only if you know how to use them. "They can add to the danger," Susan Fleck told me. "If a polar bear is injured because a person doesn't know how to use a weapon, then there's real trouble. We'd like to see people hiring guides to go with them. Inuit guides who know about bears and are familiar with firearms."

Fleck and Herrero concluded by focusing on five strategies for avoiding bear problems: alertness, avoidance, attractants, detection, and deterrents. They recommend that a person charged by a female bear defending her cubs play dead and curl in a fetal position. Once the human no longer threatens her cubs, the mother bear may lose interest. If a person is attacked by a single bear and didn't see it coming, the authors recommend trying to escape or acting aggressively toward the bear. They further recommend a change in Canadian park policy to allow visitors, under stringent provisions, to carry firearms.

Off the west coast of Ellef Ringnes Island, four men from a Canadian government seismic operation were on the ice in the summer of 1961, waiting for a helicopter resupply flight. They had a tent, but three of the men had chosen to sleep outside, because some food had been spilled in the tent. The men later speculated that they probably looked like seals, stretched out in their dark sleeping bags on the ice.

About four in the morning, one of the men, Tony Overton,

awoke to see a subadult female polar bear advancing in his direction. The bear was already close; she had walked boldly to within ten yards when Overton stuck his left arm out of the sleeping bag and fumbled for his rifle. When the bear saw Overton's arm move, she ran the remaining few yards and sank her teeth into it. Holding fast with powerful jaws, the bear began dragging Overton away. After he'd been pulled several yards across the ice, Overton was able to shout loud enough to awaken one of his companions, although it took him at least three attempts. Bill Tyrlik scrambled from his sleeping bag and grabbed the rifle. The bear spotted new movement. Dropping Overton, she charged Tyrlik, who had just enough time to swing the rifle up to his hip. He fired with the bear directly in front of him and coming fast. Tyrlik was either a crack shot or extremely lucky. His hip shot caught the bear between the eyes and dropped her on the end of Tyrlik's sleeping bag. Overton survived his ordeal with only minor lacerations and punctures to his left forearm.

Such tales of near tragedies and close calls with the white bear abound. Among the most chilling is an account from the late nineteenth century of a native hunter caught on the open ice without a weapon when a bear approached. The man played dead, lying motionless on his back. The bear came close. Fearing for his life, the man lay paralyzed with terror. He dared not even breathe. The bear sniffed him all over. Finally, Nanook pressed his steaming nostrils directly against the Eskimo's nose and lips. When the man still refused to respond, though his lungs seemed about to explode, the bear simply walked away. Later the same bear killed and ate the man's hunting companion. The hunter, who escaped—literally—the kiss of death because he lay corpselike on the ice, lived to tell the tale.

Sometimes close calls with the white bear have an element of humor, or relief, when the danger has passed. In 1980 Ken Vaudrey was studying an ice buildup known as Katie's Floeberg, about a hundred miles off Point Barrow, where the waters of the Beaufort Sea are only 40 to 50 feet deep. The shoal accumulated grounded ice floes. Because oil-drilling platforms in the Beaufort Sea might cause similar ice accumulations, Vaudrey and his partners wanted to examine the ice rubble closely. "We knew there would be bears in the area," Vaudrey told me, "because there was a wake of open water downwind from the shoal, where they could hunt seals. Because we were so far offshore, we couldn't afford the weight in the helicopter of an additional man to be a bear guard or monitor. We took a gun, but none of us had any real hunting experience.

"At our first stop, we wandered out of sight of the helicopter and were examining the stacked rubble fields when we came across fresh bear tracks. We didn't see the bear, but we thought it would be smart to head back to the copter. Retracing our footprints, we found fresher bear footprints on top of our own! Now we were really worried. We had visions of turning the corner of the rubble mound and finding the helicopter lying on its side with blood pouring out the door. What we actually found were two pilots, calmly reading books.

" 'Did you see anything?' we gasped.

" 'No. Were we supposed to?'

"The bear tracks showed that the bear had passed within fifty feet of the helicopter, while the pilots, oblivious, kept on reading."

The Naval Arctic Research Lab in Barrow, the setting of Tom Johnson's story of the two cubs, holds special memories for Ken Vaudrey as well. During the mid-1970s, when Vaudrey visited, "they had a nine hundred-pound male bear named Irish in a cage constructed from three-inch-diameter pipe. There was just enough room to fit a camera between the bars, but you couldn't get a decent picture because as soon as you approached the cage, Irish would come to investigate you. He tweaked his claws—they looked about four inches long—between the bars. We had the wall of the building behind us, with only about an eighteen-inch space for us to slither along. My pictures didn't turn out very well, because I was always moving backwards.

"They told us that one of Irish's keepers got so comfortable with him that he would scratch the bear between the eyes. After hundreds of successful scratchings, one day Irish bit off the man's finger. They may have embellished the tale for our benefit, but I suspect that somewhere in the United States there's an ex–polar bear keeper walking around with one missing finger.

"The main reason for keeping Irish was to measure his intake and output, and to calculate his metabolic rate. Once every summer, Irish would get weighed. This was accomplished using a tranquilizer, a sling, and a crane. One summer while I was there, Irish was lifted off the ground when the drug began to wear off and Irish woke up. The crane operator, startled, dropped the sling. Irish started walking around, somewhat groggy. Everyone ran in a different direction, looking for an Eskimo with a rifle. He should have been standing guard, but was nowhere around. Irish turned around slowly, looked at the scrambling, yelling mass of people. Still confused, he seemed to make a decision: he walked back to the building, and settled into his cage.

"During 1974–75, Irish's keepers tried to mate him to a recently captured female. Although he was twice her size, he didn't seem to know what to do. She didn't care for him at all— he obviously wasn't coming on strongly enough. Despite her smaller size, she just beat the shit out of him."

Polar bears are prominent in north country humor, usually because of comical human attempts to evade or dissuade them. A Danish zoologist in northeastern Greenland, for example, looked up from his notebook one evening to see a bear standing in the doorway of the tent, staring hard at its two occupants. The flustered scientist grabbed a butterfly net and began beating the bear over the head. Nanook, doubtless confused by this turn of events, beat a rapid retreat.

Also from Greenland comes the tale of a sailor surprised by a bear on an ice floe. The man started to run, with the bear in pursuit, toward his companions, who waited at the edge of the floe in the ship's boat. The sailor stripped off his jacket as he ran and dropped it on the ice. Seeing the bear stop to investigate, the man began discarding other items of clothing. Each time a garment hit the ice, the bear stopped to examine it closely. The sailor made it safely back to the boat, just ahead of the bear. By the time he got there, according to contemporary accounts, the man was totally nude.

To gain an appreciation for the damage a polar bear can inflict on his victim, I spoke with a doctor who has struggled to put such a person back together. Simmons Smith was on duty in the emergency room of a Cleveland, Ohio, hospital when the victim of a polar bear assault at the city zoo was wheeled in. Dr. Smith's patient was "completely covered in blood. It was impossible to tell whether it was a white person or a black.

"After some washing," the noted surgeon continued, "it became apparent that she was a white blonde, but no one could tell whether she had been a pretty girl or not, since her face was largely hidden by her scalp, which had been turned inside out and covered the front of her head. Every square inch was covered with blood—lots of it."

The scalp injury resembled others that Dr. Smith had repaired. "You usually see these on people who've been in car accidents—who've gone through the windshield," he told me. "Putting them back together is like putting a pillow back in a pillowcase. You fold the scalp back over the skull. There's such a good blood supply that they usually heal quickly.

"We carefully replaced her scalp and put stray pieces of tissue back in place—much like a jigsaw puzzle. Fortunately, no flesh seemed to be missing; it was just rearranged."

Once the girl's scalp was restored, the surgical team went to work on her face, which "had been raked with claws to the point where it would be difficult to assess past appearance." The rest of the girl's body looked no better: "Torn segments of skin were everywhere. If she'd been able to stand, she would have resembled a Christmas tree, with ornaments of flesh hanging from each limb. Muscles and tendons were openly exposed."

The surgeons worked into the night, washing dirt and debris from the wounds, giving more units of blood, suturing. After about six hours on the operating table, it started to look like the victim might pull through. Then the questions began. The ambulance crew who'd brought the girl in had said something about a polar bear. In Cleveland?

As the story unfolded, they learned that the girl was an art student who wanted to paint a polar bear at the zoo. She perched on the side of a hill that formed the backdrop to the bears' enclosure and dangled her feet over the edge. Dr. Smith continues the tale: "The bear showed little interest in her presence and wasn't the least interested in posing. The girl picked up a tree branch, downed in a recent storm. Using it as a prod, she reached down and provoked the creature into a more attentive posture. At this point the bear reared up on his hind legs and easily reached her dangling feet, twelve feet above him.

"After pulling her down from her perch, he took great delight in mauling her, rolling and pulling her from one side of the cage to the other. From her injuries, it seemed he had enjoyed playing with her, as a cat would play with a mouse. His claws were sharp, but there was no indication that he ever used his teeth. Apparently he'd been well fed earlier and hadn't had time to work up an appetite."

Quick action by zoo personnel and rapid response by the ambulance crew, combined with the surgical skill of Dr. Smith and his colleagues, saved the young artist's life and restored her beauty. "Within a month," the surgeon said, "it was obvious that when the scars faded, she would again be a very attractive person—and a very fortunate one."

In case of bear trouble, the residents of Churchill, Manitoba, are to call the Polar Bear Alert staff. When the phone rings, it usually signals action. That's why the workers were stymied just after midnight on November 29, 1983, when a caller reported a bear in the vicinity of the Royal Canadian Legion. Investigators sent to check found no sign of the bear. They were especially on guard, though, because the bears had been late that year in coming ashore. When they did arrive, many were ill tempered and emaciated. Apparently the ice and seals hadn't cooperated, and hunting had been poor. The Alert staff was also particularly watchful because only two days earlier Fred Treul had been attacked in his tundra buggy.

A few minutes after the first call, word came in that a man was being attacked by a bear in the burned-out ruins of the Churchill Motel. A subadult male had surprised the man on the steps of the Arctic Trading Company. The bear dragged him back to the shell of the Churchill Motel, where the man had been foraging for food in the charred remains of the kitchen. In the hotel ruins—the result of a fire nine days earlier—the bear grabbed the man by the head and shook him like a terrier killing a rat. Photographer Mike Beedell stood in the street as the bear came by. "He was running down Main Street, holding the body like a limp rag doll," Beedell says. Churchill residents arrived on the scene and began trying to distract the bear by yelling and throwing snow. The bear charged the circle of people that surrounded him. Finally, a bear-tour operator arrived with a rifle and shot the bear, too late to save the man. The cause of the attack was all too clear: in the pockets of Nanook's victim, his fellow citizens found raw meat, pie crust, and other food that he'd salvaged from the hotel freezer. The man's hunger proved his undoing.

Geologists encounter bears while out mapping the land, but few of these scientists ever meet Nanook as intimately as Gordon Cox did in the summer of 1970. Cox and his colleagues were based on Ellesmere Island studying glacial deposits when they were surprised by a bear that wandered into their camp.

"It was about three o'clock in the morning," Cox told me, "and I opened my eyes to see shadows on the tent wall over my head. At first I thought there was a fox standing on the tent. Then I realized that a bear was leaning with its forepaws right above my face.

"I'd left my gun in the kitchen tent. All I had was my sheath knife. If the bear came through one side of the tent, I was ready to cut my way out the other.

"I didn't know whether to yell loudly, whisper, or stay quiet. All I knew was I wanted out, and my sleeping bag seemed to have a million snaps down the side.

"The tent had both inner and outer walls, and I had lots of knots to untie. By the time I got out, the others in the survey party had chased the bear off. Then I turned to look at my friend's tent, which we had set up near mine. It was totally collapsed. The bear had sat on him as he lay quaking in his sleeping bag."

Another geologist with experience in the Far North is David Goodner, who tells of petroleum exploration among the islands of Svalbard, north of Norway:

"We landed a team of geologists on Edgeoya near a corrugated metal hut where two Dutch ecologists had been living for the past four months. Although there were bear tracks all over the place, the ecologists chastised us for carrying rifles, saying they weren't necessary and that we'd only wind up hurting ourselves. They didn't even have a weapon in their camp, even though it's required by law in such remote areas. They were at the end of their field season, only five days from pickup, and seemed pretty laid-back.

"A few days after we left, a bear—I'm convinced it was one that we saw nearby—wandered into their camp. One man ran out the cabin door, charging straight at the bear, yelling to shoo him away. The bear swatted him and knocked him to the ground. The second man grabbed a burning piece of wood from the stove, but the bear knocked it from his hand. The first man, lying on the ground, was badly bitten: the bear took most of his scalp off. Both men, though seriously injured, managed to crawl back inside the cabin.

"For three hours the bear tried to break through the wall of the building, then finally wandered off. The men had a genuine medical emergency but no way to reach the outside world. They had no radio—another violation of Svalbard law. Ironically, there was a thirty-foot radio mast on their cabin, but it was useless without a transmitter. The two had no choice but to wait another two days for the ship that was coming to pick them up.

"Somehow they made it. By the time our crew returned to the Norwegian mainland, their story was in the newspapers."

Goodner also tells of the day he was tracked by a bear on the south coast of Barentsoya:

"I was taking a geological party ashore in a Zodiac. We scanned the shoreline carefully before landing, because we knew bears often get stranded on those islands when the ice floes melt, and they can be hungry and foul tempered. After we'd been put ashore, the Zodiac returned to our ship, which departed for a neighboring island. We were in the most dangerous situation of our entire expedition: we had no means of escape, and I couldn't raise the ship on our radio, because the island topography blocked our signals. We took another look around, decided we were safe, and started sampling the rock layers up a river drainage.

"While the team worked, I climbed a hill to scan the beach again. A snow squall was blowing from the west. I looked into the wind and spotted four bears on the beach. I wasn't concerned: we were downwind, so they didn't catch our scent, and the bears appeared relaxed. They must have eaten recently—they were really laid-back, and the cubs were being goofy. I turned in the other direction and stopped short. A huge male was advancing up the beach.

"He'd already caught our scent with that amazing nose and was holding his head high to try to locate us. I canceled the sampling and called my team together. As we watched apprehensively, the bear found our tracks in the river drainage. He stood for a minute, trying to decide which way we'd gone. Then he turned and followed our trail toward the water, probably because that's the usual escape direction of his prey. He sniffed his way to the point where we'd brought the Zodiac ashore and entered the water.

"If he'd turned to follow our track uphill, I think we'd probably have been forced to shoot him, as we had nowhere to go. With all the adrenaline rushing through us, though, I'm not sure we could have hit him. Now I know what a mouse feels like when there's a cat in the room."

Experts agree that well-fed polar bears are usually docile and tractable; Nanook is not easily aroused. Captive bears appear to be under control, but trainers and keepers must remain alert. A performer with the Ringling Brothers, Barnum & Bailey Circus once required thirty-five stitches because her polar bears turned on her. The incident occurred during the traditional bear mating season, perhaps demonstrating that even after several generations in captivity the cycles of the wild still control behavior.

Captive bears are unpredictable. More than one zookeeper I interviewed said polar bears are the most dangerous mammals in the zoo. Although the concern in most zoos is protecting the animals from harm by the people, with polar bears the opposite is also true. Most zoo incidents, however, are caused by the stupidity of the humans involved and through no malicious intent of the bears.

In 1979 two polar bears at the Buffalo, New York, zoo were shot by police after a twenty-year-old trespasser climbed the zoo fence, drank some beer with his buddies at the edge of the bear enclosure, and then climbed down a rock wall into the bears' pit. He apparently slipped and fell to the pit floor. One of the bears threw the young man into a pool of water, then pulled him out and stood on him. Officers summoned by the man's companions fired a dozen shots into the air. The smaller of the two bears, a seventeen-year-old female named Maggie, walked away. Herman, an eighteen-year-old male bear weighing 700 pounds, knocked the man back into the pool. By this time firemen arrived and rigged hoses to drive the bears away from their victim.

Before a tranquilizer gun could be located, Herman entered the water and began shaking the man, then backed away. When Herman again moved toward the man, police opened fire and killed both bears. The man was pulled to safety but required six hours of surgery to repair his broken shoulder and badly mangled arm.

A public outcry arose at the loss of the popular zoo animals. Operators of the area's McDonald's restaurants donated funds to purchase another polar bear, and local television stations organized fund drives for a second bear.

In such incidents there are no winners. The person injured, even if he or she survives, is no hero. The bear involved is usually killed. The real loss is to the community, and to us all.

In Baltimore, Maryland, in 1976, polar bears at the zoo killed a man and tried to pull his body into their den. They were driven away from the corpse by police with tear-gas grenades. In most such zoo incidents, the human victim is described as having "fallen" into the bears' enclosure. But zookeepers know better.

A somewhat stranger incident occurred in New York's Central Park Zoo a few years later. One Saturday, zookeepers had to escort a thirty-year-old man out of the zoo after dissuading him from climbing into the elephant yard and later pulling him off the six-foot fence surrounding the lion cage. The man refused to answer questions from zoo officials. All he said was, "You have to get close to the animals."

The man was last seen alive about 2:00 A.M. Sunday near the lion cage. He was again escorted out of the zoo. Shortly after 7:00 A.M. keepers discovered the man's body in the polar bear cage. Scandy, a 1,200-pound male bear, was toying with the body, flipping it in and out of the water. The bear appeared calm. Clearly he had killed the man, but the corpse was just a plaything to him. The body bore multiple injuries, including extensive cuts on the head, hemorrhages in neck muscles, and puncture wounds on the head, chest, and arms. The intruder had apparently climbed the twelve-foot outer fence around the zoo's perimeter, the six-foot fence surrounding her bears' cage, and the twelve-foot cage bars, curved and spiked on the top. This incident was recorded as the Central Park Zoo's first fatality.

Such a statement shows a familiar bias, for it was in truth the zoo's first *human* fatality. From the bears' perspective, it had happened before. In 1975 a Central Park policeman had fired his revolver and killed a polar bear after the bear refused to let go of a derelict who had stuck his arm through the cage bars.

A few years later, a polar bear briefly terrorized a Rhode Island neighborhood. In 1979, at Slater Park Zoo, an 800-pound polar bear named Frosty was let out of his cage by vandals. The bear knocked two teenagers to the ground and wandered off toward a cluster of mobile homes. More than sixty state troopers and local police officers converged on the area and eventually shot the bear. Frosty's freedom was short-lived.

Even sadder is the report from Minnesota's Como Zoo,

where a female polar bear was beaten to death in her cage, despite her size (she weighed over 600 pounds). Her assailants escaped.

The depressing list continues. Headlines: 1977—"Zoo Bear Mauls Woman"; 1988—"Vilas [Park Zoo] Bear Killed, Man Walks Away after Being Mauled." So many beautiful bears destroyed because of the stupidity of a few of their adoring public. Zookeepers willingly state that a human life takes precedence but also agree that it is nearly impossible to design foolproof enclosures that guarantee separation of man and beast.

Modern concepts of zoo design reverse the traditional roles. "Our exhibit is based on the principle that the people are in the enclosure and the bears are outside," says John Houck, curator of mammals at the Point Defiance Zoo and Aquarium in Tacoma, Washington. Houck's polar bear display, constructed in 1981, won an award the following year as the best new zoo exhibit in the nation. It depicts a natural setting copied in detail from a section of the Alaskan coast near Point Hope. Bears share the exhibit with lemmings and arctic foxes.

"Visitors see the bears through windows," Houck told me. "This is safer for the people, as there are no open-air observation points where someone might climb or fall into the bears' area. It's also safer for the animals, because it limits large crowds, which can be quite a stress factor on the bears." Houck knows there is a practical limit to safety: "You can't build a Stalag-14. A concentration-camp mentality to keep people out of the animal enclosures just wouldn't make for a good zoo."

Safety in the zoo, however, bears little resemblance to safety in Nanook's home range. Those who live, work, and travel in arctic regions have evolved over the years a wealth of bear-safety information and guidelines: human behavioral adaptations to Nanook's firm rule over the frozen North.

Inuit wise in the ways of bears never venture onto the ice without firearms. Construction workers and exploration geologists hire armed bear monitors. Anyone entering Nanook's kingdom had best observe the rules. According to researchers Fleck and Herrero, these include (1) learning as much as you can about polar bears; (2) carrying a firearm if you know how to use one, or hiring an armed guide; (3) being alert and traveling only during periods of good visibility; (4) setting up a trip wire or other perimeter defense in camp; (5) using deterrents; (6) carrying a radio to summon help; (7) having windows in your tents so you can see the surrounding area, and spacing tents far enough apart to give a bear an escape route; and (8) keeping food and garbage in bearproof containers.

The traditional bear alarm and deterrent is a dog. Dogs, however, can cause additional problems. Bears do not like them and have been reported to walk slowly down a line of tethered dogs, killing each one in sequence. Fleck and Herrero give sobering advice: "Be prepared to lose the dog. Keep the dog staked so that it cannot run to you for protection."

When humans share territory with Nanook, the potential for conflicts multiplies. The Manitoba Department of Natural Resources must plan for such conflicts in its polar bear management program. Steve Kearney, Regional Wildlife Manager, is involved with Manitoba's Polar Bear Alert Program, which is directed at the Churchill area. "The goals of the Program are twofold," Kearney told me. "Under the Alert Program we want to minimize the opportunity for human/bear interactions in and around the town of Churchill, to prevent human injury or fatality. We also want to be sure that the bears are not unduly harassed or killed. Outside the Churchill area, we'd like to encourage tourist activities which will have minimum impact on the bears or on their environment, and to educate people on the land as to what to do if confronted by a polar bear."

That phrase, *on the land,* recurs in conversations about northern Canada. It's a useful term, because it describes the situation very well. Someone who's on the land is not safe within the shelter of an airplane, or a ship, or a tundra buggy, or even a horse. On the land means standing on your own two feet on rock or soil or tundra moss. Standing on the same land, on four furred feet, is the great white bear.

I asked Kearney how effective his programs are, especially with youngsters. "With children," he said, "so much depends on how many times they hear the same thing. When we go into classrooms and school assemblies, we try to vary the program.

We're probably most effective if they hear our message one, two, or three times. More repetition, and they'll probably start to tune us out."

The Alert Program distributes a coloring book for children that introduces polar bear safety in a fun and engaging manner. The book focuses on a north-country watchword: *the safe bear is a distant bear.* Under the heading "Let's All Be Bear Aware," the booklet lists ten important points for children:

1. *Play only in safe areas.*
2. *If you see a bear—keep away from it.*
3. *Do not play outdoors at night.*
4. *Report all bears.*
5. *Obey all signs.*
6. *Never feed bears.*
7. *Be a noisy, open area hiker.*
8. *Never explore bad-smelling areas.*
9. *Keep away from bear traps.*
10. *Learn more about polar bears.*

The book's final message, after warning kids to stay far away from bears, is, if a bear surprises you up close:

DON'T TURN AND RUN. Like a dog, the bear may chase you. He may come closer, stand upright or circle around you to get your scent.

Make the bear aware that you are there. Talk and wave your arms slowly. Try to help the bear figure out what you are. His answer might be to threaten you in bear talk . . . popping his teeth, huffing and growling . . . telling you to go away. DON'T TALK BACK!

Leave slowly, . . . always facing the bear. If the bear follows you or starts to circle you, slowly but calmly keep backing up towards help.

If you are carrying something, such as your lunch or your jacket, drop it. The bear may explore your lunch, giving you time to leave the area.

If the bear gets REALLY CLOSE AND YOU HAVE NO OTHER

CHOICE, curl up and put your hands behind your neck and play dead. Once the bear thinks you are dead he may leave you alone. Wait until the bear is long-gone before you get up and go for help.

Government publications warn that a bear that appears too familiar may pose the greatest risk of all: "Any bear that has become accustomed to people and shows no fear of them is dangerous, not tame."

As the northern lands are developed, a task of primary importance is finding an effective way to repel bears so they don't threaten life and property. Such a goal is necessary not only for human safety but also for Nanook's well-being. If workers at drill sites and communications outposts feel secure, they will view bears more as a resource to be enjoyed and less as a threat.

In 1981 biologist Gordon Stenhouse began a series of studies at Cape Churchill, Manitoba, on possible polar bear detectors and deterrents. The long-term objective of his study was "to develop safe and practical techniques, aimed at changing the behaviour of bears rather than those that result in the death of bears." During the first year Stenhouse and his colleagues tried microwave detection systems (100 percent effective in spotting approaching bears), a recording of barking dogs (ignored by 87 percent of the bears and challenged aggressively by four bears), an electrified fence (crossed without incident by 93 percent of the bears), and a strangely named weapon: the multipurpose riot gun. This last, a 38-millimeter rifle, fires an elongate rubber bullet called a baton. It was so effective in 1981—it stopped all approaching bears struck—that it warranted additional study.

Before Stenhouse's experiments workers had tried trip wires, but these caused constant false alarms resulting from wind or ice loads, required much maintenance, and had to be reset after an intrusion, exposing people to the very hazards the wires were designed to thwart. In addition, when motivated by sights, smells, or merely their own curiosity, bears quickly learned to crawl under, break through, or leap over trip wires.

Electrified fences repel bears but with varying degrees of success. Researchers at Cape Churchill tell two different sides of the story. Stenhouse showed photos of bears climbing right through an electrified barbed-wire fence. "Gordon's attempts were on a dry ridge," says biologist Chris Davies. "We were camped on swampy land, and the electrified fence around our enclosure stopped bears 100 percent of the time." The difference is one of electrical conductivity. In the dry arctic air, a dry bear standing on dry land won't be shocked. A bear slogging through muskeg, however, will get a jolt strong enough to send it searching elsewhere for food. Stenhouse responds: there are "not many places in the Arctic where people and bears meet in a swamp."

Chemical repellents and a variety of recorded sounds— including Nanook's own voice—had little effect. Gunshots and sound-and-flash devices elicited some reactions from the bears, but the results were unpredictable. In the scientists' words, such studies "demonstrate the potential danger of relying solely on these devices for personal protection during a confrontation with a polar bear."

In 1982 Stenhouse tried again. Drawing bears to a drum baited with seal and beluga carrion (anchored to a steel drum filled with rocks), he exposed them to microwave detection (again, 100 percent effective) coupled with loud sirens (which had no effect). A trip wire succeeded; another barking dog recording (this time of Inuit dogs reacting to a polar bear skin) did not. A pistol to fire rubber batons didn't work well, and bomb-shaped plastic shotgun slugs with tail fins were ineffective. More than three-quarters of advancing bears were deterred by flare scaring cartridges, which are fired from a 12-gauge shotgun and travel about 400 feet, trailing a yellow arc through the air, and then explode with a bright flash and a loud bang.

In 1983 the experiments continued. The rubber baton fired from the riot gun proved more than 99 percent effective. To the scientists' dismay, however, a year-old male bear died after being struck in the ribs. Postmortem examination suggested that the shock wave generated by the impact had damaged a ventricle in the bear's heart. According to the researchers, "Bears struck by rubber batons responded by flinching, snapping at the area of contact (sometimes accompanied by a hiss or growl), spinning around, and then galloping, trotting, or walking back from the bait site."

Stenhouse concluded that the rubber batons are useful. They do have drawbacks, however. They are inaccurate, short-range projectiles. The weapon from which they are fired is single-shot and isn't readily available to the public (nor are most civilians permitted to carry one). Plastic slugs fired from a 12-gauge shotgun may be the answer, but they haven't yet been perfected for scaring bears. Wildlife officers who have used the batons in day-to-day service, with bears of all kinds, rate their effectiveness as "good to very good." Any bears that had been hit once fled at the subsequent approach of the officer. "Officers felt that returning bears showed a dramatic change in behaviour."

In the three years of Stenhouse's research at Cape Churchill, only 1 bear out of 404 hit by the rubber batons kept coming. The researchers quit firing at that one bear after five hits, for fear of hurting him. If he had been endangering humans, they noted, no one would have stopped shooting: they are confident that he, too, would have been turned away. However, as Stenhouse wrote, "It should be recognized by all people who are faced with the task of deterring a bear that the use of deterrents is an art as much as a science."

The Canadian biologist also put his work in perspective, recognizing that it is the humans who are intruders in Nanook's world and that the bears are simply behaving naturally. He wrote, "We should not forget that deterrents should be used when an *unavoidable* bear problem has occurred. If people do not behave in a responsible and appropriate manner (e.g. storing and handling food stuffs, garbage, and other waste materials), no deterrent will solve the problem."

The experts advise avoidance of potential conflicts, but if no other options are available, the arctic traveler must be prepared to shoot to kill. Guidelines include (1) waiting until the bear is close before firing, because a shot at close range has the greatest chance of a clean kill; (2) aiming for the front shoulder if the bear is broadside, or for the base of the neck between the shoulders if the bear is head-on; and (3) avoiding the tendency to shoot at the head, because head shots often don't kill. Advice to the person, likely terrified, who holds the gun: don't stop to check the results of your shots; keep firing until the bear lies still. "Try to kill the bear cleanly and quickly, as a wounded bear is very dangerous."

If attacked while unarmed, you are advised by the Renewable Resources publications to "make every attempt to protect your vital organs. Drop to the ground and lie on your side, curled into a ball with your legs drawn to your chest and your head buried in your knees. Clasp your hands behind your neck. Keep your legs tightly together. Try to stay in this position even if moved. Try not to resist or struggle as it may intensify the attack. If a bear does try to maul you, serious injury may be reduced or prevented by keeping still."

Whenever a polar bear attack is reported, people across the Arctic sit riveted, their attention fixed on the radio or newspaper recounting the event. Following the usual clucking of tongues over the victim's bad luck, ignorance, or stupidity, the incident tucks itself deep in each person's subliminal memory, adding to the lore that generates vague dread when danger threatens.

Two British filmmakers were camped on the ice near Svalbard. During the night they awakened, fearful, at every creak that might be a bear's footsteps. Eventually they realized that the noises were caused by the shifting ice floes. Rather than worry about a crack opening beneath their tent, exposing the dark waters beneath, the two men were relieved. One of them wrote, "On reflection it amuses me that we were not concerned about the ice. Only the polar bear looms large in the wild dreams of Arctic adventurers."

ELEVEN

The Polar Bear
Capital of the World

I LIVE IN SOUTHEASTERN TEXAS, close to the meridian that marks 95 degrees west of Greenwich, England. That imaginary line is useful: it runs exactly north-south. I could follow it north to Nanook's kingdom. If I set my sights due north and started walking, hiking along that dark stripe that mapmakers drape over the earth, I'd soon leave behind the humid coastal plain. I'd cross the east Texas hills, the rugged folds of Oklahoma's Ouachita Mountains, and farmlands of the eastern Great Plains.

Following the Pole Star, just in front of the Big Dipper—like escaped slaves fleeing northward, admonished in song to "Follow the Drinking Gourd"—I'd eventually bog down in Minnesota's lakes and muskeg swamps. I'd stand knee-deep in mud at the southern edge of the great belt of dark green conifers that encircles the top of the globe like the fringe of hair on a monk's head. Pulling my feet from the sucking mud, I'd step onto some of the oldest rocks on earth, the granites and gneisses of the Canadian shield.

If I could stand the muck and mosquitoes of the muskeg, I'd press on, ever northward. By the time I reached northern Manitoba, I'd have a new vista, but one with few landmarks. With my left hand clutching the imaginary longitudinal string—stretching from my home to the Pole—I'd sweep my right hand across a broad view: a coastal plain like the one I'd left so many miles behind me. With a few scattered trees behind me, I'd stare out across taiga tundra: transition between the northern forest and the true Arctic. This gently mounded surface eases down to the waters of Hudson Bay. Off to the east would be a low promontory, an angle where the shoreline juts eastward into the bay. Cape Churchill. Between me and the cape would be the town of Churchill, Manitoba.

Lying some 1,700 miles almost due north of my home, Churchill is very different from the world I know. The town is, in fact, unique. It draws its singularity from the white bear. Churchill is home each fall to the greatest gathering of polar bears on earth. With considerable pride, the town bills itself in tourist literature as the Polar Bear Capital of the World.

Churchill is a seaport that ships grain from Canada's heartland. Located where the railroad meets the sea, the town is also the site of a much older rendezvous: it lies astride the major pathway taken by the Hudson Bay polar bear population during their annual migration. The bears follow a huge oval in their meanderings. Moving clockwise around the western half of the bay throughout the year, they trudge onto the sea ice from Cape Churchill during the fall freeze-up, hunt seals from the ice throughout the long winter, and ride the icepack southward in the spring. When the ice sheets melt in June and July, the bears swim ashore along the southern and western margins of Hudson Bay. There they stay, wandering along the coast through August and September, ambling slowly northward toward Cape Churchill. Somehow in their ancestral memories the bears know that the cape—focus of weather, tides, and currents—is a promontory where the bay's ice forms first, usually in early November. The bears congregate in its vicinity and wait. Their main goal during their time ashore is conserving energy, because they have eaten little during the ice-free months. From July through October the bears live off their fat reserves. Pregnant females that enter dens in late fall will continue their fast until spring.

Because they're hungry and occasionally ill tempered, the bears cause problems in town. For many years Churchill was portrayed in the outside press as a community that lives in fear, with polar bears stalking the streets. The truth is somewhat less dramatic. Bears do wander close, and occasionally forage in the city dump, but wildlife officials are attempting to break the pattern of bears' dependence on humans: they now tranquilize dump bears or bears found in town and lock them in a "polar bear jail" at the edge of town. Here the bears wait in twenty cells until freeze-up, when they are released onto the bay ice. Jail guards provide their furry inmates with clean water but no food, so the bears will continue their natural fasting. To reduce the likelihood that the bears might lose their fear of people, human contact is minimized: these prisoners are permitted no visitors. Inside a metal complex of Quonset huts, they pace or sleep away the days until they're freed, apparently unharmed, to begin life anew.

Churchill's main street—a modern paved road—runs parallel to the shoreline. On both sides of the road, gritty gravel parking areas surround the town's buildings like the margins on a postage stamp. At the edge of the gravel, where gray rocks jut abruptly from the soil, a row of signs bearing Nanook's image also display the telephone number of the Polar Bear Alert office. Inside the marker posts human safety comes first. Beyond them is the world of the white bear. Enter at your peril.

The present Alert system began in 1969 as the Polar Bear Control Program; its name changed in 1984 to reflect a broader mission. Operated by the Manitoba Department of Natural Resources, the Alert program has a dual objective: to protect people from bears and bears from people. In addition to educating the 1,200 residents of Churchill and some 10,000 tourists a year, the officers follow very specific guidelines that define responsibilities, equipment, and procedures to use in case of bear problems. They maintain a twenty-four-hour vigil over the living and working sections of town, a perimeter zone that includes the dump, and outlying areas. When a bear enters a defended zone, the Alert staff has many options. They may just monitor the bear's activities; they may try to scare him away using noisemakers or rubber bullets; they may try to capture him alive using culvert traps or leg-hold snares; or they may use drugs to immobilize the bear. As a last resort, they are prepared to shoot to kill.

Although the Polar Bear Alert Program puts human safety first, officers are clearly concerned about the bears' welfare as well. It wasn't always so, however. Residents tell of a conservation officer they nicknamed Speedy because he was likely to bypass most of his options and cut straight to the last choice. Speedy shot twenty-two bears before being transferred to another assignment.

Bears live-trapped in town or at the dump are locked in the Quonset hut jail, officially known as the Polar Bear Compound. Several years ago problem bears were helicoptered 200 miles up the coast, at a cost to taxpayers of $500 each. Some walked right back to Churchill. Several were repeat offenders, so familiar that officers gave them names. Officials watched mother bears introduce their cubs to the fine art of scavenging at the dump. To interrupt this pattern, bears that kept reappearing in town were eventually shipped south to zoos. Since construction of the compound in 1982, very few bears have had to be shot in the Churchill area. Local citizens approve: they recognize that increased tourism pumps at least $3 million a year into the local economy, attributable entirely to the public's fascination with the great white bear.

Churchill resembles any other northern community, but its residents do make certain concessions to their furry neighbors. At Halloween, for example, the town guards its trick-or-treaters. Children scamper from house to house under the vigilant stares of armed wildlife officers, Mounties, and other officials patrolling the streets. (I'd bet bear costumes aren't popular.) Even though bears are common in the vicinity, familiarity has definitely not bred contempt. Most Churchill residents recognize that humans are the intruders in the bears' world.

Everyone living in Churchill has a strategy or deterrent in mind for the night when the white bear comes calling. My favorite is the man who carefully planned a defense of his front door. He drove huge nails through planks so the spikes protruded about four inches out the other side. He then laid the boards, steel points up, on the front steps of his cabin to discourage approaching bears. One night the man thought he heard a bear, so he grabbed his rifle and rushed out the door, forgetting his clever invention. The resulting holes in his feet kept him in the hospital for about three months.

Downtown at midday, visitors occasionally hear cracker shells whistling and popping like the Fourth of July in small-town backyards in the United States. Somewhere nearby, a bear shuffles away from the edge of town and an officer from the Alert team breathes a sigh of relief. Another operation that went according to plan—another bear that won't be going to jail. Everyone prefers deterrence over detention.

Every year Churchill is visited by television crews from several nations. Their documentaries reveal the universal popularity of the white bears. Churchill is perhaps most firmly fixed in the minds of North American viewers by the dramatic footage showing an intrepid photographer inside a wire cage, with a bear sniffing, rearing, shoving, and biting the cage, apparently to get to the tasty human inside.

"Absolute rubbish!" snorts a man who was present during the filming. "Irresponsible reporting! The bear wasn't aggressive in the least. To enhance the action, the film crew lathered the steel cage with whale oil. The bear wasn't trying to eat the man—he was just licking the oil off the bars. Any bear in the vicinity could have flattened the cage if it had wanted to, but we didn't see any aggressive behavior. This was done strictly for sensationalism, and it gave the bears a bad rap. Polar bears are so fascinating that this type of coverage isn't needed to get the public's attention."

My projects in eastern Canada, northwestern Greenland, and the Alaskan Beaufort Sea had involved a relatively small group of geologists, engineers, and oceanographers. I wanted to gauge the reactions of other southerly people to the frozen world, and to the white bear, so I headed north to Churchill during the prime bear-watching weeks at the end of October and joined a polar bear photo tour led by Mike Beedell, a world-class adventure photographer whose epic journeys and dramatic images—reproduced in posters, calendars, books, and magazines—have made him something of a north country legend. His passion for high adventure has already led him through the Northwest Passage in an open catamaran and across northern Canada to Greenland on a 120-day dogsled expedition (during which a polar bear pressed its nose against Mike's cheek through the tent wall and hissed in his ear). Mike's motto is "If you can dream it, you can do it." A weeklong photo safari must seem pretty tame to Mike Beedell.

Once a day at the height of the fall season, a Canadian 737 jet from Winnipeg lands at the Churchill airport to disgorge about a hundred passengers eager to see bears. Like tourists everywhere, they're easy to spot. Cameras dangle, tripods clatter, bags full of film and lenses pile up in corners of the airport waiting room. Bear watchers carry every imaginable picture-taking device from Kodak Instamatics to professional video cameras that barely fit in the aircraft's overhead compartments. Other bear enthusiasts arrive by train, after a two-day ride.

Accommodations in Churchill are limited and usually booked several months in advance. (Bear watching is an activity that few people choose at the last minute.) I did, however, meet tourists flying in without room reservations, tundra buggy reservations, or firm plans of any sort. One was a perky South African stewardess, eager to see the northern wilderness. She wanted to see the bears, of course, but seemed more interested in simply having an adventurous good time. While around her tourists struggled with carry-on luggage in the airport lounge—stuffing in parkas, wool shirts, and heavy sweaters—she sat demurely, dressed fashionably, as if she were bound for a cocktail party.

Like many other communities scattered across the Arctic, Churchill is a rough mix of tumbledown shacks, modern modular buildings, and the slowly disintegrating remnants of a former military installation: dusty windows with broken panes, radar domes missing a few triangular panels, and roadside signs bearing cryptic warnings of radiation sources and no-entry zones. The military base—Fort Churchill—was a training post and rocket range. Weathered reminders of both activities dot the landscape, although the soldiers are long gone. Observation towers once used by officers to evaluate troop movements across the tundra in arctic survival exercises now make superb bear-watching platforms. The rocket range command facility—built to study the weather and the auroral displays, and closed in 1985 after more than 3,400 launches—has become the Churchill Northern Studies Center, a two-story complex of gray buildings that cling tenaciously to the rocky soil east of town.

The center lies at the end of a paved road heaved into bone-jarring unevenness by the freeze and thaw of the thin soil that overlies permafrost. Viewed from the gravel parking area, the center appears to be some sort of prison, more like a penitentiary, in fact, than the polar bear jail closer to town. Crossed steel bars form a grid over each window. Powerful floodlights illuminate the surrounding gravel. Doors to the outside trigger alarms when opened. Within this secure compound, however, there are no criminals but rather an international mix of scientists, technicians, professors, and students. The buildings contain spartan but functional research facilities: laboratories, classrooms, sleeping and eating areas, a library, and teaching collections. A Plexiglas rooftop dome provides superb views of nighttime auroras. Inside, the emphasis is on science. Outside— and often peering in the windows—is the white bear.

At the Northern Studies Center I encountered Dr. Malcolm Ramsay, a polar bear specialist on the biology faculty of the University of Saskatchewan. Dr. Ramsay and his colleagues seek out bears using helicopters, tranquilize them, and withdraw tissue and fluid samples as part of a continuing study of bear physiology. Although it's focused on polar bears, their project may eventually pay big dividends in human medicine.

"When polar bears are fasting, they don't produce urine or feces," Ramsay explained. "The bears are able to recycle the wastes that result from the breakdown of proteins—wastes that in our own bodies must be removed by our kidneys—and re-form them into proteins again. We'd like to understand how the bears do this, with the hope that someday we might induce a similar process pharmacologically in people suffering from kidney disease. We might spare those patients the elaborate mechanical dialysis that they now must undergo in order to stay alive. We'd also like to understand the medical implications of a continuous diet that is almost exclusively saturated fat—this is higher in polar bears than in any other animal. We ask the same questions about the Inuit, who eat mostly saturated fats but have very low incidence of heart disease."

Ramsay travels to Churchill four times a year in search of bears. He sees Nanook in all seasons of his life. When I asked him to describe a typical field day, he began with effusive praise for Steve Miller, his helicopter pilot. "Steve is the best in the world, without question. He's worked more than 2,000 bears. Steve maneuvers the helicopter sideways and gets us about ten feet from the bear. In order to do this, he has to keep track—simultaneously—of the bear, the trees, the altitude of the helicopter, and the wind. With most pilots I just close my eyes; with Steve Miller I can concentrate on the bear."

Once a bear is darted with a syringe of Telazol (a drug that biologists say offers wide margins for safe dosage), Ramsay's ground team goes to work. In his words, "First we look for identifying marks, tags, or tattoos, to determine if this is a recapture. Then we inject the bear with tracer compounds—liquids containing stable isotopes of oxygen and hydrogen—that allow us to calculate the bear's percentage of body fat, its metabolic rate, and, in the case of mother bears, rates of milk transfer to the cubs. We draw blood samples to study hormones and other indicators of the bear's feeding-fasting condition. Also, the white blood cells contain DNA that we use to estimate the discreteness of bear populations.

"Next we inject urea tracers, tagged with stable isotopes of carbon and nitrogen. None of these harms the bear in any way. We look for the tracers to show up—a few hours to a few weeks later [if the same bear is recaptured]—in body tissues as part of our studies of protein breakdown and waste recycling."

The biologists collect other samples from the bear as it lies sprawled in the snow, including adipose (fatty) tissue that accumulates toxic compounds and also indicates the bear's biochemical condition; milk, if the bear is a lactating female; and exhaled bear breath, collected in a gas bag through a mask and one-way valve slipped over the bear's mouth. Pointing to a compact unit sitting on the laboratory bench, Ramsay explained, "We run the breath sample through an oxygen and carbon dioxide analyzer to determine what substrates—fats, proteins, or carbohydrates—are being metabolized."

The bear, still tranquilized, is weighed on a tripod scale, and its girth, length, and head size are measured with tapes. (The largest bear Ramsay has captured weighed 1,980 pounds.) The scientists clip ear tags in place and tattoo a unique number on an inner lip. In past years researchers painted large numbers on bears with Lady Clairol hair dye: this practice aggravated photographers hoping for pictures of immaculate "natural" bears and concerned the biologists themselves, who worried that the painted numerals might interfere with a bear's ability to stalk seals by making Nanook more visible to his prey. The practice has since been abandoned, although bears can be found on Cape Churchill with a discreet code of letters and numbers painted along the spine behind the shoulders.

Reaching into the fearsome mouth, the workers remove a premolar tooth: after its calcium has been dissolved in the laboratory, the tooth's remains will be cut and ground to a transparent slice only one-thousandth of an inch thick. Microscopic examination of the tooth section will disclose the bear's age, although the field biologists make fairly accurate assessments on the spot based on body size, shape, and characteristics. While all this is going on the scientists also monitor their patient's rectal temperature and breathing rate.

With daily air service, a concentrated bear population, and a well-equipped research station, Churchill ranks high on the list of field areas chosen by wildlife biologists. "I prefer to work with the Churchill bear population because the logistics are easier and less expensive," Ramsay said. "In the western Arctic, our costs run about $2,000 per bear. Here, it's more like $1,000."

When I mentioned my initial encounters with, and fear of, bears on the sea ice, Ramsay concurred. "There is no question in my mind that polar bears behave far differently toward people on the sea ice than they do on land. On the ice, they're hunting, and people may be among the hunted. Ashore, they're resting, conserving energy, and generally just want to be left alone."

Malcolm Ramsay faces a paradox in his work: "I put a great deal of stress on bears, and that bothers me a lot. However, I have to believe that my work will ultimately be for the bears' benefit."

On the subject of tourism, the scientist is equally ambivalent: "The more people know about any animals, the more likely it is that people will take a stand to protect them. Therefore, tourism plays an important role. At the same time, tourists do add to the stress on the bears. The Manitoba government made a wise move in restricting viewing to a few areas, so that any bear that doesn't want to face tourists doesn't have to."

In downtown Churchill it's hard to escape the emphasis on Nanook: the white bear is ubiquitous. The complex of buildings known as Town Center features a hockey rink with a bear design in the face-off circle. A nearby snack bar displays a mounted trophy bear rearing menacingly above patrons munching hamburgers. Beside the tables a huge wooden bear, rough-sculpted from two-by-four lumber, resembles the Trojan horse. It's a children's slide: brave bear challengers enter beneath Nanook's tail (no doubt evoking some primal symbolism) and escape by sliding out the mouth. Mounted bears, bear skeletons, preserved bear fetuses, and other bear artifacts are displayed in the Churchill Museum. Welcoming signs at the city limits feature a stylized black-and-white bear. In the stores—the Arctic Trading Company, The Hudson's Bay Company ("The Bay"), and Northern Images, the native handicraft cooperative—shoppers admire Inuit carvings of polar bears in soapstone, bone, and ivory. They paw through polar bear prints, polar bear place mats, polar bear pins, polar bear patches ("Churchill Household Pests"), polar bear postcards, polar bear posters, polar bear puppets, and beer mugs labeled "Polar Bear Piss." Miniature polar bears line the store shelves in too-cute fluffy or ceramic poses. There are polar bear T-shirts, polar bear sweatshirts, polar bear nightshirts, and polar bear neckties.

And in one corner (sadly, think conservation-minded tourists; legal and proper, think civic boosters intent on improving Churchill's economy), the white bear himself is for sale as rugs or loose skins, with prices in the thousands of dollars. Shop cashiers carefully explain to U.S. citizens that they won't be able to take any bear parts back across the border (nor can they bring back bears carved from walrus ivory or any other marine mammal products).

Down the street from the stores, visitors to the Kelsey Lodge see claw marks in the narrow hallway, where a polar bear (too big to reverse direction on all fours) stood up to turn around after coming in through the kitchen door. Around the corner they can hear a resident describe the bear that broke into his kitchen while he was cooking steaks. In the center of town a bronze statue of a mother bear and her cub in front of the city's information center provides a focal point for tourism. In almost every restaurant diners eat beneath polar bear photos. The white bear is clearly the most famous resident of Churchill.

Churchill's recorded history begins in 1619 with Captain Jens Munk and his expedition of two ships and sixty-four men. Exploring the western reaches of Hudson Bay, they came ashore where the Churchill River flows into the bay's salt water. Forced to winter there, they suffered terrible cold, sickness, deprivation, and the occasional marauding polar bear. By the following summer only Munk and two men were alive to sail back to Denmark.

In 1689 England's Hudson's Bay Company made an unsuccessful attempt to establish an outpost on the Churchill River, hoping to defend their claim to the riches of the Northwest. The area remained in dispute long after the Treaty of Utrecht in 1713 established English control over all of Hudson Bay. Among the problems of administering this vast region were traditional hostilities among the Chipewyan, Cree, and Inuit bands that lived along the shoreline. Eventually, through the diplomacy of a remarkable Chipewyan woman named Thanadelthur, a peace was negotiated with the natives, but another danger remained, in the form of the French.

Fort Prince of Wales, a wilderness outpost as sturdily built as any European gun battery, was constructed at the mouth of the Churchill River to protect the fur trade against French incursion. Samuel Hearne of the Hudson's Bay Company began work on the fort in 1732. Because of its remote location, chronic understaffing, and the prevalence of scurvy and frostbite, the fort wasn't completed until 1771. It flourished briefly as a center for trading with the Inuit but never produced the riches that its financial backers were seeking.

Eleven years later the fort fell to the French without a shot. A naval force under Compte de La Pérouse sailed into the mouth of the river in 1782; Samuel Hearne surrendered his garrison, numbering fewer than forty men, realizing they could never repel a major assault. La Pérouse spiked the cannon, blew up the stone walls, and set fire to the gun carriages and buildings. Fort Prince of Wales passed into history (but may be seen today, in reconstructed form, across the water from the Churchill docks).

In 1783 the Hudson's Bay Company established an outpost known as Churchill Factory, several miles upriver from the ruins of the fort. That trading post remained in operation until 1932, when it closed as a concession to modern technology: the railroad had come to Churchill in 1929, and the present townsite was becoming a grain-shipping port.

Today the major Churchill landmark is a five-million-bushel grain elevator that rises above the town's low skyline. Wheat and barley from farms in Saskatchewan, Alberta, and Manitoba are loaded at the Churchill pier into ships bound for Europe, the Soviet Union, Egypt, Greece, Iran, and other exotic markets.

Outside the town lies the taiga tundra, a changeling landscape, part forest and part barren land of the Far North. A sky the color of burnished pewter slants oppressively toward the horizon. Low, misty clouds spit a drizzle that is not quite rain, not quite snow, not quite ice. Tufts of grass and mounded moss punctuate shallow lakes scattered randomly across the land. In October thin skins of ice cover the smaller ponds—soon they will freeze solid. Larger lakes and the great blue-gray waters of Hudson Bay are still ice free or wear lacy frozen necklaces, strands of flattened pearls, along their shorelines.

Trees, decades old but only three to four feet tall, march in ranks through the mist. Dense shrubs of willow line the shores of ponds. Conifers grow on elevated patches, with branches decorating only their southeastern sides, making the trees appear flattened in one plane, narrow as feathers. Better than any weather vane, they show the direction of the prevailing winds from the northwest. Many of the trees have died at the top: their uppermost branches point gray, spindly fingers skyward. Luxuriant green boughs spread low, taking advantage of the slightly warmer microclimate near the ground, where sheltering snow covers their needles throughout much of the year.

The highest points of land are barren gravel ridges that parallel the shoreline. Former beaches and offshore bars, these rocky lineations emerged from the sea as the land rose after the last glaciers melted. From the crests of these fossil beach ridges, would-be bear photographers scan the shorelines, ponds, and willow thickets.

Before freeze-up the bears are most often napping or lounging casually. They seem indifferent to the approach of a tundra buggy rolling across the ponds, rocks, and mosses. From the safety of windows seven to eight feet off the ground, visitors peer into the world of the white bears. Often the bears peer back.

Our vehicle is a short school bus, mounted high on a 1947 truck frame salvaged from military left-behinds. It rides on four huge tires, each representing an investment of almost $2,000. The roof of the yellow bus is ten feet from the ground. Bears can reach the windows and doors. Dwight Allen, driver and buggy builder, swings a heavy welded frame across the folding school-bus door, just in case. He's built a wooden-walled observation deck onto the back of the bus. On one wall is a black button, just in case. If a photographer feels uncomfortable with a bear's behavior, the button sounds a two-tone warbling horn, and the bear, we're assured, will back off. No one really wants to try it.

On a typical fall day buggies of various shapes and colors carry from ten to forty passengers each through the bleak landscape. They cruise ponderously across the tundra like buffalo grazing. They're searching for bears. Inside the vehicle, passengers sway from side to side like fronds of kelp in a tidal current. The huge tires creep over rocks and through ponds, or churn slowly through the black muck in lowest low-range four-wheel drive. The engine whines a constant accompaniment, recalling hordes of mosquitoes, two months gone. Looking out over the tundra, we watch the nestlike masses of willow shrubs that fringe the ponds, scanning for yellow-white lumps amid the branches. Often these prove to be only tan rocks the same size and shape as sleeping bears. About one out of ten, however, is the real thing. "Sleeping bear at three o'clock," someone shouts above the engine noise, "just at the edge of the pond." We gently lower the bus windows for clear photography. Dwight shuts off the engine and opens the door but leaves the heavy steel frame in place, in case the bear should decide to come in.

Scattered around the vehicle are Mike Beedell and his ten charges. During a quieter moment of the bear hunt, we learned one another's backgrounds. I'm impressed by the variety: people from all walks of life are fascinated by polar bears. Ben is a geologist from Oklahoma. Bill distributes auto parts in Vancouver. Pete is a retired engineer from Indianapolis. Rod and Betty flew in from England, where they recently sold their wood-products business. There are two Marilyns, good friends, from farms outside Toronto; one raises vegetables, the other, trotting horses. Rebecca is a photographer from Washington, D.C., where she takes publicity pictures of dignitaries. Wanda is a lively, well-traveled eighty-year-old from the San Francisco area. I introduce myself and immodestly claim two occupations: geologist and writer.

What we all share is a desire to see and photograph polar bears and their surroundings. We take pictures—lots of them— each time the vehicle lurches to a stop, whether it's foggy, cold, windy, sunny, or raining. Mike, as instructor, is patient and creative. Where I see gloom, fog, and a terrible day for photography, Mike seeks opportunities: "See how those trees are silhouetted in the mist! Look at the sensuous curve of the rocks—how they gleam when they're wet! Capture the motion of that grass as the wind whips it!"

As the days of cramped togetherness pass, the group becomes a tight-knit clan. Between bears, our jokes grow increasingly ribald. We share special moments: a bear yawns and stretches; another pries up a log, hoping to catch a tiny lemming for a snack. We savor every bear, every movement, every moment.

Some days we travel on foot. In blustery mists along the shores of Hudson Bay, we move cautiously among huge outcrops of mouse-colored rock, exclaiming over metamorphic swirls of pink and gray minerals. We set up tripods to photograph orange and green lichens. We climb back aboard, laugh at one another's jokes in the warmth of the bus, reload our cameras, and head out again into the cold fog, back to the glistening, beckoning rocks. Always in our minds—even when we're focusing on a tiny berry or a single leaf—are the white bears. We've seen how they lie, so rocklike and almost invisible, among the willows. Here, Mike explains, he's found them sleeping between the rounded rock ridges that ascend, tier on tier, like smooth-backed gray whales frozen as they rose to breathe in a sea of tundra. Over each rise, around each corner, Nanook could be dreaming, and each of us—much as we hope to see bears—doesn't want to be the one who wakens him.

About ten years ago a trapper working near Churchill stepped on a sleeping bear. "The bear awoke," says Mike, "not aggressive, but upset. It ripped the man's arm off at the shoulder with a biff of its paw. The trapper managed to get back to town, where doctors had only to snip a little skin—otherwise, it was a clean amputation." The story grabs our attention and ensures that we'll follow Mike's instructions.

The bears in this area are mainly subadults, the age-group responsible for most human injuries. Reason enough for caution. Before we leave the bus, Mike surveys the area. Before we clamber up the rocks, he takes a look around. Before we wander out of sight, he assigns buddy pairs and blows a whistle so we'll recognize the danger signal. Before any of this, Mike has selected one or more deterrents for the day: hand-launched cracker flares, short-range thunderflash grenades, or a gun that fires rubber bullets. About the grenades Mike says, "They're very effective. You do have to be careful, however, not to throw them too far. If one goes off behind the bear, it'll start him running toward you."

One day all the bears we encounter seem interested solely in sleeping. They lie, sprawling or demure, and yawn and stretch every five to ten minutes in the glorious warmth of the sun. In the buggy murmurs of "his head's coming up!" blend with whispered encouragement: "That's it, turn back this way!" The pose most often adopted seems to be mooning the bus. The bears think that if they turn their backs, we'll go away. We photograph a lot of rumps and make the obvious jokes about bear backsides. We cluster repeatedly at the open windows, bumping elbows, trying not to interfere with one another's photography. The group has become so cohesive that we laugh about the inconvenience, rather than jealously guarding the narrow openings.

Bears can be seen near Churchill without the need for tundra vehicles. One day ten of us crowd the windows of a small school bus as it pulls to a stop on a gravel ridge where sled dogs are tethered. The owner has thrown out food for them, but the scent of the whale meat also draws Nanook. Five polar bears prowl the area. Photographers murmur, then shout in their enthusiasm: "There's a big one on the ice! Look, he's broken through!"

In the golden light of late afternoon we watch the big male struggling to climb out of a pond and back onto the ice. The edge of the sheet where he's broken through is too thin to support his weight. His churning forepaws break away the rim, and he half-climbs, half-swims his massive way toward shore, leaving a wake of broken ice rubble, just as a powerful icebreaker opens a channel for other ships. The sunlight glows warm on his magnificent pelage, the creamy coat that sets him apart from lesser bears. As the male climbs out of the water at last, he shakes in a long, satisfying, full-bodied ripple that sends cold spray flying a good ten feet in all directions. Advancing up the shore, he challenges the nearest dog in a hissing, growling confrontation. All the dogs are crazy with the bear scent. We sense their excitement but surprisingly little fear. Their yapping, barking, and lunging never stop during the entire two hours that we remain in the vicinity. Occasionally, their feints and leaps connect: the dog usually loses the argument and limps quietly away. In one encounter, though, a dog jumps to the full extent of its chain and snaps its jaws for a fraction of a second on a bear's ear. Other dogs don't get so close but are rebuffed by a toss of the bear's open-jawed head, by a throaty, bellowing growl, or by a brief rush and paw swipe. Except for an occasional fast gobble by a dog, the food all seems to be disappearing into the bears. A few dogs are sufficiently brave or foolish to grab the meat while a bear has it in his teeth, and try to wrestle it out of his grip. This tug-of-war has a truly primal quality: bears and dogs have been enemies far longer than humans can remember.

Photographers lurch from window to window, laden with equipment. We juggle lenses, wrestle with windows that refuse to open, load more film, slip out the bus door, cluster nervously around the front grille of the bus, and jostle quickly back aboard when a bear turns in our direction. Bear spotters who aren't snapping pictures keep us advised: "There's one coming up behind. Another on the left, but he's turning away—woops, he's coming back!" Shutters click, motor drives whine, and people clamber awkwardly over one another, but the bears are interested only in the dogs' food.

"The owner of the team says he's just feeding his dogs, and that he has put down extra food because the bears take some," a Churchill resident told me, "but he's really baiting the bears. It's illegal to feed bears. Last week the conservation officers caught two tour groups with lard in their vans. It's not right—we don't like it," she added emphatically.

About thirty-five miles east of town lies Cape Churchill, famous as the site of numerous polar bear research projects. From a perch high above the ground—in an enclosed structure built from the salvaged parts of a fire-watch tower—Ian Stirling and various students and colleagues watched, measured, marked, and described hundreds of bears. It was here that deterrents were tested and means of tagging and marking bears were perfected. Some of these involved unusual activities, such as this scene described by biologist Gordon Stenhouse: "Unmarked bears approaching the observation tower were struck with dye-filled eggs thrown by the researchers." In an earlier year, Stenhouse wrote, "One bear was marked when he opened an equipment box and bit into a pressurized tin of blue acrylic spray paint."

Stenhouse spent long hours watching bears from the top of the tower during his study of deterrents that might drive away problem bears. I asked whether he had had any unusual encounters.

"At one point," he responded, "we'd lived on the tower for about two months. We desperately needed hot showers and supplies, so we caught a lift back to town aboard a helicopter. When the pilot took us back to the tower, we noticed an old 'bag of bones' bear—in very poor condition—camped right at the base of the tower. As the helicopter landed, the bear moved away. We told the pilot we'd be okay, and he lifted off. We began walking nonchalantly toward the tower with our supplies. Suddenly the old bear made a beeline straight for us.

"All our firearms were at the top of the tower. When the bear charged, all we could do was drop everything, run for the tower, and jump for the ladder. We scrambled up to our weapons and got the 38-millimeter riot gun that fires rubber bullets. Aiming from above, however, we couldn't get far enough from the bear to be certain that we'd just smack him and not hurt him—especially considering how skinny he was.

"We spent the next two or three days trying everything we could think of, dropping pails of rocks or whatever else we could get our hands on. Meanwhile, the bear, who could smell the seal meat that we used as bait—locked away, out of reach— ripped into the supplies we'd abandoned, took our food, a tent, and other gear. We were most concerned about our fuel supply, which was on the ground for safety reasons. Without a stove, it gets mighty cold on that tower.

"Every time we'd set foot on the ground, he'd charge. Eventually, he moved off a little way and we were able to use the gun. We hit him three or four times with rubber bullets before he finally ran off."

Northern veterans like Stenhouse—especially those who've worked in the Churchill area—almost always have a favorite bear story and a polar bear joke. Their sense of humor is strongest when danger threatens: it's a way to relieve the stress. Typical is Canadian wildlife biologist Chris Davies: "We tell stories about the white rocks that grow legs and stand up, or the bears that turn into white rocks. There are far too many white rocks in the north country. We used to joke about hiring someone to paint red *x*'s on all the real ones. At Churchill a graduate student asked me about a white lump in the distance. I assured her it was a familiar white rock we all knew very well. About that time, the 'rock' stood up. A polar bear had been lying right in front of the familiar rock."

In town as well everyone has a bear story. Two involve bears and aircraft. One bear wandered into the taxiway in full view of an approaching pilot. He was directly behind a member of the ground crew who was guiding the aircraft with the lighted wands used at air terminals the world over. The worker had no idea there was a bear in the vicinity; he was concentrating on his job. The pilot tried to get the man's attention by alternately revving his engines and weaving the plane from side to side. The man kept waving his arms. The bear seemed to find the whole performance amusing: he sat down about ten feet behind the man and just watched.

Another bear surprised a helicopter pilot while he was sitting in his aircraft on the cape east of town. The bear smashed in the clear windows and climbed into the cockpit. The pilot ducked quickly out the other side and cowered on the floor of a nearby plane while the bear ate the seats out of his helicopter. The man's survey team arrived and chased the bear away. The pilot climbed into the windowless, seatless helicopter, flew it to the Churchill airport, boarded a commercial flight heading south, and was never seen again.

Cape Churchill doesn't look like much: somehow you expect the site of world-acclaimed research to be more imposing. It looks just like a thousand other parts of the Hudson Bay shoreline, except that it sticks out into the bay, forming something of a right angle. Ian Stirling wrote, "The place can seem decidedly unremarkable except for the fact that it is not at all uncommon to get up on an October or November morning and see thirty or more polar bears." From his work here and elsewhere, Stirling has come to be acknowledged as Canada's foremost polar bear specialist. His expertise is much in demand. As he wrote in his 1988 book, *Polar Bears,* "In our lab, we always know when it is fall because the geese start to fly south, the leaves turn color, and the photographers begin to phone for information about polar bears at Churchill."

Is the polar bear capital unusually dangerous? Researcher Malcolm Ramsay told me, "Any place has its dangers. In downtown Boston, you look both ways before you cross the street. Here you don't worry about traffic, but you do have to remember to turn on the lights and look outside before you step out."

The greatest danger in Churchill may not be *to* the tourists but *from* the tourists. Their tundra buggies churn the black, muddy soil like tractors, plowing furrows that will scar the land for centuries. The drivers are careful to follow one another's tracks to minimize the impact, but restricting traffic to a narrow lane only concentrates the damage. Ideally, visitors would drive out over the tundra only after it freezes, but by then the bears are offshore, heading for good seal hunting.

Bears don't appear outwardly stressed by tourists, so long as the visitors obey the regulations about not feeding or harassing them. Buggy drivers are sensitive to Nanook's need for rest and privacy and usually advise their passengers when it's time to move on. In late fall the bears can't afford much stress: their bodies are already biologically stressed by enforced starvation.

The tour operators live in Churchill and have economic incentive to ensure the bears' welfare. Doing so won't be easy, though—plans for Churchill's future are unsettled. Several things *are* certain: that the town won't just pack up and move, as I heard one tourist suggest; that the garbage dump will continue to attract bears; and that the Alert program and its Polar Bear Compound will continue to be needed. Beyond these certainties Churchill's strategies for coping with bears are still evolving. For the present, the relationship between man and beast seems to have reached a stalemate. Nor is new technology likely to help: for example, a modern incinerator at the dump hasn't worked since the first day it was fired up. What Churchill needs most is a long-range plan that will guarantee both the bears and the human residents the peace and security they need to coexist.

Since 1978 some 6,500 square miles of shoreline, tundra, and forest have been protected as the Cape Churchill Wildlife Management Area. Various plans have since been put forward to convert the area east of Churchill into some kind of national park, with entry restrictions and fees for off-road vehicles. Any proposal to restrict tourism irritates some Churchill residents, who cite the depressed economy and the need for outside dollars. Others think the bears deserve all the protection the law can afford them.

I share Malcolm Ramsay's view: although tourism could eventually expand to damaging levels, it presently does more good than harm. Churchill's annual influx of polar bear watchers produces a continuing stream of outbound enthusiasts, headed home with memories, stories, and photographs of the great white bears. Having met Nanook in his chilly kingdom, they become his ambassadors to their own world. Though a truly majestic ruler, the white bear sits atop a shaky throne: he is powerless and mute when confronting human establishments and depends on the voices of others—mine included—for his very survival. I hope we are equal to the task.

TWELVE

Nanook Today

Pɪᴄᴋ ᴜᴘ ᴀ ɢʟᴏʙᴇ. Look at the top. Converging toward the North
Pole are lines of longitude. The Arctic draws them in toward
the center. Toward the axis—toward the Pole. The Pole draws
the earth together, like the drawstring that closes a net.

Even the nations of the earth, scattered across the planet,
going their separate ways, are drawn together by the polar
regions. Facing the cold, men and women forget their differ-
ences. One of the first multinational accords had an arctic focus: after the *Titanic's* fatal scrape alongside an iceberg drifted
south from Baffin Bay, the International Ice Patrol was organized in 1915. For over seventy-five years its ships and aircraft
have kept North Atlantic sea-lanes safe from the peril of floating
arctic ice. At the other end of the earth, nations are likewise
drawn together as the lines converge toward the South Pole.
The Antarctic Treaty, signed by twelve nations in 1961, reserves the southernmost continent for peaceful and scientific
endeavors.

Nations are also drawn together in support of the white
bear. The boundaries of five countries—the United States, Canada, Denmark (Greenland), Norway (the Svalbard Archipel-

ago), and the Soviet Union—enclose shorelines and snowbanks marked by polar bear pawprints. In 1973 representatives of these nations met in Oslo to complete a remarkable agreement that had been discussed for years. Affirmed by each of the five nations by 1978 and unanimously reaffirmed in 1981, the International Agreement on the Conservation of Polar Bears and Their Habitat is the first document concerning a common resource to be signed by the arctic nations. It commits the five countries to the protection of polar bears and their habitat and to cooperative research that will ensure the bears' survival. The agreement was prepared by a group of polar bear specialists acting under the auspices of the International Union for the Conservation of Nature and Natural Resources; these specialists continue to meet every two years to share the results of their research.

The agreement recognizes each nation's right to manage polar bear populations along its own shoreline. It prohibits hunting from ships and aircraft, and restricts hunting to areas where bears have been taken by traditional methods in the past. The document focuses protection efforts on denning and feeding areas, and on migration routes. It allows, however, a sustainable annual harvest. (Such terms seem incongruously bucolic: *harvest* has warm, gentle connotations, but there's nothing pastoral about a once beautiful bear lying silent in the blood-soaked snow. The word elicits the same response when it's used by transplant surgeons—I shudder to hear them speak of "harvesting" lungs, or kidneys, or hearts.)

The historic document prohibits the taking (hunting, killing, or capturing) of polar bears except for (1) scientific or conservation purposes; (2) safety (but the body of a bear killed to protect life or property must be forfeited); (3) hunting by local people using traditional methods; or (4) hunting by other citizens using traditional means (usually interpreted as requiring nonmechanized transport but permitting modern firearms). It also prohibits importation of any part or product of a polar bear into any of the five nations.

The international agreement includes a provision that each nation may, if it chooses, enact more stringent controls. Their governments and native groups have done so, and in one instance the native peoples of two nations joined hands to establish their own polar bear management program.

Within each nation polar bears are protected to varying degrees. In the United States the international agreement was implemented and augmented by the Marine Mammal Protection Act (MMPA), developed simultaneously with the international accord and passed by Congress in 1972.

Because this act allows native subsistence killing throughout the year, without a hunting season, without limits, and with no distinction among adult male bears, subadults, or mothers with cubs, some bear experts question whether it qualifies under the international agreement as a "more stringent control." While the MMPA led to an overall decrease in the number of polar bears killed in Alaska, the proportion of females and cubs taken—the most valuable portion of the population, according to one biologist—increased substantially.

Administered by the U.S. Fish and Wildlife Service (USF&WS), the MMPA is a wide-ranging statement covering whales, dolphins, porpoises, seals, sea lions, sea otters, walrus, manatees, dugongs, and polar bears. Of these, only the polar bear and the walrus are not listed as threatened or endangered species. These two mammals therefore don't benefit from the additional protection offered to the others under the Endangered Species Act.

The MMPA forbids the taking (defined as harassing, hunting, capturing, collecting, killing, or attempting any of these) of marine mammals, and the importation, possession, transport, or sale of such animals or their products. Exceptions are made for (1) pre-1972 specimens; (2) pre-1972 international agreements (these deal primarily with Pacific fur seals); (3) Alaskan natives; (4) permits granted for scientific research, public display, and incidental capture in commercial fisheries—the last a topic of current controversy over dolphins caught in tuna nets; and (5) waivers granted by the federal government (to be used if animal populations recover sufficiently to permit hunting).

Polar bears are also specifically protected under the Convention on International Trade in Endangered Species (CITES). The CITES regulations control international traffic in certain species and stipulate both import and export permits. Because they're not on the Endangered List, however, polar bears are on a secondary list, known as CITES Appendix II, and command less strict control. In many countries permits aren't difficult to arrange. Canada, especially, exports many polar bear skins. Jonathan Blackmer, special assistant U.S. Attorney from the Land and Natural Resources Division of the Department of Justice, summarizes the situation: "One of the problems with a legal hunting system in only one nation is that other countries allow imports that the United States doesn't. You can take a bear legally in Canada and import your trophy into many other countries. West Germany, in particular, seems to get a lot of polar bear rugs and mounts. Because they're covered by CITES, you'll need a permit, but because they're Appendix II animals, the paperwork is easy."

The MMPA contains a provision that grated hard on the nerves of Alaskans already sensitive to the power of the federal government, some 6,ooo miles away, to intrude in their lives. "No State may enforce, or attempt to enforce, any State law or regulation relating to the taking of any species . . . of marine mammal within the State unless the Secretary [of Interior] has transferred authority for the conservation and management of that species . . . to the State." In one swift stroke the federal government brushed aside Alaska's jurisdiction and permitting system, replacing it with regulations that, according to some experts, offer polar bears *less* protection, not more.

The provision of the MMPA for Alaska natives is written to encompass "customary and traditional uses by rural Alaska residents of marine mammals for direct personal or family consumption as food, shelter, fuel, clothing, tools, or transportation, for the making and selling of handicraft articles out of nonedible byproducts . . . and for barter, or sharing for personal or family consumption." The act also specifies that these native uses be "not accomplished in a wasteful manner." Such handicraft articles may not be "sold or otherwise transferred to any person other than an Indian, Aleut or Eskimo, or delivered, carried, transported or shipped in interstate or foreign commerce" without federal permits.

According to a publication of the Fish and Wildlife Service,

"Approximately 75 percent of meat parts are salvaged and consumed by the Eskimos. Although traditional practices vary by village, one trait which is practiced universally is the sharing of meat with other village residents. Sharing is generally based upon the immediate and secondary family. However, the older and more needy receive greater consideration when sharing meat."

Presently in Alaska about 130 polar bears are taken each year by the residents of a dozen villages. The bears can be hunted year-round, but most are killed between November and January, when the pack ice is frozen firmly to the shoreline. According to the publication just mentioned, "The harvest appears to be sustainable and polar bear populations are stable and healthy." Biologists I spoke with are enthusiastic. Said one: "We have the luxury of studying a stable population of healthy animals. One of the best indications is that we're now seeing the older, larger bears that were missing a few years ago—those that were preferentially sought by sport hunters."

Still, the native harvest generates controversy. The Fish and Wildlife Service has been assigned the dual role of protecting the bears and providing data that enable native hunters to kill them. "Of the five polar bear nations," says Gerald Garner, a research biologist in Alaska with the USF&WS, "we have the only unregulated harvest: the natives are not restrained in any way, shape, or form. You can debate the merits of this system, but the fact remains that very few Eskimos go out on the ice to hunt bears in the traditional way."

The law permits natives to use snowmobiles, motorboats, and even aircraft. The MMPA, while not addressing methods and means of harvesting marine mammals, does specify that taking should be nonwasteful and from nondepleted, healthy populations. Subsistence hunting is a very delicate issue among conservationists. A bear still brings much prestige to a native hunter. When Alaskan Eskimos encounter bears, they may kill none, or they may kill them all. Some hunters take only large males, others avoid the big males. Throughout Alaska hunters agree, however, not to kill females with cubs of the year in the spring. In general, though, the native harvest is difficult to predict or regulate because each hunter follows his own ethical and traditional guidelines.

Researchers are frustrated by such attitudes. One biologist tranquilized a bear and painted a big number on its side while an Eskimo watched the operation. About thirty minutes later, as the drug began to wear off, the native shot the bear. Only later did he begin worrying that the painted number made the hide worthless and that the drug in the meat might poison his family. The result was a useless bear carcass left in a biologist's front yard.

Biologists charged with the dual responsibility of protecting the resource and facilitating a sustainable harvest don't find those duties contradictory. "I support the harvesting of marine mammals, so long as it's done wisely and populations are not placed in jeopardy," USF&WS biologist Scott Schliebe explained. "There's a need for authorities to regulate the harvest before populations become depleted. The law that we enforce, the Marine Mammal Protection Act, specifies that hunting for subsistence is permitted, and it's our job to ensure that the harvest is at the proper level and not forcing populations to decline." Managers of the polar bear population use a businesslike vocabulary that contrasts with the wild majesty of the bears themselves. They speak of hunters as "users of the resource" and of the annual kill as the "removal rate," as if Nanook were a commodity traded in some far-off exchange. I almost expect to hear a daily report: "Polar bear futures were up slightly today in heavy trading, on reports of a new agreement. . . ."

I asked Schliebe how USF&WS representatives are treated by the native hunters. "I think they accept me," he replied. "There's a certain degree of trust. I have developed a number of good friendships with hunters in various villages over the years. Hunters are profoundly interested in our studies on polar bears and are very willing to discuss their impressions about the biology of the bears. The service's harvest data acquisition program requires that this partnership of cooperation exist.

"We try not to interfere with the hunt," Schliebe continued. "We do indicate, however, that we'd prefer to see hunters not taking entire family groups of polar bears. Hunters are opportunists: if they see bears only rarely, they won't pass up the chance to shoot them.

"To gauge the effect of the unregulated harvest on the bear

population," Schliebe said, "you have to look at the net removal rate. Under state management, adult females comprised 25 percent of the harvest. That percentage is larger today, but the overall take is way down, so fewer females are being taken." There is no doubt, however, in Schliebe's mind that mother bears deserve protection. "From the viewpoint of modeling population dynamics," he said, "the most important animal is the female just entering the den to have her first litter."

For a twenty-five-dollar fee anyone can apply to become a marine mammal registered agent and assist natives in processing raw polar bear materials to be used for handicrafts. Special Agent George Elkins of the USF&WS Branch of Investigations said, "If a marine mammal is taken by a subsistence hunter, its parts can be used in handicrafts rather than be thrown away. I don't think there's much handicraft trade in polar bear products, though, other than perhaps some trimming or fringing on clothing." Biologist Schliebe elaborated: "In the case of polar bears, handicrafts usually means mittens, ruffs for parkas, mukluks, and trimming on other items. The actual number of hides used in handicrafts hasn't been determined.

"Registered agents act as intermediaries. For example, a taxidermist who's a registered agent can send a hide to a tannery in the lower forty-eight states and then deliver it back to a native. For the most part, though," Schliebe explained, "natives tan the hides themselves in the traditional way. After fleshing the skin completely, the hide is left outside all winter, stretched flat on a frame or tied over a beam. Essentially, the skin is freeze-dried. Then the hide is scraped in the spring to make it supple."

Many such skins find their way south in violation of the MMPA. I asked Agent Elkins about the success of his branch at stopping illegal trade in polar bear products. "We have about two hundred agents, scattered from the Arctic Circle to the Mexican border," he replied. "Each one of them knows to look for polar bear items. We conduct about fifteen thousand investigations a year, with all sorts of objectives. One day we may focus on illegal alligator skins in Louisiana; the next day it may be polar bear hides coming in from British Columbia. There's usually at least one polar bear investigation under way at any given moment. Usually it involves a trophy hunter who's trying to smuggle in a whole mount or a bearskin rug. Occasionally, someone will try to bring in a raw hide and have it processed in the United States."

A recent case, investigated jointly by U.S. and Canadian authorities, involved Jerome Knap, an Ontario hunting guide and prominent outdoor writer. Knap organized Canadian polar bear hunts for American sportsmen. Under Canadian law the hunts were legal. What the Americans couldn't do legally, however, was bring their trophies back across the border. "There is absolutely no question that the American hunters knew they were breaking the law," said prosecutor Jonathan Blackmer. "Knap's brochure even mentioned the Marine Mammal Protection Act and its prohibitions against import. He'd imply to his customers, however, that the law might be changed soon. Then, after you'd shot your bear, he'd hint that for an additional thousand dollars or so, he'd get your trophy back across the border. Some hunters, though, chose to abide by the law, and told Knap to keep the bear they'd shot. Some are still paying him an annual storage fee, hoping the law will change."

I asked Blackmer how likely such a change would be. "The Canadians tried to make it part of the recent trade discussions," the prosecutor said. "We said no—it's an environmental issue, not a trade issue."

According to Ann Haas, a representative of the USF&WS, Jerome Knap had been in business as a guide for many years and was well respected. "He was even scheduled to serve as a tour guide for delegates attending a CITES meeting," she told me. "That changed once this story broke.

"Knap was good at what he did," she conceded. "He described how to make a sales receipt appear old, so the bear would appear to be pre-act, by putting the paper in the window and letting the sun turn it yellow. He had it all figured out—almost."

Jonathan Blackmer resumed the story: "Because we have no extradition agreement with Canada concerning these specific crimes, we had to arrest Knap in this country in order to prosecute. We followed his movements and arrested him on one of his visits here, at a hunting convention. He and his wife, who helped get the bears across the border, pled guilty to an additional charge after a conviction in Corpus Christi, Texas. Knap was also charged and pled guilty on Canadian charges and agreed to cooperate with investigators after a conviction by trial jury. He spent two months in jail and received a five-year suspended sentence in addition to more than $100,000 in U.S. and Canadian fines. To date, we've prosecuted twenty-two of his hunters. The key to the case was the seizure of Knap's business records by Canadian officials. The Justice Department worked closely with the Canadians on this one, and the cooperation paid off."

"In addition to the fines," said Special Agent Tom Mason, who handled the case from his Corpus Christi office (located, appropriately, on Bear Lane), "Knap retained two attorneys in Corpus Christi, one in Washington, and one in Canada, and he bore the cost of paying for several witnesses to assist in his defense." I asked Mason why Knap was tried in U.S. District Court in Corpus Christi. "It all began in 1986," he replied. "Special Agents Pete Nylander and Bill Reynolds spotted a mounted polar bear on display in a Texas boat dealer's showroom. The owner maintained that the bear had been killed in 1970, and he had a faked document to prove it. The bear turned out to have been killed in 1984 on a hunt with Jerome Knap, arranged through an outfitter in Corpus Christi, so the case wound up here.

"South Texas is probably not the assignment where a fish and wildlife agent would expect a lot of polar bear work," Mason continued, "but we do get some. Some wealthy Texas hunters try to bring back their trophies. We suspect black-market smugglers fly polar bear hides nonstop from Montreal to Mexico City under legitimate CITES permits and then try to smuggle the skins across the United States–Mexico border. We have only one agent for the entire Rio Grande Valley, and we're spread pretty thin all along the southern border. Most polar bears, though, still come in across the Canadian border."

Polar bear trophies, rugs, and other items seized by federal investigators are subject to forfeiture. Such material is turned over to the government for educational and scientific purposes. "For items that have such a sad beginning," said Haas of the USF&WS, "this is a great recycling program. For example, we have a beautiful mounted two-year-old polar bear [seized in the Knap case from an American hunter] that we use to educate the public. He just made a trip to the national Boy Scout Jamboree in Virginia, where I'm told he was a real showstopper."

These federal officials are dedicated to their mission. Regarding the Knap case, Jonathan Blackmer said, "It's basically smuggling. It's not the drug trade, but it is serious business. The sanctity of our borders was broken by this act."

In Alaska a sizable black market exists for polar bear hides. As agents describe the typical situation, an Eskimo kills a bear legally. Some months later a white trader visits the village, sees the dried or tanned bear hide, and offers to buy it. In a financially depressed village it doesn't take long for word to get around that someone is in town who will pay cash or drugs for bear hides. A few days later a bear hide that was being saved to make mukluks and trim clothing is on its way to a collector in the lower forty-eight states or Europe.

The illegal traffic in polar bear products operates at a high-dollar level. Reports of $25,000 being paid for a bearskin rug are not uncommon. Federal agents investigating these activities must depend on tips from alert citizens. Otherwise they go undercover. This cloak-and-dagger work includes electronic transmitters secretly attached to polar bear hides, which can then be tracked by agents driving unmarked cars. The federal investigators encounter some very shady characters. A big sting operation in Alaska involving polar bears caught one of the major drug dealers in the area. He was arrested for illegal possession of polar bear hides and walrus ivory, but officers also recovered a huge drug shipment.

Pressure is intense from big-game hunters to rewrite the law or to force changes in the funding and activities of the Fish and Wildlife Service. In 1982, for example, the Safari Club International approached the USF&WS with a request to waive the MMPA moratorium on polar bear hunting. The issue was dropped because of insufficient data on bear populations.

The big-game hunters' associations have a powerful lobby

and are influential in Washington. Some members of these groups may think they've been unfairly singled out for investigation or prosecution, but that's just not true. "We investigate individuals based on information we receive," Special Agent Mason explained, "many times from their peers or other people they come in contact with—and we try to enforce the law regardless of an individual's background, because we're out here to protect the resource."

How big is the problem? Does illegal hunting and black marketeering make a significant impact on polar bear populations? Mason thinks so: "There are a number of polar bears missing from Alaska—and probably from Canada, too—and it's hard to know where they're going. As to how big the problem is, I know that if we did permit open trade in bear products with Canada, it would hurt the Alaskan polar bear population. We wouldn't be able to tell if a skin or mount was a Canadian bear or an illegally taken Alaskan bear at this time."

The high price commanded by a polar bear skin, according to Mason, "makes it extremely lucrative to set up a smuggling ring or a false-permit scheme. These folks can put out the word that a polar bear skin—covered by a false document—'might be available.' Then they sit back and wait to get rich."

In the Canadian Arctic in the nineteenth century, it was common practice to kill all polar bears encountered. As the trade in fox pelts brought more dollars to the north country, there was a gradual awakening to the fact that polar bears are essential to a healthy fox population. Without the food that they scavenge from the bears' kills, the foxes could never survive the long winter. Protection of polar bears acquired an economic impetus: to profit from fox furs, hunters had to change their attitudes toward bears. Suddenly the ice bear was valuable alive.

Today hunting is permitted from October to May in the Northwest Territories and in part of the Yukon. Cubs are protected if they are so small that their stretched, dried skins would be less than 1.8 meters (6 feet) long, and females with such cubs are also covered. The quota system works, at least on paper. The kill in some years is slightly over the allotted quota; in other

years, slightly under. The numbers are difficult to interpret, however, because the total killed includes native hunters'
subsistence kills, sport kills, problem kills, discovered illegal
kills, bears found dead, and deaths that occur during capture,
tagging, or other handling. An export permit costs from one to
five Canadian dollars, and a government seal must be affixed
to the hide. Fur dealers and taxidermists are licensed and must
abide by stringent regulations requiring proof-of-origin documen-
tation.

Most Canadian bearskins are sold at auction: the principal
buyers are Japanese and Europeans. The system is closely monitored. A Canadian fur official assured me that "if an identifi-
cation [back to the source of a hide] cannot be made, the skin
either cannot be sold or it cannot be exported." He added, however, that "the existing CITES system is not as effective as it
should be. It is understaffed and too centralized; our border
with the United States is the longest in the world and the least
controlled. The potential for abuse has been demonstrated; polar bears have entered the United States illegally, and in large
numbers."

Marion Love is married to an Inuit hunter and lives in Coral
Harbour, a town with a population of about 575 in Canada's
Northwest Territories. Each November 1, she told me, bear season opens, and other activities in her village come to an abrupt
halt. About sixty bear tags are assigned to the community and
are allocated to various individuals by the Hunters and Trappers Association. As many as 150 hunters, both men and women,
are eligible. "Depending on the number of bears in the area—
and we have a lot of bears—the hunt may last only ten days,"
Love said. "Some years it may stretch all the way to April."

The village also gets five sport tags that may be sold to non-
Inuit hunters as part of a $15,000 package that includes a ten-
day dogsled hunt. The white hunter claims the skin; his Inuit
guide keeps the meat. "We eat a lot of bear meat," Love told
me. "We cook it long and slowly, like pork.

"We're trying to keep alive the old skills and traditions," she
said. Although she's employed in adult education that stresses

job training for a technical world, Love knows the value of the older Inuit ways in their unforgiving world. "For example, when you're on the land, it's essential for survival that you know how to build snow houses. My husband learned as a child in Igloolik and is quite skilled at building them.

"Last year was my husband's first hunt. He came over a rise and spotted sixteen bears, all together in one spot. Like most hunters, he selected a large male, because it provides more meat and a skin with higher value. The skins are sold at auctions regulated by Renewable Resources and bring prices of $1,000 to $4,000, depending on the time of year and the bidding that day.

"A bear is still the true sign of a great hunter. My husband was so proud—I couldn't get him down off the ceiling for weeks after."

Mike Beedell, Canadian adventurer, sees an advantage to a system that mixes native and sport hunters. He explained, "The $15,000 fee that a white hunter pays not only provides income to the communities that so desperately need it, but it also preserves traditional ways—it allows the Inuit to maintain a lifestyle closer to the land."

This question isn't restricted to Canada; the issue arises worldwide wherever native groups hold values that differ from those of the governing populace. "The entire issue of native subsistence comes into play," said U.S. Agent Mason, "with the complications added by modern methods, modern weapons, and modern equipment. It's an issue for those of us in the United States as well, and we're going to have to deal with more of it in the future. I think a very positive sign is that the natives seem to be agreeing that the resource is finite and must be managed. Public opinion in these areas is coming around. I just hope it comes around in time."

Today there are probably between twenty thousand and forty thousand polar bears. They are scattered in discrete subpopulations and keep to specific areas within the circumpolar region. The various arctic nations have set aside parks, nature reserves, and wildlife management areas where the white bear is protected from hunting and harassment.

In Canada, Nanook has his own playground: along the shores of Hudson Bay and James Bay, in northern Ontario, lies Polar Bear Provincial Park. Encompassing 9,300 square miles it is one of the world's largest parks. Established in 1970 the park preserves a vast expanse of transitional forest (muskeg swamps and stunted trees at the edge of the northern tree line) and large areas of treeless tundra. This "arctic" environment is 800 miles south of the Arctic Circle. It owes its existence to the harsh local climate, caused by the frigid waters of the two bays, and by the abundant ice, snow, fog, and clouds that reflect the sun's warming rays back into space.

Polar Bear Provincial Park, already the size of New Hampshire, is growing, but not by executive fiat, nor by donations from philanthropic landowners. Rather new land—about three square miles each year—is a gift from the Ice Age. Relieved of the mass of ice that this region supported during the millennia when vast continental glaciers covered the Canadian shield, the land is relaxing, rising. Out of the sea it emerges, gaining about half an inch of elevation each year. Because the topography is so flat, a half-inch rise exposes large areas of seabed, which become new park land.

Some four hundred polar bears live in and around the park named for them. Black bears also frequent the area, even wandering north of the tree line. The two don't mix, according to resident biologists. Nor are bear-human interactions much of a problem. "Our coast is so low-lying that it's swampy and not a very pleasant place to live," Chris Davies, district biologist, explained. "Our villages are located some fifteen miles inland. The bears keep to the shoreline most of the year, so we have few problems."

Like tourists, bears visit the park seasonally: the smallest number of polar bears are recorded during late spring. The count increases as ice melts on the bays. By late October large groups of bears congregate along the shoreline and at headlands, waiting for the fall freeze-up so they can again hunt seals from the frozen surface. Pregnant females walk inland during the fall to dig maternity dens (some birth chambers are found more than ninety miles from the shoreline).

The bears of this region form a discrete subpopulation. Their annual migration appears limited to the southern portion of

Hudson Bay. Because this area has abundant food resources and a somewhat gentler climate than other bears must face, the bears of this group appear well fed and healthy. Better yet, their numbers seem to be increasing.

Humans may not do so well in this setting. A brochure about Polar Bear Provincial Park describes the landscape as "challenging," and notes that "the area is flat and unscenic except in a wild, languorous way. Dry land for camping can be difficult to find. The lakes are shallow and very often swampy. Weather during the 'warm' season, late June until mid-September, is often an unpleasant combination of low temperatures, strong chilling winds, and overcast skies. . . . Possibly, there is nowhere else on earth where biting and sucking insects are more of a nuisance than in the lowland. Because of the park's isolated nature, there is an element of danger associated with camping there. In spite of such challenges, Polar Bear offers adventurous visitors some exceptional recreational opportunities."

Canada has other wildlife preserves and management areas, including Cape Churchill and Bathurst Island in the high Arctic. In national parks throughout northern Canada, bears are protected, but growing numbers of visitors make bear-human interactions increasingly probable.

Greenland, which achieved self-government in 1979, remains a part of the Kingdom of Denmark and sends two representatives to the Danish parliament. Under the home rule government, a Department for Wildlife Management conducts research on the size of the annual polar bear harvest, the incidence of trichinosis in bears, and environmental issues affecting Nanook.

Visitors to Greenland may apply to the home rule government for licenses to hunt hare, birds, reindeer, or foxes. Other animals, including polar bears, musk-oxen, eagles, falcons, and snowy owls, are protected. Permanent residents of Greenland, however, can apply for polar bear licenses issued by their municipal councils, certifying that hunting is their primary occupation. About 10 percent of the 55,000 Greenlanders make their living as hunters, but most of these hunt only seals.

Stringent restrictions apply to polar bear hunts. Forbidden

are airplanes, helicopters, and motor vehicles, including snow-mobiles. Greenland is the last place on earth where the traditional Inuit dogsled hunt continues (although it is making something of a comeback in northern Canada, where similar regulations now control hunting). Greenlanders may not use poison, foothold traps, set guns, shotguns, or automatic weapons. Keeping or exporting live bears requires special permits, and buying or accepting the meat, skin, or other parts of illegally taken bears is prohibited.

Present regulations, enacted in 1988, include protection of cubs under two years of age and mothers with such cubs. Exceptions are made near a few villages, where only first-year cubs and their mothers are protected. Adult male bears may be taken year-round, a provision requested by local hunters, who claim that male bears pose a risk to cubs and denning females. Hunting was recently prohibited from the decks of ships larger than forty tons in an attempt to stop the shooting of bears from large fishing vessels that operate each spring near the edge of the Baffin Bay icepack. Because Greenlanders rely on Denmark for defense, the Danish Navy protects the coastal waters and, among its other tasks, enforces fishing regulations. A common sight in Greenland waters is the Danish patrol vessel *Hvidbjør-nen* ("Polar Bear").

Between eighty and one hundred eighty polar bears are killed each year by Greenlandic hunters. In northwestern Greenland, Nanook is still an important element in traditional native culture. Bearskins are still used to make clothing, and bear meat forms part of the native diet. The annual take in this region is not known but is estimated at thirty to forty animals. Neither is the bear population known: aerial surveys suggest that perhaps 1,000 to 2,000 bears walk back and forth on the sea ice between Canada's Ellesmere Island and northwestern Greenland. However, many bear experts say aerial surveys are ineffective: looking for a white bear on a snowy surface isn't easy at any speed, but in a moving airplane it's even harder. Biologists want to estimate population densities and to document the effectiveness of setting aside as a nature reserve the central portion of the Melville Bay coast. This area was preserved in 1980 because the local Inuit said it was an important polar bear denning area, but thus far no den sites have been studied.

According to one expert who has lived, traveled, and hunted with both Canadian and Greenlandic natives, it is common for Greenlanders to cross the sea ice to hunt bears on Ellesmere Island. Such boundary-crossing hunts may go unreported in either nation.

In southeastern Greenland polar bear hides are sold or used as clothing, and bear meat is eaten. In a typical year over forty bears are taken in this region. As on the west coast very little is known about bear populations on the eastern side of the world's largest island.

An immense national park occupies the entire northeastern quarter of Greenland. This park—the largest on earth, covering an area the size of Texas and California combined—is a nature preserve established in 1973, in which the taking of bears is permitted only within a one-day dogsled range of the park boundary. Nanook wanders unmolested along the shoreline bordering the remaining 400,000 square miles. The towering coastal peaks and wild, glacially scoured fjords form a majestic backdrop for the white bear, symbol of the Far North. Nanook is symbolic also of Greenland and has graced its crest since 1666. The present heraldry depicts a sitting white bear, forepaws raised, on a field of blue. The symbolism is appropriate, for white bears are more at home than humans in this region of stark beauty, a land that is mostly no land at all but rather huge fields of ice and snow.

In Norway's Svalbard Archipelago, about 40 percent of the land area was set aside by royal decree in 1973 to form three national parks, two nature reserves, and fifteen bird sanctuaries. The area includes significant polar bear denning sites. Additional protection for the northeastern Svalbard nature reserve was added in 1976, when it became a biosphere reserve protected by the United Nations under UNESCO's Man and Biosphere Program. Special permits are required for scientists to enter the area to study the bears. Throughout Svalbard polar bears may be killed only in self-defense.

There is, however, continued pressure to resume hunting, and not just from would-be sport hunters. Nanook has become a nuisance. After several years of protection, the bears of Svalbard have apparently lost their fear of humans. They arrive with increasing frequency in villages and weather stations, and several are shot each year as problem bears. As biologist Ian Stirling has observed, "Just stopping all killing of these animals is not a guaranteed means to save the species . . . those responsible for their management must have a variety of options open to them. These options must include the authority to remove individuals when the occasion demands it."

Wrangel and Herald islands, north of the Soviet Union, are important polar bear denning areas and have been designated state reserves. Visitors are not allowed. Any human activity in the area must take second place to the welfare of the bears.

The Wrangel Island bear population is shared with western Alaska, in an annual exchange far older than détente or *glasnost*, across the Bering and Chukchi seas. As the water warms and the ice edge retreats northward in late spring, bears move to the north and northwest. By midsummer the majority of bears are concentrated along the edge of the remaining pack ice between Wrangel Island and Barrow, Alaska. In late fall pregnant females enter dens, usually on land, but in the spring the new mothers take their cubs southward onto the icepack in search of seals. The bears, ignoring human boundaries, follow their food supply and the ice they need to hunt.

Managing the bears as a joint resource has brought the United States and USSR closer. "We're setting up a cooperative research program with the Soviets," American biologist Gerald Garner explained. "In the spring of 1989 we had two Soviet biologists in Alaska to learn our marking and capturing techniques. During the spring of 1990 three of us will go to Wrangel Island to work alongside their scientists.

"We estimate that the western Alaskan bear population is stable, but we don't know how much of its recovery is due to the cessation of hunting in the Soviet Union. In the USSR," Garner continued, "bears have recovered sufficiently to be a nuisance problem in the northern villages. They're talking of reinstituting a regulated harvest. Part of our cooperative research is aimed at allocating the shared resource between the two nations so they could set a reasonable quota under the International Polar Bear Agreement."

In January 1988 another historic document was signed concerning the white bear. The natives of Alaska's North Slope, known as Inupiat, met with the Inuvialuit of northwestern Canada, and the two groups hammered out a joint management plan for polar bears in the southern Beaufort Sea. Radio-tracking studies show that bears wander back and forth across the U.S.-Canadian boundary and that the mainland coast bear population is thus a common resource. Before 1988 it was, however, a population subject to very different hunting regulations on opposite sides of the border. With the Alaskan native hunt essentially unregulated, females with cubs could be taken on the U.S. side. This practice was forbidden in Canada. The situation worried the Inuvialuit, who were concerned about its effect on the long-term harvest. The Inuvialuit persuaded the Inupiat that it would be in their best interest to adopt the Canadian quota system. The wording of the 1988 agreement protects both denning bears and mothers with cubs. Hunting tags are allocated to each village, and the use of aircraft is prohibited. Harvest information will be compiled, shared between the two groups and used to set future quotas. Game management officials call this document precedent setting and express hopes that similar measures will be adopted by other Alaskan native groups and perhaps extended to other animals, such as beluga whales.

This is a model agreement, for under it everyone wins. Bear stocks will remain undepleted, and the native hunters of both nations will retain their traditional rights. If all human agreements were the product of such common sense, not only polar bears would benefit. In many ways the white bears have brought the separate races and nations of mankind closer together.

THIRTEEN

Nanook Tomorrow

WHAT DOES THE FUTURE HOLD for the white bear? His continued well-being—perhaps his very survival—depends on research (both on captive bears and in the wild) and on preservation of his arctic habitat. Captive breeding programs in various zoos around the world offer hope, but they'll never replace the natural system. "The real battle is in the wild," says John Houck, curator of mammals at the Point Defiance Zoo and Aquarium in Tacoma, Washington. "Zoos are merely an adjunct to preservation in the wild. In terms of the long-term survival of polar bears, habitat must be set aside. We have no illusions that zoos are going to save the polar bear."

"On an international level," says Mark Rosenthal, curator of mammals at Lincoln Park Zoo in Chicago, "people have gotten their act together, both politically and scientifically. The five-nation polar bear agreement is truly exceptional.

"Zoos find themselves in less of a role as recreational exhibitors of exotic animals," Rosenthal continues. "We have a new role in preserving species through captive management and breeding. Whether it's a holding action, time will tell. We can point to some successes, though. If it hadn't been for expertise in captive breeding, animals like the black-footed ferret or the California condor wouldn't have survived. There's a philosophical question that underlies captive studies: what is a captive animal? If you fence animals in a national park, are they still in the wild? Are they in the 'wild zoo'? A proper role for zoos is to develop techniques that can be applied in the wild, to help save the species."

Many zoos now feature cubbing dens, where pregnant females feel secure and human intrusion is minimized through the use of closed-circuit television. Keepers can monitor mothers and newborn cubs without upsetting them. It's not an easy task. As Houck says, "Bears of all kinds are hard to breed in captivity, but polar bears are notoriously difficult."

In a cubbing den, a mother bear—seen on a television screen—cuddles her newborn, holding it against her chest with a massive forearm. She looks down at her baby. With her muzzle close to the tiny bear, she breathes gently on the cub to keep it warm. Such little ones are vulnerable: many zoo records list cubs born dead, or cubs that lived only a few days.

"It would be different if we were talking about antelope," Rosenthal explains. "They go off to have their babies and then quickly return with them to the herd. It's a matter of group survival. Polar bears are not group animals," he emphasizes. "They're born in an underdeveloped form. They have to develop in isolation while their mother cares for them. A zookeeper has to do certain things, and do them *well*, or the cubs won't survive."

According to captive breeding experts, there are three requirements for a polar bear cubbing den: (1) isolation in a small, dark area simulating the natural den; (2) strict privacy—no human contact is permitted—whether sight, odor, or sound; and (3) prebirth fasting, to simulate confinement in the natural den. Even with such precautions, it is a rare zoo that successfully raises newborn cubs. Clearly more art than science is involved.

Wanting to get close to captive bears, I accompanied a zookeeper into the cages behind a zoo's polar bear exhibit. My first impression of the holding area was of security. Every door was doubled: behind the sheet steel creaked a stout second door of welded bars. Resting my hand at the edge of an open rectangle in the solid door, a window no larger than a slice of bread, I peered through to see the bears at play in their outdoor grotto. I drew back suddenly as a huge black nose thrust its way into the open window. The keeper laughed. "I was about to warn you that they *can* reach in a little way!" The wet probe sniffed expectantly. Two dark nostrils in a jet black leathery square, surrounded by a white muzzle. Clouds of steaming bear breath dampened my sleeve. Harkening back to my arctic experiences, I felt a brief twinge of absurdity. I was two inches from the business end of Nanook. In the arctic icepack my position would mean almost certain death. Here, with a confident keeper beside me and a stout steel door in front of me, I was still unnerved. As if on cue, a thunderous banging threatened to rip the steel door beside me off its hinges. I jumped. Five hundred pounds of polar bear wanted in. An excellent idea, I thought, these double doors.

In a modern zoo bears have room to move about, pools of water, and shelters where they can retreat from the crowds of people. Zoo standards have been raised in response to the Marine Mammal Protection Act in areas such as water quality and facility design. Zoos have come a long way from the iron cages and bear pits of a few decades ago.

What is it like to be responsible for polar bears? Tacoma's John Houck replies: "It's not a whole lot different from being responsible for Gila monsters, or any other animals. Your main concerns are the same: social groupings, social behavior, diet, medical care, lighting, temperature, off-exhibit holding areas, maternity dens."

In a zoo setting polar bears must be monitored continually for parasites, especially intestinal worms. They also have problems with hair loss: some bears have gone completely bald for more than a month, for reasons that were never determined. Another concern is the broken teeth that result from fierce play or chewing on the steel bars. Boredom is a real problem and leads to neurotic behavior in many zoo animals. Polar bears are no exception; they need room to roam and pools big enough to swim in. If a zoo bear requires medical attention, a veterinarian arrives with a tranquilizer syringe on the end of a long pole. Minor medical needs are attended to in the cage. Otherwise, the unconscious animal may be carried away on a plywood stretcher to an infirmary. One time when a bear *must* be removed is if a female enters the cubbing den and there is a mature male on display—a mother may kill her own cubs if she hears or smells the male and thinks he might get to them.

Animals in the zoo live long, comparatively easy lives. Their wild cousins face a harsh struggle and an uncertain future. The greatest threat to Nanook's survival is probably an environmental change that is all the more insidious because it's invisible. Unseen in the clear arctic air are chemicals that sow the seeds of environmental disaster. The first is carbon dioxide, an everyday compound that we exhale with each breath. That colorless, odorless gas—so innocuous that we laugh as its nose-tickling fizz dances over a glass of soda—is all around us and perfectly safe in the concentration we encounter daily. The problem is that the carbon dioxide content of the earth's atmosphere is increasing. Because it's a product of combustion, carbon dioxide wafts into the air whenever we burn a fireplace log, generate electricity from coal, draw water for a bath from a gas-fired heater, or drive the family car to a Sierra Club meeting. We may even think we're doing the trees a favor: after all, they take in our carbon dioxide and give us precious oxygen in exchange. The equation, however, is becoming lopsided. We're generating more carbon dioxide all the time and cutting down the world's forests at an alarming pace. The natural system is falling behind, and carbon dioxide is becoming a bigger and bigger fraction of the air we breathe.

It is ironic that the evidence for this increase is found in the ice bear's frozen kingdom. The snow that settles in the interior of Greenland contains abundant air pockets trapped between the settling flakes. It is this air that makes snow such an efficient thermal insulator and gives warmth to the Eskimo snow house.

As more snow falls, the lower layers compress and recrystallize, becoming the blue-white ice of the great Greenland icecap. The trapped air is enclosed as bubbles in the ice. It remains locked in place as the ice flows into glaciers, breaks apart, and calves into icebergs, until the icebergs eventually melt. At least one arctic entrepreneur has capitalized on this imprisoned air by chipping away at floating icebergs and then selling exotic fizzing ice cubes to enliven the cocktails of the social set.

The air bubbles preserve a fossil record of past atmospheres. By analyzing the air trapped in different layers of the ice— annual layers that can be reliably dated by their volcanic ash content and correlated to known major eruptions—scientists conclude that the carbon dioxide increase began with the onset of the Industrial Revolution and its demand for coal-fired boilers, furnaces, mills, and factories. More dramatic is the increase in the ice layers representing the past two decades, when more fossil fuels have been burned and the destruction of forestland has escalated.

Why should a few bubbles in the ice or a few trees in the tropics matter to the white bear? The answer lies in the way carbon dioxide (and other gases, such as methane, which compound the problem) transmit solar radiation. In the air these invisible gases drape an insulating blanket around the earth. This transparent mantle allows the shortwave radiation of inbound sunlight to pass through to warm the earth's surface but doesn't permit the escape of longer waves of heat reflected back toward space. The atmosphere becomes a one-way gate, a heat trap. Just as a hotbed or greenhouse holds in heat, a carbon dioxide–laden atmosphere causes global warming. The phenomenon has been dubbed, with complete logic, the greenhouse effect.

It is far from certain that the earth is yet warming appreciably. The greenhouse effect as a global catastrophe is still an unproven theory. Short-term and local weather conditions complicate the issue. Computer models of climatic shifts predict that the high Arctic will feel the most pronounced changes, but just what these changes will be, no one is yet willing to forecast. What is certain, however, is that significant global warming would have dire consequences for polar bears. At first the area covered by ice would shrink, restricting the bears' range, be-cause—in the language of biology, both they and their prey are *obligate ice creatures*—the bears need floating ice to hunt seals, and the seals need the ice to give birth. At worst, the polar icepack might melt completely, as it has done several times in the geologic past. For the bears there would be nowhere to go, no ice, and no seals. Such manmade changes would occur at a pace that would outstrip evolution: bears wouldn't have time to revert to the land-based life-style of their ancestors. Loss of the polar ice cover would mean extinction of the polar bear. "Even if the ice doesn't melt completely," one biologist warned me, "the result of a warmer climate would still be disastrous. If the 'window' of feeding opportunity—the bears' time on the ice—were to shrink by a week or more, the stress on the bears might be extreme."

Also borne on the arctic wind are chemical signals of human activity, dangerous agents that insinuate their way into Na-nook's bloodstream, muscle tissue, and insulating fat. Because he's at the top of the arctic food chain, the polar bear concen-trates pollutants found in small quantities in the bodies of his prey. Pesticide residues, polychlorinated biphenyl compounds (PCBs), and toxic heavy metals are found in the flesh of polar bears killed in areas remote from industrial or agricultural ac-tivity. Most organic toxins wind up in an animal's fatty tissue, so polar bears—with their entire life organized around fat stor-age—are particularly vulnerable. The PCBs found in bears are approaching dangerous quantities. "You shouldn't eat polar bear meat because PCB levels are so high," says biologist Malcolm Ramsay. "The concentrations are close to the thresholds that inhibit egg and sperm production. In five or ten years we may see polar bear reproduction stopping, even though the bears will appear healthy."

Once such pollutants reach the Arctic, they are long-lived. Biological and chemical breakdown processes operate very slowly at low temperatures, and many of them shut down com-pletely for months at a time. Poor soil drainage and slow water movement exacerbate the problem. Most of these chemicals and metals, at their present levels, probably don't pose a risk to the bears, but knowing that they're in Nanook's tissues somehow gives wilderness travelers a gut-level sense of personal violation. The fact that our waste—the effluent of the affluent—travels so far, so easily, diminishes us all.

Heavy metals?" asked federal prosecutor Jonathan Blackmer. "Would you include lead bullets in 'heavy metals'?"

"I think the real threat to polar bears is continued 'sport' hunting. Anyone with the money can get a permit in Canada. For $25,000 they get a sleigh ride, a couple of nights in an igloo, and an almost guaranteed kill. With dogs, Inuit guides, and high-powered rifles, the bear doesn't have a chance.

"I've been to fur auctions in Toronto," Blackmer told me, "where I've seen piles of polar bear hides stacked floor to ceiling. I just can't believe the quota system is working."

Canadian bear expert Ian Stirling outlined the problem with a simple but sobering statement of fact: even after all the protective legislation, "death by gunshot is probably the greatest single cause of mortality in wild polar bears."

Nanook's own curiosity and rapacious scavenging from human dump sites create problems for individual bears. In bear droppings or the stomach contents of killed bears, hunters find fragments of plastic and auto parts, especially battery elements. Another hazard is glycol antifreeze. Like dogs, bears will lap this substance up because it tastes sweet. It's poison, however— and kills them quickly. Bear researchers have warned northern construction engineers who mark ice runways with glycol-based dye that their efforts to make human activities safer may be unsafe for polar bears.

Does northern oil exploration pose a risk to Nanook? Almost certainly, but experts are divided on the severity of the problem. Most feel that the threat is small. An oil spill in arctic waters, for example, would be a very localized phenomenon. Unlike the oil that spread across Prince William Sound from the Exxon *Valdez*, oil in colder water would congeal to the consistency and appearance of chocolate mousse and would be fairly easily recovered in the open sea, even during the warmest months of summer. Only bears in the immediate vicinity might be affected.

To determine the consequences of bears becoming oiled in a possible spill, Canadian researchers conducted an experiment that had disastrous results and embroiled the scientists in a long-lived public controversy. Because bears are attracted to seal oil and whale oil, biologists were concerned that they might eat oiled birds or preferentially swim through floating oil. Ian Stirling, Canada's foremost polar bear authority, described the results of allowing three bears to swim through a pool with oil on the surface: "It was winter when the studies were done. The oiled bears began to shiver and then to lick the unrefined crude oil from their fur in the same manner they lick seal oil from their fur when out on the sea ice. Two of those bears suffered kidney failure and died. The third was treated . . . it fully recovered and now lives in a zoo in Japan."

This experiment became a media sensation. "When news of the deaths became public, the press vilified the scientists for weeks for their perceived inhumane behaviour," Stirling wrote. "The large amount of valuable information that was obtained was ignored. While regretting the fate of the two animals that died, I feel their sacrifice was of great importance to the conservation of the species."

Clearly, oil and bears should not be allowed to come together.

Canadian experts predict they will have five options in the event of a major oil blowout or spill: (1) monitor its effects but take no action; (2) attempt to scare bears away from the oil; (3) transport bears away from the oil; (4) capture oiled bears, clean their fur, and treat them for ingested oil; or (5) euthanatize oiled bears. Option 4 would be the most costly but would almost certainly be demanded by the public.

Steve Amstrup, a research biologist with the U.S. Fish and Wildlife Service, is responsible for the bears of the Beaufort Sea—the bear population that has the greatest potential for interaction with U.S. oil explorers. Commenting on the "polar bear plans" that must be filed by offshore operators, Amstrup told me, "I'd like to see a great deal of flexibility in requirements. For example, different types of drilling platforms call for different polar bear plans. Vessels with tall vertical steel sides are virtually impossible for bears to scale. The chance that a bear or human will be endangered is relatively small. Such a vessel does alter the environment, however. Rather than hire a monitor whose job is to guard worker safety and shoot problem bears if necessary, it would make more sense to hire a biologist who could record quantitative data about the bears that come to the site.

"On the other hand," Amstrup continued, "a gravel island drilling site has very different needs. Bears can simply walk right up onto it. Planners need to consider lighting, ground configuration, pathways, and other layout patterns as well as, where indicated, polar bear guards, in order to minimize man-bear interactions."

On the question of the risk of such activities in the Beaufort Sea, Amstrup cited the need for more information: "The worst possible scenario would be a major spill on or under the sea ice. If such a spill occurred, it would be uncontrollable and could be a catastrophe beyond anything we could imagine. Fortunately, there appears to be a very low likelihood of a major spill. Other hazards associated with hydrocarbon exploration and development can't yet be evaluated or managed, because we don't have enough data. As an example, the creation of habitat that isn't otherwise there, such as the open lead on the lee side of a drill rig: we know such open water attracts both seals and bears. Is that bad? We just don't know. Such a phenomenon might prolong the productivity of the ocean in a local area by admitting more sunlight, and it might produce feeding sites that wouldn't have occurred otherwise. Is that good? Again, we need more data."

Sea-ice specialist Ken Vaudrey believes petroleum activities, except for the possibility of a tanker accident or a well blowout, will have minimal impact on polar bears. He told me, "Just as shrimping and fishing are better in the Gulf of Mexico around oil-drilling platforms, bears should actually benefit in winter from the open-water wake downwind from the arctic platform

in the otherwise tight icepack. I don't see the Arctic ever becoming so financially attractive that you'll have platforms as
dense as in the Gulf of Mexico. There'll probably never be more
than ten or fifteen platforms in any large area of the Arctic. In
addition, bears don't congregate in any particular spot. You
can't really destroy their habitat on a local scale, because they're
not local creatures. They're so independent, so wide-ranging."

Some biologists express a different view of the same setting:
that bears drawn to drilling rigs by the easy seal hunting might
become accustomed to humans and lose their fear of them. Bears
unafraid of workers and attracted to their worksites might be a
deadly combination for both human and bear. "Current drilling activity in the Chukchi Sea," says federal biologist Gerald
Garner, "is restricted to the ice-free summer months. If wintertime drilling should increase human density in the area, there
may be problems. The goal then will be to avoid creating
human-bear encounters, which the bear is, ultimately, going to
lose."

Other development activity worries wildlife specialists. They
fear that drilling, seismic exploration, aircraft overflights, ship
traffic, and road building might cause females to avoid traditional denning areas. The U.S. Minerals Management Service,
together with oil companies active in the Arctic, works on ways
to minimize such disruptions. Before a well is drilled, in addition to the thousands of pages of documents required to ensure
protection of the fragile arctic environment, oil companies must
file a polar bear plan. Nanook has entered the world of bureau-
cracy, of revised draft environmental impact statements, of
plaintiffs and counselors and class-action suits, of interminable
hearings, objections, and appeals.

The great majority of men and women who work in the
Arctic adhere to a strong preservation ethic, despite the rocky
relationships with conservation groups that may have charac-
terized their projects in past years. Whether their jobs involve
searching for oil, forecasting the weather, or defending the top
of the world, such people appreciate the frozen North as one of
the last remaining truly wild places on earth. Typical is Ken
Vaudrey, whose studies of sea ice are designed to facilitate oil

exploration. He has enough problems with Nanook that it would be easy for him to imagine the bear as an adversary: "I try to reduce the exposure of my instrumentation, like the positioning buoys. Bears like to use the instrument boxes as hockey pucks. We've also apparently left a lot of back scratchers on the ice. I've left two-by-four timbers and come back to find them snapped like twigs.

"I once had an eighteen-inch whip antenna on an aluminum canister. The canister was buried in the ice, but the antenna stuck out. A bear apparently gnawed on it after urinating on it, but we didn't lose any data. The foxes are worse. I try to make our equipment more foxproof. They gnaw the insulation off cables: we have to cut slots in the ice with a chain saw, bury the cables, and freeze them in place. When the bears move farther offshore in winter, the foxes are truly starving; they eat anything they can."

Despite these difficulties with the denizens of the North, Vaudrey remains committed to the wild beauty of the arctic lands and seas. High on his list of worthy creatures is Nanook: "One day while flying," he recalled, "we passed a mother with two first-summer cubs. She was teaching them how to hunt the seals that lay hauled out on the ice. We dropped lower for a closer look, and suddenly, for the bear family, it was 'circle the wagons' time. The mother gathered her twins close. One of them dropped to the ground, rolled over, and began scratching his back, legs waving. His mother whirled around and told him, in no uncertain terms, to get up and stand behind her. It was obvious that he wasn't taking this as seriously as she thought he should, and she intended to put him in his place.

"The pilot asked if I'd like another low pass. I told him to fly on. I had no intention of bothering such a close-knit family."

Beyond the enthusiasm of zoo patrons, beyond the exclamations of tundra-buggy photographers, beyond the fearful admiration of workers trudging through northern snowdrifts—beyond all of these lies another category of human interaction with the white bear, one with far greater long-term consequences. As I interviewed biologists, wildlife officials, and legal experts, I began to appreciate the fragile nature of the balance—both ecological and bureaucratic—that exists between the modern world and the empty reaches of the Arctic. Many of us call ourselves, in smug self-satisfaction, environmentalists. Our efforts are feeble, however, compared with those of the small but dedicated cadre of men and women whose actions in behalf of the white bear may influence his ultimate survival. Those who measure his metabolism in the face of a polar blizzard, those who negotiate his freedom in the vaulted halls of diplomacy, and those who argue his case in stuffy human courtrooms far removed from the windswept icepack are the real heroes of modern arctic life, and they deserve both Nanook's thanks and our own.

I am pleased that the future of the great white bears is in such hands. The individuals whose stories are told in these pages are polar bear enthusiasts. All want to see the ice bear thrive in an unspoiled Arctic. The bears' survival, though, isn't just an arctic problem, any more than it's a Canadian or a U.S. problem. It doesn't belong solely to industrial nations, nor to East or West. Nanook is a citizen of the world. Ultimately, his fate lies in the hands of all of us who live on this planet, because the future of the polar bear mirrors the future of earth itself.

I once watched a superb performer whose message from the stage had a profound ecological theme. Among other props he juggled a large ball colored with bright continents and blue oceans. At the close of his performance, he pretended to fumble one object, then another, so they fell and rolled across the stage. Then, just as the lights went out, he caught the blue ball with a deft maneuver and left his audience with a dead-serious closing: "And whatever you do, *don't drop the earth*."

Epilogue

Atop the Churchill Northern Studies Center is a large, clear plastic dome. It's a popular gathering place on nights when the Northern Lights put on a good display. Recently, though, I had the show all to myself on a clear October night. I savored the solitude.

Overhead a curtain of light undulated, gently swaying against the blackness. The diffuse top of the auroral drapery glowed faintly rosy. The middle portion was green, and its lower fringe blue. Hanging as a filmy sheet, it made a pale rainbow in the dark sky. Suddenly, pulses of brighter color rolled along the curtain at regularly spaced intervals like so many soldiers passing in review. Inuit spirits of the dead, I remembered. Then the pattern stabilized. Fingers of light pointed downward at the drape's lower hem. The meandering sheet closed in on itself to form a ring in the sky—a cylinder of light—and hung motionless.

I forced myself to look away, to scan the ground. Lights from the buildings illuminated a ring around the compound to match the sky's ring overhead. Past the fringe of light I could see the faint outlines of trees, indistinct in the darkness. Beyond, only the black forest, seeping away into the black night.

In the dark, though I couldn't see them, I knew there were bears. Bears curled into balls sleeping. Bears walking purposefully. Bears wandering aimlessly. Bears oblivious to humans. Bears protected by human laws. Bears that would be killed by human hunters. Bears wearing scientists' ear tags and tattooed numbers. Bears with young cubs. Bears with unborn cubs just beginning to form inside them.

As the aurora shifted silently overhead, I realized that the magnificent display wasn't for me but rather for the bears. Not spirits of the dead, not charged particles of the solar wind— instead it was a chorus, a celebration, an outpouring of the soul of the Arctic, paying homage to the king.

It was an appropriate gift, an honor deserved, the only possible tribute befitting his dignity. Nothing in the sky compares with the splendor of the aurora; nothing on the ice can match the majesty of Nanook, the white bear.

End Notes

ONE: NORTH OF THE NORTH SLOPE

Stefansson's quotation is from Vilhjalmur Stefansson, *The Friendly Arctic* (New York: Macmillan 1921). *Nanook* is also spelled *Nanuk*. The Eskimo language and its various dialects are spelled phonetically. Thus how a word is spelled depends on where you are: *angakok*, the Alaskan shaman, is *angaqoq*, the same wise man, in Greenland. The quotation about arctic traveler Etienne is from B. C. Imbert, "Solo Man-Hauling Journey to the North Pole," *Polar Record*, vol. 144 (1986).

TWO: LAND AND SEA OF THE MIDNIGHT SUN

I am indebted for many of my arctic experiences to the officers and men of the United States Coast Guard icebreakers *Westwind*, *Southwind*, and *Polar Sea*, and to numerous north country pilots, whose flying prowess is legendary wherever northern veterans gather to swap stories.

Farley Mowat's *The Snow Walker* (Boston: Little, Brown, 1976) is the source of the quotation about snow.

THREE: WHITE BEARS IN A WHITE WORLD

A concise summary of polar bear characteristics and ecology is D. P. DeMaster and Ian Stirling's *"Ursus maritimus," Mammalian Species*, no. 145 (1981), pp. 1–7. The paper on green polar bears is R. A. Lerwin and P. T. Robinson's "The Greening of Polar Bears in Zoos," *Nature*, vol. 278 (1979), pp. 445–447. Descriptions of the behavior of polar bear skin with respect to infrared and ultraviolet radiation are found in D. M. Lavigne and N. A. Øritsland, "Black Polar Bears," *Nature*, vol. 251 (1974), pp. 218–219.

The information on Nanook's nonskid treads is found in D. P. Manning, J. E. Cooper, Ian Stirling, C. M. Jones, M. Bruce, and P. C. McCausland, "Studies on the Footpads of the Polar Bear (*Ursus maritimus*) and Their Possible Relevance to Accident Prevention," *Journal of Hand Surgery*, vol. 10-B, no. 3 (1985), pp. 303–307.

The Barry Lopez quotation on polar bear milk comes from his *Arctic Dreams* (New York: Scribner's, 1986).

Ian Stirling's hypothesis about polar bears' sense of smell comes from his wonderful *Polar Bears* (Ann Arbor: University of Michigan Press, 1988). The Schumacher quotation appears in T. Larsen, "Polar Bear: Lonely Nomad of the North," *National Geographic*, vol. 139, no. 4 (1971), pp. 574–590.

FOUR: LIFE AMID THE ICEPACK FLOES

The description of research on the caloric value of seals is from Ian Stirling and Eoin McEwan, "The Caloric Value of Whole Ringed Seals (*Phoca hispida*) in Relation to Polar Bear (*Ursus maritimus*) Ecology and Hunting Behavior," *Canadian Journal of Zoology*, vol. 53 (1975), pp. 1021–27. Ian Stirling's *Polar Bears* is the source of the quotation about the ultimate arctic carnivore.

The description of polar bears killing beluga whales is found in M. M. R. Freeman, "Polar Bear Predation on Beluga in the Canadian Arctic," *Arctic*, vol. 26 (1973), pp. 163–164, and L. F. Lowry, J. J. Burns, and R. R. Nelson, "Polar Bear, *Ursus maritimus*, Predation on Belugas, *Delphinapterus leucas*, in the

Bering and Chukchi Seas," *Canadian Field Naturalist*, vol. 101, no. 2 (1987), pp. 141–146.

FIVE: BEAR BEHAVIOR

The Stirling citations are from his *Polar Bears*. The Bruemmer quotation comes from his "How Polar Bears Break the Ice," *Natural History*, vol. 93, no. 12 (1984), pp. 38–46. The Nyholm passages are from his fascinating account of his life among Svalbard's bears, *"Isbjørnundersøker på Nordaustlandet* [On polar bears' behavior in Spitsbergen]," *Norwegian Polar Yearbook* 1975–76, pp.12–29. Hugh Miles and Mike Salisbury, *Kingdom of the Ice Bear* (Austin: University of Texas Press, 1986). The Fleck and Herrero quotation is from a government report described in the notes for Chapter 10.

SIX: FROM THE ICE AGE TO THE STONE AGE

The best guide to the polar bear's evolutionary history is Björn Kurtén, "The Evolution of the Polar Bear, *Ursus maritimus*, Phipps": *Acta Zoologica Fennica*, vol. 108, pp. 3–30. Ian Stirling on the subject of grizzly bears hunting seals is from his *Polar Bears*. The Sam Hall quotation comes from his *The Fourth World: The Heritage of the Arctic and Its Destruction* (New York: Knopf, 1987). The Pierre Berton quotations are from his *The Arctic Grail* (New York: Viking, 1989).

SEVEN: PEOPLE OF THE BEAR

I have used the words *Eskimo* and *Inuit* almost interchangeably but usually in a geographic sense. Eskimos live in Alaska. Inuit live in Canada and Greenland, although in Greenland they prefer to be called Greenlanders or *Kalâlek*. In the USSR the northern people are officially *Eskimosy*, but they call themselves *Yugyt*.

John Dyson wrote about the continuity of Eskimo culture

in *The Hot Arctic* (Boston: Little, Brown, 1979). Richard C. Davids's *Lords of the Arctic* (New York: Macmillan, 1982) contains the passage about bears discussing humans. The tale of the "Big Nail" is from Frederick Cook's *Return from the Pole* (New York: Pellegrini & Cudahy, 1951). The Peter Freuchen quotations are from *Arctic Adventure: My Life in the Frozen North* (New York: Farrar and Rinehart, 1935). The tale of Anoritoq comes from Roald Amundsen's *My Life as an Explorer* (New York: Doubleday, 1927).

Descriptions of eating polar bear meat are taken from Doug Wilkinson's *Land of the Long Day* (New York: Henry Holt, 1956) and Viljhalmur Stefansson's *The Friendly Arctic*.

Eskimo legends are paraphrased from accounts by arctic explorers and traders such as Knud Rasmussen, *Greenland by the Polar Sea* (London: William Heinemann, 1921), p. 327, and from Lawrence Millman's *A Kayak Full of Ghosts* (Santa Barbara: Capra Press, 1987).

EIGHT: ENTER THE KABLOONA

One of the best guides to the history of arctic exploration is Berton's *The Arctic Grail*. The early history of European interaction with polar bears is summarized in T. J. Oleson, "Polar Bears in the Middle Ages," *Canadian Historical Review*, vol. 3, no. 50 (1950), pp. 47–55. Roald Amundsen told the tale of his icepack encounter with a mother bear in *My Life as an Explorer*. The Richard Davids quotation about the diplomatic trade in polar bears is from his *Lords of the Arctic*. Frederick Cook's description of his near-starvation comes from *Return from the Pole*. Viljhalmur Stefansson's *The Friendly Arctic* is the source of the bear tale that ended with a prolonged hunt. Donald MacMillan's cub story is from his *Four Years in the White North* (Boston: Medici, 1925).

Also quoted is Roald Amundsen, *My Life as an Explorer* (New York: Doubleday, 1927).

The account of the bear named Marion is found in P. D. Trask and N. G. Ricketts, *The "Marion" Expedition to Davis*

Strait and Baffin Bay, Under the Direction of the United States Coast Guard, Part 1 (Washington, D.C.: U.S. Government Printing Office, 1932). The story that ends the chapter is from Naomi Uemura's "Solo to the Pole," *National Geographic*, vol. 154 (1978), pp. 298–325.

NINE: THE COLD WAR HEATS UP THE ARCTIC

The Peter Freuchen quotation is cited in E. Stafansson, *Here is the Far North* (New York: Scribner's, 1957). The tale of Jacko the hunter is found in Doug Wilkinson's *Land of the Long Day*. John Dyson wrote about the modern world's impact on Eskimos in *The Hot Arctic*.

TEN: BEAR ATTACK!

The descriptions of polar bear attacks on humans have been taken from interviews or media accounts. Government documents quoted include a very informative report by Susan Fleck and Steve Herrero, *Polar Bear–Human Conflicts*, prepared in February 1988 for Parks Canada and the Department of Renewable Resources. I thank Susan Fleck for her cooperation. The wonderfully written lines on "the trouble with being a polar bear" are taken from Richard Davids's *Lords of the Arctic*, and the quotation about problem bears and their success as carnivores comes from Ian Stirling's *Polar Bears*. Gordon Stenhouse's research on deterrents is summarized in reports titled *Bear Detection and Deterrent Study, Cape Churchill, Manitoba* for the years 1981, 1982, and 1983, prepared for the Northwest Territories Wildlife Service, and used by permission of Gordon Stenhouse. The quotation that closes the chapter is from Miles and Salisbury, *Kingdom of the Ice Bear* (Austin: University of Texas Press, 1986).

ELEVEN: THE POLAR BEAR CAPITAL OF THE WORLD

To learn more about polar bear viewing in Churchill, contact Adventure Canada, 920 Yonge Street, Toronto, Ontario M4W 3C7 (phone 800-387-1483); Churchill Wilderness Encounters, P.O. Box 9, Churchill, Manitoba ROB OEO (phone 204-675-2248); Northern Expeditions, P.O. Box 614, Churchill, Manitoba ROB OEO (phone 204-675-2793); Tundra Buggy Tours, Ltd., P.O. Box 662, Churchill, Manitoba ROB OEO (phone 204-675-2121). Tundra buggy trips cost between $100 and $600 per person per day, depending on how many share the vehicle.

Studies at Cape Churchill are described in Gordon Stenhouse's government reports cited in Chapter 10. Ian Stirling's quotation about the fall season is from his *Polar Bears*.

TWELVE: NANOOK TODAY

For the full text of the international agreement on polar bears, see Jack Lentfer, "Agreement on the Conservation of Polar Bears," *Polar Record*, vol. 17, no. 108 (1974), pp. 327–330. Ian Stirling is quoted from his *Polar Bears* about the necessity of being able to remove problem bears. The U.S. Fish & Wildlife Service document cited is *Fish & Wildlife Facts* (FWS-044), obtainable from the Department of Interior, Washington, D.C. 20240. The Jerome Knap case is described from interviews, media accounts, and court documents.

Information about Polar Bear Provincial Park is available from the Ontario Ministry of Natural Resources, P.O. Box 190, Moosonee, Ontario POL 1YO.

THIRTEEN: NANOOK TOMORROW

Special thanks go to the zoo experts and wildlife biologists who shared their views on the long-term outlook for polar bears. The experiment involving bears and crude oil is described in Ian Stirling's *Polar Bears*.

Selected Bibliography

Amundsen, Roald. *My Life as an Explorer* (New York: Doubleday, 1927).

Berton, Pierre. *The Arctic Grail* (New York: Viking, 1989).

Cook, Frederick A. *Return from the Pole* (New York: Pellegrini & Cudahy, 1951).

Davids, Richard C. *Lords of the Arctic* (New York: Macmillan, 1982).

Dyson, John. *The Hot Arctic* (Boston: Little, Brown, 1979).

Hall, Sam. *The Fourth World: The Heritage of the Arctic and Its Destruction* (New York: Knopf, 1987).

Lopez, Barry. *Arctic Dreams* (New York: Scribner's, 1986).

MacMillan, Donald. *Four Years in the White North* (Boston: Medici, 1925).

Miles, Hugh, and Mike Salisbury. *Kingdom of the Ice Bear* (Austin: University of Texas Press, 1986).

Millman, Lawrence, *A Kayak Full of Ghosts* (Santa Barbara: Capra Press, 1987).

Rasmussen, Knud. *Greenland by the Polar Sea* (London: William Heinemann, 1921).

Stafansson, E. *Here Is the Far North* (New York: Scribner's, 1957).

Stefansson, Vilhjalmur. *The Friendly Arctic* (New York: Macmillan, 1921).

Stirling, Ian. *Polar Bears* (Ann Arbor: University of Michigan Press, 1988).

Wilkinson, Doug. *Land of the Long Day* (New York: Henry Holt, 1956).

Index